THE MARY FLEXNER LECTURES

Established in 1928 at Bryn Mawr College to
promote distinguished work in the humanities

Experiments in Ethics

KWAME ANTHONY APPIAH

HARVARD UNIVERSITY PRESS
Cambridge, Massachusetts · London, England

First Harvard University Press paperback edition, 2009

The author is grateful for permission to reproduce two stories by Lydia Davis.
"Trying to Learn" first appeared in *Conjunctions* 21 (Fall 1993), 359–360, and
was republished in the collection *Almost No Memory: Stories* (New York: Farrar,
Straus and Giroux, 1997; Picador, 2001), copyright © 1997 by Lydia Davis.
"Happiest Moment" appeared in *Samuel Johnson Is Indignant* (New York:
McSweeney's Books, 2001; Picador, 2002), copyright © 2001 by Lydia Davis.
Both stories are reprinted by permission of Lydia Davis and of Farrar, Straus and
Giroux, LLC.

LIBRARY OF CONGRESS CATALOGING-IN-PUBLICATION DATA
Appiah, Anthony.
Experiments in ethics / Kwame Anthony Appiah.
p. cm.—(The Mary Flexner lectures)
Includes index.
ISBN 978-0-674-02609-4 (hardcover : alk. paper)
ISBN 978-0-674-03457-0 (pbk.)
1. Ethics. I. Title.
BJ37.A67 2007
170—dc22   2007017984

THE MARY FLEXNER LECTURESHIP was established at Bryn Mawr College on February 12, 1928, by Bernard Flexner, in honor of his sister, Mary Flexner, a graduate of the College. The income from the endowment is to be used annually or at longer intervals, at the discretion of the Directors of the College, as an honorarium for a distinguished American or foreign scholar in the field of the humanities. The object of the lectureship is to bring to the College scholars of distinction who will be a stimulus to the faculty and students and who will help to maintain the highest ideals and standards of learning.

Henrico

CONTENTS

Experiments in Ethics

Prologue

This little book is an attempt to relate the business of philosophical ethics, which is my professional bailiwick, to the work of scholars in a number of other fields and to the concerns of the ordinary, thoughtful person, trying to live a decent life. There are philosophers aplenty in these pages; but there are, as well, many other practitioners of what used to be called the moral sciences—psychologists, economists, anthropologists, and sociologists.

The relevance of the social sciences to our ordinary lives is fairly straightforward. Since what we should do depends on how the world is, our everyday decisions can draw on knowledge from any sphere. It is less obvious that empirical research could have any bearing on our specifically moral judgments. Yet in making our choices we must sometimes start with a vision, however inchoate, of what it is for a human life to go well. That was one of Aristotle's central insights. It is my argument that we should be free to avail ourselves of the resources of many disciplines to define that vision; and that in bringing them together we are being faithful to a long tradition. In the humanities, I think, we are always engaged in illuminating the present by drawing on the past; it is the only way to make a future worth hoping for.

The burden of the disciplinary genealogy with which I will begin is that "experimental philosophy," rather than being something new, is as old as the term "philosophy." The commonplace I want to challenge is that philosophy, in having relinquished those inquiries that now belong to the physical and social sciences, has somehow become more purely itself. The second chapter pursues a case study in empirical moral psychology—focusing, in particular, on the challenge that so-called situationist research has posed to the revival of virtue ethics. The putative confrontation should, I think, help to show what is and isn't of value in "virtue." In the third chapter, I consider more broadly the vexed status of intuition in moral philosophy, focusing on the distinction between explanations and reasons. The fourth chapter takes seriously the proposal that a certain array of distinct "moral emotions" may be a deep feature of human nature, and explores the concordances between our traditions of explicit moral reflection and these posited primitives. In the last chapter, I'll be relating these inquiries to the project of ethics in its capacious, classical sense. (In the notes, you'll find, in addition to source citations, some suggestions for additional reading and the occasional ancillary argument or observation. You may treat this endmatter like the "extras" on a DVD: please be assured, in other words, that you needn't ever flip there if you're not so inclined.)

The experiments of my title are, in one sense, not mine. Throughout the chapters that follow, I touch upon a range of experimental work that seems to bear on our moral makeup. I do so as a philosopher, convinced that our discipline has a role to play in these discussions, and interested, I admit, in the philosopher's angle more than the psychologist's or the economist's. Though I want the insights and the discoveries of other disciplines to be taken up in mine, I don't think that, in taking them up, we philosophers are losing a distinctive voice. Philosophy should be open to what it can learn from experiments; it doesn't need to set up its own laboratories.

But I want to ask you to think of the whole book as experimental, in another sense. The stimulus for this book was the invitation to give the 2005 Flexner Lectures at Bryn Mawr, which allowed me to explore—in the tentative way that the word "experimental" connotes—the significance of work that is very much ongoing for my own developing views about the values that guide us. The result is in the nature of a preliminary report from that laboratory of reflection; a report that is addressed, as the Flexner committee asks, to a nonspecialist audience . . . to anyone, in fact, who is engaged in—or by—the "moral sciences."

Introduction: The Waterless Moat

The study of history confirms the reasonings of true philosophy.

—DAVID HUME, *A Treatise of Human Nature*

The Partition

At least since Homer, in the European tradition—but surely everywhere and everywhen in societies both oral and literate—communities have fashioned themselves around stories of the past, chronicles that constitute "us" as Hellenes or Yorubas or Americans. This is, by now, a familiar idea, famously expressed more than a century ago by Ernest Renan in his essay "Qu'est-ce qu'une nation?" (What Is a Nation?) It is not as often remarked that the communities that engage in this practice are not just ethnic and national: one of *my* communities, the league of Western philosophers, has constructed histories that reach back two and a half millennia, assigning to the ancients the very problems we now claim to be working through ourselves.

"Forgetting, and I would even say historical error, is an essential element in the creation of a nation," Renan noticed, rather more provocatively, "and that is why the progress of historical studies is often a danger for the nation itself."[1] His observation could just as easily have been made about disciplines: there is the same likelihood of forgetting and historical error here, too. Offering an account of the past, in disciplinary histories as in ethnic and national ones, is in part a way of justifying a contemporary practice. And once we have a stake in a practice, we shall be tempted to invent a past that supports it. Disciplines are shaped by what Kant once called the conflict of the faculties—the struggle among the different traditions associated with different departments. And, in those conflicts, incompatible stories are often told about how we got to be where we are. If they are incompatible, one of them must be wrong. So we can agree with Renan both that such conflicts are constitutive ("essential," as he says) and that the truth (the "progress of historical studies") may be threatening.

It's often said that psychology has a short history and a long past. Might the opposite be true of philosophy? In what follows I want to invert some common assumptions about the continuity of my discipline. Philosophy is now typically defined by what it is *not* (psychology, physics, anthropology, etc.), and if you want philosophers to engage more eagerly with practitioners of other disciplines, it's helpful to see how newfangled that disciplinary self-conception really is. What's novel isn't the experimental turn; what's novel was the turn away from it.

Looking back at our putative ancestors with an attempt at historical objectivity, one is struck by how much of what Renan

6

called "forgetting" the construction of a philosophical canon has required. We have had to ignore so much of what they wrote. Plato and Aristotle had almost physiological theories about the nature of the soul and the nature of life, which invoked reason and various kinds of passions to explain the way people behave and more general faculties, shared between humans and other animals, to explain, say, the workings of the senses.

Is Descartes, whose "mechanical philosophy" aimed to overturn Aristotelianism, our true forebear? Then you should wonder at how selectively most of us read him. Much of his attention, after all, was devoted to geometry and optics, and for a period, he was revered among scholars as, principally, a sort of mathematical physicist. (The only reference to him you will almost certainly know of, if you don't do philosophy, is in talk of the "Cartesian" coordinates he pioneered.) He also spent time and energy dissecting cows and other animals. Only later was he repositioned as, centrally, a theorist of mind and knowledge, whose primary concern had to do with the justification of belief. In his *The Passions of the Soul* (1649), he discusses the way the "movements of the muscles, and likewise all sensations, depend on the nerves, which are like little threads or tubes coming from the brain and containing, like the brain itself, a certain very fine air or wind which is called the 'animal spirits.'"[2] Descartes aimed to solve what we think of as the canonically philosophical puzzle about the relation between the soul and the body by appeal to an empirical hypothesis about the brain: "On carefully examining the matter, I think I have clearly established that the part of the body in which the soul directly exercises its functions is ... the innermost part of the brain, which is a certain very small gland situated in the middle of the brain's substance and suspended above the passage through which the spirits in the brain's anterior cavities communicate with those in its posterior cavities."[3] That "very small" gland (the pineal, which sits near the hypothalamus) is not an incident of the theory. Without it, Descartes has no story of how mind and body are functionally integrated.

"The true philosophy," Robert Hooke wrote in his *Micrographia* (1665), is "to *begin* with the Hands and Eyes, and to *proceed* on through the Memory, to be *continued* by the Reason; nor is it to stop there, but to *come about* to the Hands and Eyes again, and so, by a *continual passage round* from one Faculty to another, it is to be maintained in life and strength, as much as the body of man is by the *circulation* of the blood through the several parts of the body, the Arms, the Feet, the Lungs, the Heart, and the Head."[4] It's a lovely image—but he was simply describing what he took to be the basis of any sound learning. The term "philosophy" hewed to the curricular contours of the medieval university, in which it was a general designation for systematic knowledge, typically subdivided into the natural, moral, and metaphysical (the last—in the scholastic mode— being largely confined to typologies of substance and accidents, form and matter).

I don't want to overstate the case: before the disciplinary rise of modern philosophy, one can readily trace distinctions— between, say, reason and experience, speculation and experiment—that seem cognate to our way of organizing knowledge. When Thomas Hobbes denied that Robert Boyle's air-pump research deserved the name "philosophy," one element of his brief was the intrinsic superiority of demonstrative findings (à la Euclid) to experimental findings. But another was simply that the pump was leaky.[5] Descartes gives us hope when he refers to "first philosophy," and he famously maintained that "all philosophy is like a tree, of which the roots are metaphysics, the trunk is physics, and the branches, which grow from this trunk, are all of the other sciences, which is to say medicine, mechanics, and morals."[6] Yet even here, we can see that his taxonomy isn't quite ours: morals, to us a division of philosophy, is to him a practical endeavor on a par with medicine. Margaret Cavendish, early in her *Observations upon Experimental Philosophy* (1668), urged that "the experimental part of philosophy" was not to be "preferred before the speculative," for "most experiments have their rise from the speculative, so the artist or mechanic is but a servant to the student."[7] Still, it's significant that, at the time, there were virtually no thinkers who confined themselves to the realm of unsullied abstraction; Cavendish, in later chapters of her *Observations,* went on to offer opinions about how wood got petrified and whether snails have blood. John Locke's inquiries into the origins of ideas involved consideration of facts about savages and children.

By the eighteenth century, the growing prestige of experimentation was apparent everywhere. The encyclopedist Jean D'Alembert praised Locke for reducing metaphysics to what it should be: "la physique expérimentale de l'âme"—the experimental science of the spirit.[8] And Hume subtitled his great *Treatise of Human Nature,* as we do not sufficiently often recall, *Being an Attempt to Introduce the Experimental Method of Rea-*

soning into Moral Subjects. The point is not just that the canonical philosophers belong as much to the history of what we now call psychology as to the genealogy of philosophy. It is that their "metaphysical" and their psychological claims are, insofar as we insist on distinguishing them, profoundly interdependent. Their proper place as ancestors of both modern disciplines is reflected in the fact that many of the claims they make about the mind—including those claims that *are* thought to be of current philosophical relevance—are founded in empirical observation, even if they are not often founded in experiment. They depend on stories about the actual doings of actual people, on claims about how humanity actually is. Hume's *History of England*—five volumes of empirical information, elegantly organized—has rightly been seen as expressing ideas about morality and politics and psychology. For him, it was an extension of the project of a work like the *Enquiry concerning Human Understanding,* where, in a famous footnote, Hume identified and rebutted an emerging tendency:

> NOTHING is more usual than for writers, even, on *moral, political,* or *physical* subjects, to distinguish between *reason* and *experience,* and to suppose, that these species of argumentation are entirely different from each other. The former are taken for the mere result of our intellectual faculties, which, by considering *a priori* the nature of things . . . establish particular principles of science and philosophy. The latter are supposed to be derived entirely from sense and observation, by which we learn what has actually resulted from the operation of particular objects . . .

But notwithstanding that this distinction be thus universally received, both in the active and speculative scenes of life, I shall not scruple to pronounce, that it is, at bottom, erroneous, at least, superficial. . . . It is experience which is ultimately the foundation of our inference and conclusion.[9]

A case has been made that the modern conception of the discipline is presaged in the epistemological preoccupations of Thomas Reid and Immanuel Kant.[10] But Reid himself was emphatic in his suspicion of mere conjecture. Every real discovery, he says, is arrived at by "patient observation, by accurate experiments, or by conclusions drawn by strict reasoning from observation and experiments, and such discoveries have always tended to refute, but not to confirm, the theories and hypotheses which ingenious men had invented."[11]

It is anything but historically anomalous that Kant, to whom we owe the analytic-synthetic distinction, worked avidly on both sides of the putative divide. The founder of "critical philosophy" elaborated theories of the winds and of the earth's rotation, and dispensed advice about the training of the young ("games with balls are among the best for children"); the author of A Critique of Pure Reason was also the author of Concerning the Volcanoes on the Moon.[12] Kant possessed the resources for a conceptual partition between what we think of as philosophy and psychology, but not those for a vocational partition.

One artifact of philosophy's striking modernity—it is almost too obvious to remark—is that twentieth-century reference books almost invariably give pre-twentieth-century philosophers compound designations: this person is a philosopher and mathematician, that a philosopher and littérateur, the other a philosopher and political economist. The trailing conjunction signals the shrunken disciplinary rump state to which we have retreated. To retrace the old boundaries, we might give particular attention to books that call themselves histories of philosophy, because, as Renan would have expected, the contours of the discipline are shaped by such narratives. In this sense, the history of philosophy is the history of its histories. Thomas Stanley's *History of Philosophy* (its four volumes, published in the 1650s and 1660s, "containing those on whom the attribute of Wise was conferred") focused entirely on "barbaric" and classical figures; Jacob Brucker's *Historica Critica Philosophiae*, from the 1740s, included, in its survey of modern philosophers, the natural philosophy of Copernicus, Kepler, Galileo, Newton, and so on. Hegel's *Lectures on the History of Philosophy* (published in 1832, a year after his death) contained the now-commonplace distinction between rationalism and empiricism, but placed Locke together with Descartes in the first camp. And though Hegel chastised Newton for his dictum "Physics, beware of metaphysics," it was in part because he thought that this led to bad science: "Regarding matters as he did, Newton derived his conclusions from his experiences; and in physics and the theory of color-vision, he made bad observations and drew worse conclusions. . . . A miserable kind of experience like this itself contradicts itself through nature, for nature is more excellent than it appears in this wretched experience: both nature itself and experience, when carried a little further, contradict it. Hence, of all the splendid discoveries of

Newton in optics, none now remain excepting one—the division of light into seven colours."[13] (The point is not that Hegel is right, here: it is that these remarks reveal his sense of disciplinary geography.) Even through much of the nineteenth century, by which time physics was a well-defined separate profession, you could routinely replace the term "philosophy" with "philosophy and psychology" without loss of precision.

About a decade after Hegel's *Lectures* appeared, and about the same time that George Henry Lewes was publishing his immensely popular *Biographical History of Philosophy*, Charles Dickens was publishing his novel *Martin Chuzzlewit* and taking gleeful notice of the ways of self-improving Americans:

> "What course of lectures are you attending now, ma'am?" said Martin's friend, turning again to Mrs. Brick.
> "The Philosophy of the Soul, on Wednesdays."
> "On Mondays?"
> "The Philosophy of Crime."
> "On Fridays?"
> "The Philosophy of Vegetables."[14]

The novelist knew that the term "philosophy" breathed uplift, whatever its purview (which he only slightly exaggerated). The historical ambit of the noun, plainly, is no more a guide to its current disciplinary contours than the Macedonian empire is to the present-day republic of Macedonia. You would have had a difficult time explaining to most of the canonical philosophers that *this* part of their work was *echt* philosophy and *that* part of their work was not. Trying to separate out the "metaphysical" from the "psychological" elements in this corpus is like trying to peel a raspberry.

Psychologism and Anti-Psychologism

Did psychology calve off from philosophy? You can make a strong case that it was the other way around. Hobbes, Locke, and Hume spent a great deal of energy elaborating an account of associationist psychology, in order to explain how faculties of the human mind processed sensations and ideas; for John Stuart Mill, logic was "not a Science distinct from, and co-ordinate with, Psychology. So far as it is a science at all, it is a part, or branch, of Psychology."[15] It was as a professor of philosophy at the University of Leipzig that Wilhelm Wundt established the first institute for experimental psychology, in 1879. (He aimed in part to prove Kantian ideas, and disprove Kantian skepticism about the methods by which he did so.) And the psychology labs at Harvard are in William James Hall because its inhabitants rightly think of James (who migrated from Harvard's Physiology Department to its Philosophy Department in 1881) as one of their ancestors, just as we contemporary philosophers claim him for ourselves. His colleague Josiah Royce was elected president of the American Psychological Association in 1902, and president of the American Philosophical Association in 1903. The common lineage is visible in the history of our professional journals too. The quarterly *Mind* has long been considered a premier journal of philosophy, and is one of the oldest; but when it was founded, in 1878, and for a couple of decades afterward, it just as often published articles we would now consider to be psychology. Even in the years following the rise of experimental psychology, a habit of intimacy was presumed. The *Journal of Philosophy* was founded, in 1904, as the *Journal of Philosophy, Psychology, and Scientific Methods*. This was, it might be worth underlining, little more than a century ago.

It's significant, then, that the two great founding figures of twentieth-century philosophy, Edmund Husserl and Gottlob Frege, were marked by their vehement *anti*-psychologism. (If you want to adjust the story for modern Continental philosophy, demote Frege and promote Heidegger.) In an often-repeated formula, a pupil of Wundt's, Theodor Lipps, had proposed that logic was "nothing if not the physics of thought"—and that was the grievous error that subsequent generations of theorists sought to stamp out. For Frege, even "the thought," *der Gedanke*, wasn't a mental event, but an abstract object. To have thoughts without thinkers: it's hard to get more anti-psychological than that! Philosophy was struggling to define itself, crucially, by contrast with psychology.[16] That took time. Experimentalists and pure speculators coexisted in Harvard's Philosophy Department until the mid-1930s, and, give or take a few years, you find a similar pattern at other universities. I was educated at Cambridge University, where the degree in philosophy had not long before been called the Moral Sciences Tripos, and experimental psychology was still one of the fields in which you could choose to be examined for that degree. To see when entities that we'd recognize as philosophy departments came into existence, look to see when psychology departments came into existence.

Much the same point could be made, of course, about the

distinction between economics and moral philosophy. Adam Smith, whom many economists regard as among the founding fathers of their discipline, is also one of the major moral theorists of the Scottish Enlightenment. Everybody knows this. But John Stuart Mill, who was the greatest of the British moral philosophers of the nineteenth century (with the possible exception of Henry Sidgwick), was also the author of a foundational work in classical economics, *The Principles of Political Economy*. Indeed, it can be argued that Mill was the first person to use the idea of "economic man," the rational wealth-maximizer—a central explanatory ideal type in almost all of what we now call economic theory. John Maynard Keynes, who revolutionized economics in the first half of the twentieth century, wrote *A Treatise on Probability*, which is one of the leading philosophical treatments of the concept. And his friend and contemporary Frank Ramsey, one of the most influential (if not one of the best known) philosophers of that century, invented the modern foundations of formal decision theory, which underlies almost all twentieth-century attempts at a unified and general mathematical account of human economic behavior. Ramsey, we philosophers say, was a philosopher: but the Ramsey Chair at Cambridge is quite plausibly occupied by the distinguished economist Sir Partha Dasgupta. Economists have developed increasingly sophisticated methods of taming the massive torrents of statistics generated in the modern world and discovering orderly patterns within them; and, more recently, they too have turned away from the a priori psychological theories of rational behavior in the market toward a more realistic understanding of the mind that draws on the work of modern experimental psychology. The dismal science has turned its attention to behavioral economics, even to neuroeconomics, as it continues to try to understand the patterns of human social life.

In bringing the empirical entanglements of canonical philosophers back into view, I am only doing what I said we always do. I am crafting a genealogy that supports a conception of the subject to which I am sympathetic. In deciding what story to tell of philosophy's past, those who were convinced of the importance of the distance between philosophy and the human sciences picked their way through the past accordingly: as I say, they have tended to skirt things like Aristotle's careful report of the dissection of an octopus, or Descartes' interest in optics and meteorology, or Hume's account of history as "so many collections of experiments," or Mill's vast accumulation of data in the development of his arguments about economic theory.[17] Experimental facts may illustrate philosophical truths, in this view, but they aren't usually evidence for them. When modern philosophers, whether analytic or Continental, need a story, what usually matters isn't whether it *is* true but whether it *could be* true. And the "could" here is a logical or metaphysical "could," not a psychological or historical one.

So what was this philosophy, disembarrassed of the experimentalists? *Qu'est-ce qu'un philosophe?* In the high heyday of analytic philosophy—the decades before and after the Second World War—the answer went like this. Philosophy is now what the best philosophy has always been: conceptual analysis. This is a matter of elucidating concepts or exploring meanings. But meanings are what speakers know in understanding a language, so any speaker of a language knows already, without looking beyond her own linguistic competence, what she needs to know to do the analysis. Philosophical claims—that knowledge is justified true belief, say—are true (*if* true) in virtue of the meanings of the words they contain. They are what Kant had dubbed "analytic" truths, where, as he put it, the predicate is "contained (though covertly)" within the concept of the subject. This way of doing philosophy presupposed a certain theory of meaning.

"Conceptual analysis" was the examination of important concepts, most of them familiar from the earlier history of philosophy, among them: knowledge, existence, truth, time, meaning, mind, and body, and, with perhaps slightly less urgency, such normative concepts as good, right, beauty, freedom, and justice. These concepts were explored in an essentially a priori way. You didn't do experiments or even usually attend very much to the details of the actual world. And if you did think about experiments, you thought not about how they turned out but about what you should *say* if they turned out one way or another. You considered, then, not how things are but how we think about them, more or less however they are; and the only access you really had to how we *think* was to notice some of the patterns in what we *say* (or don't say).

Though the "we" here was meant to be all those who had a native-speaker's grasp of the language, the actual conversations were naturally discussions among philosophers. W. H. Auden once wrote:

Oxbridge philosophers, to be cursory,
Are products of a middle-class nursery:

Their arguments are anent
What Nanny really meant.[18]

Now, Auden, like most poets, had a wonderful ear for other people's language; so what he had in mind, no doubt, was the *sound* of philosophers at Oxford, when he was Professor of Poetry there from 1956 to 1961. And, though comic verse does not aspire to be either accurate or fair, he had a point. "Suppose I did say 'the cat is on the mat' when it is not the case that I believe that the cat is on the mat, what should we say?" asked J. L. Austin, one of Auden's leading philosophical contemporaries in the Oxford of those years, in his William James Lectures, given at Harvard in 1955.[19] "What is to be said of the statement that 'John's children are all bald' if made when John has no children?" For Austin, "What is to be said?" was not an invitation to collect ethnographic data about how a given population of persons might make sense of these statements. It would have been a diversion because the answer was supposed to be obvious. What a person knows in knowing her language, in knowing English, say, is what everyone competent *should* say in a certain situation; and so, being competent myself, I know what everyone else *would* say if they were competent. That is why it wouldn't matter if we found individuals who *didn't* say it: it would just show that they weren't competent. In section 21 of the *Philosophical Investigations*—not in Oxford but over in Cambridge, the other branch of Auden's Oxbridge—Wittgenstein wrote: "We do in fact call 'Isn't the weather glorious to-day?' a question, although it is used as a statement." Until recently, philosophers in my tradition would have thought it impertinent to ask who the "we" is here, and pointless to go out and inquire of people in the street whether someone who said these words was really asking a question.

Philosophy, in the modern sense of the term, had finally gained an institutional aerie all to itself. Unfortunately for this happy consensus, however, by the early 1960s the theory of meaning on which it was based had been subjected to sustained assault by leading exponents of the analytic tradition itself; most influentially in the work of W. V. O. Quine, who persuaded many people that the idea of an analytic truth, the idea that a sentence could be true in virtue solely of the meanings of the words it contained, was mistaken. Belief in analyticity was, Quine argued, one of the "dogmas of empiricism"; epistemology, in his view, "simply falls into place as a chapter of psychology and hence of natural science."[20]

Anti-psychologism, which enabled philosophers to hive themselves off from other disciplines, is now just one position in philosophy among others. The Great Partition succeeded as an institutional project, but faltered as an intellectual one. The Oxford philosopher Michael Dummett has written that certain errors of Frege and Husserl "have left philosophy open to a renewed incursion from psychology, under the banner of 'cognitive science.' The strategies of defense employed by Husserl and Frege will no longer serve: the invaders can be repelled only by correcting the failings of the positive theories of those two pioneers."[21] Lower the portcullis! The bellicose rhetoric, albeit tongue-in-cheek, suggests a genuine measure of unease, but no such strategy for repelling the marauders has gained widespread acceptance. *Anti*-anti-psychologism is now perfectly mainstream. Indeed, philosophers of mind have, for decades, been working closely with their peers in psychology and psycholinguistics; there has been an effort to ground the philosophy of language, too, in naturalistic theories of the mind (an effort to which my first two books belong); and evolutionary models have become commonplace in areas of philosophical inquiry ranging from political theory to the theory of knowledge. Philosophy, after Quine, remains in the peculiar situation of having surrounded itself with a moat—only to have drained it of water.

Moral and Nonmoral

One might suppose that, at least when it comes to moral inquiry, philosophy should be impervious to the Cavalry of the Contingent. One reason for philosophical skepticism about the relevance of empirical moral psychology is a conviction, which is usually traced to Western intellectual traditions flowing from the Enlightenment, of the deep metaphysical and epistemological significance of a distinction between facts and norms. We remember Hume's remark that the step from "is" to "ought" is "of the last consequence,"[22] meaning "of the utmost importance."

Yet Hume himself never supposed that a disjunction between "is" and "ought" was a reason to recoil from evidence and experiment. "'Tis no astonishing reflection to consider, that the application of experimental philosophy to moral subjects should come after that to natural," Hume wrote in his *Treatise of Human Nature*. "For to me it seems evident, that the essence of the mind being equally unknown to us with that of external bodies, it must be equally impossible to form any notion of its powers and qualities otherwise than from careful and exact experiments, and the observation of those particular effects, which result from its different circumstances and situations."[23]

Now, many philosophers these days are inclined to think that moral judgments have the same objectivity and "truth-aptness" as nonmoral ones; to them, an "ought" is an "is," and the fallacy was to have supposed otherwise. For our purposes in this book, it won't much matter what position you take on this issue; so let me simply sidestep it for the moment. Even if you couldn't derive an "ought" from an "is," facts would still be relevant to moral life. Morality is practical. In the end it is about what to do and what to feel; how to respond to our own and the world's demands. And to apply norms, we must understand the empirical contexts in which we are applying them. No one denies that, in applying norms, you will need to know what, as an empirical matter, the effects of what you do will be on others. An opponent who denied that would be a straw man. But there are real opponents who deny that psychology can be relevant to the question of what values we ought to be guided by and what sorts of people we should aim to be. To such opponents, one can reasonably put such questions as these.

What would be the point of norms that human beings were psychologically incapable of obeying? After all, normative reflection suggests, in a philosopher's formula, that "ought" implies "can." (Which means: if you say somebody *ought* to do something, you must be supposing that it is something they *can* do.) And even if impossible norms had some sort of ideal force, how should we actual humans respond to them? If moral philosophy is to connect with moral life—if it is not to be, in the pejorative sense, "merely theoretical"—it must attend, in articulating and defending norms, to how they can come to bear in actual lives. When Hume set out, in his *Enquiry*, to make the ideas of his *Treatise* more widely available, he began by distinguishing two sorts of moral philosopher. One sort, he said, makes "us *feel* the difference between vice and virtue; they excite and regulate our sentiments"; and, he goes on, so long as "they can but bend our hearts to the love of probity and true honour, they think, that they have fully attained the end of all their labours." The others "regard human nature as a subject of speculation; and with a narrow scrutiny examine it, in order to find those principles, which regulate our understanding, excite our sentiments, and make us approve or blame any particular object, action, or behaviour."[24] But it is hard to see how we can pursue the first project (of moral exhortation and reform) if what we learn in the second (speculative) project suggests that our recommendations are hopelessly unrealistic. At the very least, then, we would owe the psychologists a hearing in our moral lives, even if there were a kind of speculative philosophy that could ignore them. As Hume once wrote in a letter: "I found that the moral philosophy transmitted to us by Antiquity, laboured under the same inconvenience that has been found in their natural philosophy, of being entirely hypothetical, and depending upon more invention than experience. Every one consulted his fancy in erecting schemes of virtue and of happiness, without regarding human nature, upon which every moral conclusion must depend."[25]

This complaint is more fairly made against the moral philosophy of the late twentieth century than it was against Aristotle. (Aristotle, after all, had read his Herodotus, and knew, like Dionysius, a later son of Halicarnassus, that history is philosophy taken from examples.) If we are, in Aristotle's founding formula, to consider "what the good life is and how to get it," what we are cannot be irrelevant to what we should be.

In the past half-century, moreover, we have been treated to no shortage of arguments for how factual-sounding propositions might yield normative- or evaluative-sounding propositions (as well as arguments against those arguments). Alasdair MacIntyre, in a paper from the late 1950s, argued that Hume himself, in his account of justice, derives an "ought" from an "is." Hume's position, in MacIntyre's rendering, is: "We ought to obey the rules [of justice], because there is no one who doesn't gain more than he loses by such obedience." And the claim that we ought to do what's in everyone's long-term interest isn't an evaluation, but a definition, a necessary truth that underlies morality. In this account, the reason Hume wanted us to be alert when moving from "is" to "ought" was that we should be on guard against the insinuations of religious morality, a foundation he sought to replace with one based on human flourishing.[26]

Other arguments draw on the ways in which our language works—the rules and institutions that undergird the terms we use. Philippa Foot, also in the late fifties, noted that "rude"—an evaluative term, expressive of disapproval—was correctly used of behavior that "causes offense by indicating lack of respect." Assuming that you're willing to discuss the issue of rudeness, then, accepting the (nonevaluative) proposition that those conditions were met requires that you accept the (evaluative) proposition that the behavior was rude. "Anyone who uses moral terms at all, whether to assert or deny a moral proposition, must abide by the rules for their use, including the rules about what shall count as evidence for or against the moral judgment concerned," she concluded.[27] A few years later, John Searle offered another argument enlisting the ways that norms and institutions were built into our language. If Jones tells Smith, "I promise to pay you five dollars," he has (ceteris paribus) taken on the obligation to do so, and the conclusion follows, fairly swiftly, that Jones *ought* to do so.[28] In a later chapter, I'll return to the significance of the fact that moral language is, indeed, language—something public, social, and open for inspection.

But now let me toss up another argument—one whose form I have an idea I learned in college long ago. Its conclusion is that you *must* be able to derive a moral claim from a nonmoral one, at least if you grant two plausible assumptions. This argument has the rhetorical virtue of being cast in exactly the abstract style of those defenders of a pure conceptual analysis whom it aims to convert.

Here are those two modest-looking assumptions. Assumption 1 is that *every claim is either moral or nonmoral.* Assumption 2 is that *if a claim is nonmoral, then its denial is nonmoral, too.* Once you grant these two assumptions and some very elementary logic, you can show that it must be possible to derive a moral claim from nonmoral ones. Here's how.

Take a moral claim, "John is a good man"; and a nonmoral claim, "Mary hates John." Imagine that Mary has announced that she hates people who aren't good and knows a great deal about John. In those circumstances you might find yourself saying,

>   A: *Either John is a good man or Mary hates John.*

From Assumption 1, it follows that A must make either a moral or a nonmoral claim. Since this way of parceling things out isn't one that I have much sympathy with, I don't have an inkling which it will be. But fortunately, in philosophy, you can sometimes get the conclusion you want without settling a disputed question. Because sometimes you can show that the conclusion follows whichever way you settle the question. So let's explore the two options. (This is called "arguing by dilemma.")

Suppose, first, that A is nonmoral. Notice that by Assumption 2, if "Mary hates John" is nonmoral, so is "Mary doesn't hate John." That's plausible enough anyway. Now consider the following argument:

>   A: *Either John is a good man or Mary hates John.*
>   *Mary doesn't hate John.*
>   So: *John is a good man.*

This form of argument is valid by a very, very elementary principle of sentential deductive logic (namely, *disjunctive syllogism*). Since we're exploring the situation on the assumption that A is nonmoral, and "John is a good man" was stipulated, by contrast, to be moral, we have just deduced a moral claim from two nonmoral ones.

You might suspect this problem is the result of our having supposed that A is nonmoral. So, suppose, instead, that A is moral. Then we can derive a moral truth from a nonmoral one as well, and this is much quicker. Because, this time relying on an equally elementary logical principle (namely, *addition*),

> *Mary hates John.*
> *So: Either John is a good man or Mary hates John.*

is a valid argument; and "Mary hates John" was, by stipulation, not moral.

I don't expect you to take this argument all that seriously. It has more than a whiff of sophistry about it. Notice, just to suggest one way to begin undermining its appeal, that it's not clear you could actually *get* to that moral conclusion by the first route, because to have reason to believe one premise, A, you'd probably have to have either good evidence that Mary hated John or good evidence that John was a good man. Now we can argue, as before, by dilemma.

Suppose you believed A because you had good evidence that Mary hates John; then, if you came to believe that she did not hate him, you'd lose your reason to believe A, and so you would no longer have the first premise to rely on. Now, suppose you believed it because you had good evidence that John was a good man. Then, in some obvious sense, your belief in the truth of A would be (let's say) "grounded" in a moral claim. And this suggests that you can't tell whether a sentence makes a moral claim simply by looking at the sentence itself. Whether we want to say that it makes a moral claim or not may depend on your grounds for believing it.

So, as I say, I don't urge you to take this argument very seriously—though, as with many apparent sophisms, we may learn a fair amount by disentangling it. What it does suggest, at the very least, is that it isn't entirely clear what we mean when we say that you can't derive a moral claim from nonmoral ones. And until we *understand* the claim, I think we are justified in not allowing anyone to rely on it too heavily.

The Psychology of Virtue

Writing in 1961, when the Great Partition was little more than a couple of decades old, Richard Wollheim ventured, "It is a very marked feature of the moral philosophy of the recent past that it has sedulously separated questions of philosophy from questions of psychology. This has been a very important thing to do, and has resulted in the careful distinction of differences traditionally obscured. But now that the differences have been firmly noted, it may well be the task of the moral philosophy of the immediate future no longer to hold apart the two aspects of human nature so distinguished. Moral philosophy, in other words, may revert from the tradition of Kant to that of Aristotle and Hume."[29]

The tradition Wollheim was invoking has come to be revived under the rubric "virtue ethics," and his call echoed one of the most influential papers in postwar Anglophone ethics, Elizabeth Anscombe's "Modern Moral Philosophy," which some have suggested was largely responsible for the resurgence of this approach. Anscombe argued that "it is not profitable for us at present"—the date was 1958—"to do moral philosophy; that should be laid aside at any rate until we have an adequate philosophy of psychology, in which we are conspicuously lacking." She went on to make a series of apparently devastating attacks on moral philosophers "from Butler to Mill." Of Joseph Butler (1692–1752), the English divine who taught that conscience was the leading faculty of the human mind, she wrote: he "appears ignorant that a man's conscience may tell him to do the vilest things." About Kant (1724–1804), she complained that he "introduces the idea of 'legislating for oneself,' which is as absurd as if in these days, when majority votes command great respect, one were to call each reflective decision a man made a *vote* resulting in a majority, which as a matter of proportion is overwhelming, because it is always 1–0." The rule utilitarianism of John Stuart Mill (1806–1873) was "stupid, because it is not at all clear how an action *can* fall under just one principle of utility." Henry Sidgwick (1838–1900), that great Victorian sage, was "rather dull" and even "vulgar." And, in general, Anscombe's own contemporaries were lost in the shadows cast by what she called a "*law* conception of ethics," which explains what it is right to do by appeal to a divine law. (You should not think that this diagnosis reflected any hostility to theism on Anscombe's part: she was an active and devout Roman Catholic.) Modern moral philosophers spoke of a special moral sense of the word "ought," but they had forgotten that the identification of this special sense presupposed the law conception. Anscombe wrote:

> It is as if the notion "criminal" were to remain when criminal law and criminal courts had been abolished and forgotten. A Hume discovering this situation might conclude that there was a special sentiment, expressed by "criminal,"

which alone gave the word sense. So Hume discovered the situation in which the notion "obligation" survived, and the word "ought" was invested with that peculiar force having which it is said to be used in a "moral" sense, but in which the belief in divine law had long since been abandoned.[30]

In the course of this slashing indictment, Anscombe threw out the suggestion that, rather than pursuing ethics in the way that had led to these various intellectual disasters, we should instead get back to basics, investigating, first, such notions as "'action,' 'intention,' 'pleasure,' 'wanting.'" Anscombe was here preaching what she had already practiced: the previous year, she had published her own book *Intention*, which Donald Davidson described (on the cover) as "the most important treatment" its subject had received since Aristotle. (A plausible commendation, if you set aside Saint Thomas Aquinas.) "Eventually," Anscombe wrote in her sketch of a possible future, "it might be possible to advance to considering the concept of a virtue; with which, I suppose, we should be beginning some sort of study of ethics."[31]

In the course of the essay, Anscombe made various approving noises about Aristotle—though even he did not escape tongue-lashing: she observed, early on, that the concept of pleasure was a "difficult" concept that had "reduced Aristotle to sheer babble about 'the bloom on the cheek of youth.'"[32] In the years that followed, both Anscombe's enthusiasm for Aristotle and her recommendation that we could return to moral philosophy by way of a psychology of virtue were taken up by a new generation of philosophers. (We can be grateful, perhaps, that they did not all share her caustic turn of phrase.) The enthusiasm of the new moral philosophy was for a psychology conceived, as Anscombe had suggested, in terms of an exploration of the *concept* of virtue; virtue, in the spirit of those times, was to be scrutinized by conceptual analysis. Nearly half a century later, there are now many explorations of such virtues as honesty, courage, and compassion. These are thought of as psychological dispositions. And, in recent years, such character-based theories have invited empirical scrutiny. They seem to incorporate—or at least to presuppose—psychological claims. Are those claims true?

In Chapter 2, I'll take the new virtue ethics as an opening case study in our post-post-psychological philosophy. Having abandoned the dogmas of empiricism, Quine had said, we would see "a blurring of the supposed boundary between speculative metaphysics and natural science." In a later paper, "Epistemology Naturalized," Quine went on to propose that the theory of knowledge abandon its normative aspirations and become "contained in natural science," even as he acknowledged that there would be a "reciprocal containment, though containment in different senses: epistemology in natural science and natural science in epistemology."[33] The prospects—indeed, the meaning—of what Quine had in mind continue to be debated; but it has become abundantly clear that moral philosophy, in which normativity is a central concern, has not been exempt from such reciprocal containments. The Great Partition granted the pure analyst a reprieve—but only a temporary one.

And so my project in these pages is, in part, to engage those who are working today to bring economics, psychology and philosophy back together—who seek, in a sense, to reconstitute the "moral sciences." Over the past couple of decades, growing numbers of philosophers have not confined themselves to "what Nanny really meant." Many seek to learn what Nanny, or a given population of nannies, would actually *say*, under specified conditions. Others, as we'll see, are busy stuffing nannies into MRI machines in order to study patterns of neural activation while the nannies contemplate various moral conundrums. These research methods—for which the centuries-old designation "experimental philosophy" has been revived—can sometimes seem rather remote from our accustomed habits, as if they're an attempt to return the philosopher's stone to philosophy.[34]

The "new philosophy calls all in doubt," John Donne wrote of the post-Galilean era; and the newer philosophy, too, generates questions more readily than answers. What happens when moral theory is called before the tribunal of psychology—when fact interrogates value? Will the blurring of boundaries advance the aims of ethics or lead to its eclipse? There are many such questions, but they funnel into one. Can moral philosophy be naturalized?

2

The Case against Character

Les circonstances sont bien peu de chose, le caractère est
tout; c'est en vain qu'on brise avec les objets et les êtres
extérieurs; on ne saurait briser avec soi-même.

(Circumstances don't amount to much, character is everything; there's no point breaking with exterior objects and
things; you cannot break with yourself.)

—Benjamin Constant, *Adolphe*

The Virtue Revival

Lydia Davis, the fiction writer, once published a short story
entitled, significantly, "Trying to Learn"—and if you know her
work, you won't be surprised to learn that it's a *very* short story
indeed. Here's how it goes, in its entirety:

I am trying to learn that this playful man who teases me is
the same as that serious man talking money to me so seriously he does not even see me anymore and that patient
man offering me advice in times of trouble and that angry

man slamming the door as he leaves the house. I have often wanted the playful man to be more serious, and the serious man to be less serious, and the patient man to be more playful. As for the angry man, he is a stranger to me and I do not feel it is wrong to hate him. Now I am learning that if I say bitter words to the angry man as he leaves the house, I am at the same time wounding the others, the ones I do not want to wound, the playful man teasing, the serious man talking money, and the patient man offering advice. Yet I look at the patient man, for instance, whom I would want above all to protect from such bitter words as mine, and though I tell myself he is the same man as the others, I can only believe I said those words, not to him, but to another, my enemy, who deserved all my anger.[1]

That's the story. It's also the story, more or less, of a growing body of research in the social sciences: we have met that man, many social scientists say, and he is us. In this chapter, then, I'd like to focus on the seeming clash between two different pictures of character and conduct: the picture that seems to underlie much virtue ethics, on the one hand, and the picture that has emerged from work in experimental psychology, on the other.

What does the first picture look like? The power core of virtue ethics is the idea of the virtuous person. A virtuous act is one that a virtuous person would do, done for the reasons a virtuous person would do it. Character is primary; virtues are more than simple dispositions to do the right thing. Those who draw on Aristotle's ideas are likely to stress, with Rosalind

Hursthouse, author of a recent book entitled *On Virtue Ethics,* that the dispositions in question are deep, stable, and enmeshed in yet other traits and dispositions. The character trait of honesty, for instance, is "a disposition which is well entrenched in its possessor, something that, as we say, 'goes all the way down,'" and "far from being a single track disposition to do honest actions, or even honest actions for certain reasons, it is multi-track." For the disposition "is concerned with many other actions as well, with emotions and emotional reactions, choices, values, desires, perceptions, attitudes, interests, expectations and sensibilities. To possess a virtue is to be a certain sort of person with a certain complex mindset."[2]

How complex? Well, Hursthouse explains, an honest person "chooses, where possible, to work with honest people, to have honest friends, to bring up her children to be honest. She disapproves of, dislikes, deplores dishonesty, is not amused by certain tales of chicanery, despises or pities those who succeed by dishonest means rather than thinking they have been clever, is unsurprised or pleased (as appropriate) when honesty triumphs, is shocked or distressed when those near and dear to her do what is dishonest and so on."[3]

Virtue ethicists also claim that having a virtue, which is something that comes by degrees, contributes to making one's life a good one—to what Aristotle called *eudaimonia,* or flourishing. A life that exhibits the virtues is for that very reason a better life: not because the acts of the virtuous have good consequences (though they may); not because they lead to satisfaction or give pleasure to the agent (though, for Aristotle at least, learning to take pleasure in what is virtuous is one component of moral development). Virtues are intrinsically worth having. Being virtuous is part, at least, of what makes a life worthwhile.

Corresponding to the virtues, as their antitheses, are the vices. They are to be shunned, just as the virtues are to be developed. And their presence in a life makes that life correspondingly less worthwhile. Vices, too, are seen as multi-track, deeper than mere habits. They are certainly multifarious; more so, it seems, than the virtues. Hursthouse, our stalking horse, offers a list of dispositions to avoid; we should not be "irresponsible, feckless, lazy, inconsiderate, uncooperative, harsh, intolerant, selfish, mercenary, indiscreet, tactless, arrogant, unsympathetic, cold, incautious, unenterprising, pusillanimous, feeble, presumptuous, rude, hypocritical, self-indulgent, materialistic, grasping, short-sighted, vindictive, calculating, ungrateful, grudging, brutal, profligate, disloyal, and on and on."[4]

Virtue ethics, to be sure, comes in a Baskin-Robbins array of flavors; I take Hursthouse's avowedly neo-Aristotelian account to be representative, because it succeeds in capturing elements that are shared by many of the doctrinal variants in circulation: the basic cream, sugar, and eggs, so to speak. The core of the basic theory, as she formulates it, lies in three claims.

1. The right thing to do is what a virtuous agent would do in the circumstances.
2. A virtuous person is one who has and exercises the virtues.
3. A virtue is a character trait that a person needs in order to have *eudaimonia*—that is, in order to live a good life.

The task of ethics, then, will be to discover what traits of character we need to live well.

This will be as convenient a place as any to announce a terminological convention. Here and elsewhere, I'll generally follow Aristotle in using "ethics" to refer to questions about human flourishing, about what it means for a life to be well lived. I'll use "morality" to designate something narrower, the constraints that govern how we should and should not treat other people. Terminological stipulations of this sort are useful only if they allow us to track distinctions that matter. There are crucial issues that come into view only if we keep in mind the distinction between two general questions, "What is it for a life to go well?" and "What do we owe to other people?" Using the words "ethics" and "morality" in this way will help illuminate the connections between the answers to these two questions. So in making this distinction I wish emphatically to avoid the impression that I think these questions are unconnected.

This may seem obvious enough in virtue ethics, where the rightness of actions is conceptually dependent upon the goodness of lives; and where the goodness of one's life consists, at least in part, in having certain complex traits of character. Its modern practitioners urge us to determine, first, what we must be like to live well (for someone like that is virtuous), and then decide what to do on any particular occasion by deciding what a virtuous person would do. Aristotle wrote that, while everyone agrees that *eudaimonia* is the "highest of all the goods," there is no such agreement as to what it requires; the "popular account of it is not the same as that given by the philosophers."[5] Virtue ethics aims at the wisest answer to the question of what *eudai-monia* requires. Its first answer is: the development of a virtuous character.

Wrongful Attributions

Anscombe, recall, wanted us to become better acquainted with psychology before resuming our moral philosophizing. What sort of psychological findings might prove relevant to the virtue ethics she helped resurrect? The underpinning conception of character shared by most virtue ethicists, including Aristotle, is what the philosopher John Doris calls "globalist," which is to say, it involves consistent dispositions to respond across contexts under the guidance of a certain value;[6] and many philosophers have also held some version of Aristotle's thesis of the unity of the virtues, according to which you fully possess one virtue only if you have them all. But just as modern moral philosophers were rediscovering the virtues, social psychologists were uncovering evidence that most actual people (including people ordinarily thought to be, say, honest) don't exhibit virtues of this sort. The reason wasn't the one that most moralists would have suspected: that vice far exceeds virtue. The reason was that most people simply didn't display such multi-track, context-independent dispositions at all, let alone in a unified ensemble.

It's not so surprising to find the unity-of-virtues thesis, in its stronger forms, called into question. Oskar Schindler—as portrayed in the film *Schindler's List*—is mercenary, arrogant, hypocritical, and calculating; but he is also courageous and compassionate. How many of Jane Austen's young women are kind but a little bit vain, too? We all know that such traits aren't served up in a fixed combination like a characterological Happy Meal. (Indeed, a reader of ecclesiastical hagiography might conclude that the virtues of the saints are sometimes less spectacular than their vices.) At the same time, there are *some* reasons for thinking that the virtues would have to be integrated in a virtuous person: for compassion without courage, say, will too often leave you not doing the compassionate thing. So there may be, at least in this straightforward way, something to be said for Aristotle's view. (As there usually is for Aristotle's views.)

No, the surprising challenge is to the core claim: that character, conceived of in terms of the virtues we ordinarily speak about, is consistent. Yet that is exactly what many social psychologists today would deny. They find that character traits simply don't exhibit (in the current argot) cross-situational stability. These psychologists are not globalists but "situationists": they claim—this is a first stab at a definition—that a lot of what people do is best explained not by traits of character but by systematic human tendencies to respond to features of their situations that nobody previously thought to be crucial at all.[7] They think that someone who is, say, reliably honest in one kind of situation will often be reliably dishonest in another. They'd predict that Oskar Schindler was mercenary, arrogant, hypocritical, and calculating sometimes . . . but not always; and that his courage and compassion could be elicited in some contexts but not in others. The playful man, the serious man, the patient man, and the angry man: same fellow, different circumstances.

Now, to ascribe a virtue to someone is, among other things, to say that she tends to do what the virtue requires in contexts where it is appropriate.[8] An honest person, for example, will resist the temptations to dishonesty posed by situations where, say, a lie will bring advantage, or where failing to return a lost wallet will allow one to buy something one needs. Indeed, our natural inclination, faced with someone who does something helpful or kind—or, for that matter, something hostile or thoughtless—is to suppose that these acts flow from their character, where character is understood in the way that "globalism" suggests: as a trait that is consistent across situations and, therefore, insensitive to differences in the agent's environment, especially small ones. But situationists cite experiments suggesting that small—and morally irrelevant—changes in the situation will lead a person who acted honestly in one context to do what is dishonest in another.

This result has been known since the earliest days of modern personality psychology. In the late 1920s, the Yale psychologists Hugh Hartshorne and Mark May studied some ten thousand American schoolchildren, giving them opportunities to lie, cheat, and steal in various academic and athletic situations.[9] What they found is that deceit was, to a surprising extent, a function of situations. It didn't track at all with measurable personality traits or assessments of moral reasoning, and the data gave little support to cross-situational predictions; the child who wouldn't break the rules at home, even when it seemed nobody was looking, was no less likely to cheat on an exam at school. Knowing that a child cheated on a spelling test didn't even tell you whether he would cheat on a math test, let alone in a sporting event.

In the past thirty years or so, broader psychological evidence against globalism has been accumulating. Back in 1972, Alice M. Isen and Paula Levin found that when you dropped your papers outside a phone booth in a shopping mall, you were far more likely to be helped by people if they had just had the good fortune of finding a dime in the phone's coin-return slot. A year later, John Darley and Daniel Batson discovered that Princeton seminary students, even those who had just been reflecting on the Gospel account of the Good Samaritan, were much less likely to stop to help someone "slumped in a doorway, apparently in some sort of distress," if they'd been told that they were late for an appointment. In a 1975 study, people were much less likely to help someone who "accidentally" dropped a pile of papers when the ambient noise level was 85 decibels than when it was 65 decibels. More recently, Robert Baron and Jill Thomley showed that you were more likely to get change for a dollar outside a fragrant bakery shop than standing near a "neutral-smelling dry-goods store."[10]

Many of these effects are extremely powerful: huge differences in behavior flow from differences in circumstances that seem of little normative consequence. Putting the dime in the slot in that shopping-mall phone raised the proportion of those who helped pick up the papers from 1 out of 25 to 6 out of 7— that is, from almost no one to almost everyone. Seminarians in a hurry are one-sixth as likely to stop and act like a Good Samaritan.[11] Knowing what I've just told you, you should surely be a little less confident that "she's helpful" is a good explanation next time someone stops to assist you in picking up your papers (especially if you're outside a bakery!).[12]

But, the research also suggests, you will probably go on ascribing good characters to people who do good things and bad ones to those who do bad things, anyway. (Lydia Davis, recall, entitled her story *"Trying* to Learn"—not "I Have Learned.") Experimental research into what psychologists call "attribution theory" shows that people are inclined to suppose that what someone does reflects her underlying character even when you explain to them that she is just putting on a performance. In one classic study, which dates from 1967, subjects were asked to read essays that were either pro- or anti-Castro and decide whether their authors favored or opposed Fidel Castro's regime. People supposed that the writer was pro-Castro if the piece was pro-Castro (and anti-Castro if the essay was anti-Castro, too), even when they had been told both that the authors had been *instructed* to write pro or con, and that whether they were assigned to write for or against Castro was decided by flipping a coin. This tendency to ignore the role of context in determining behavior and to suppose that what people do is best explained by their traits rather than their circumstances is known, in the social-psychology literature, as Correspondence Bias (the supposed correspondence, here, is between conduct and character), or sometimes, more disparagingly, as the Fundamental Attribution Error.[13]

Nor do we go wrong only when we're explaining the actions of other people; our self-accounting is often untrustworthy. Remember those helpful people who picked up your papers after getting a free dime, or who made change outside the fragrant bakery. Who—buoyed by that dime, cheered by that fragrance—would explain what they themselves had just done by saying, "I helped him because I was feeling cheerful because I got a dime," or by thinking, "Hey, I did that mostly because I was in a terrific mood brought on by the wafting smell of croissants"? And, indeed, when experimenters asked people why they did what they did, they seldom mentioned these critical variables . . . just as you would have expected.

Now, one rationale for not mentioning these facts is that they don't seem relevant: ask people *why* they do something and they'll expect that you want not a causal explanation of what they did, but their *reason* for doing it—that is, what it was about the choice that made it seem a good thing to do. The fact that there's a splendid aroma of croissants in the air doesn't make offering change more reasonable; so it wouldn't do as an answer, especially if you're one of those philosophers who take moral theory to be centrally concerned with offering justifications for action. But, of course, you fail to mention it not because it seems like the wrong sort of answer; you fail to mention it because you have no idea that the aroma is having this effect on you. The researchers, faced with these data, may hypothesize that when you're cheerful, you're more inclined to do what you think is helpful; that is, the fact that offering change is helpful will strike you as a particularly strong reason for doing it when you're feeling particularly cheerful. But this is not something that the agent herself will notice in the ordinary course of things. So, even though she's doing what's helpful, and even though she might give that as her explanation—"He needed help," she might say—there remains another sense in which she doesn't understand why she's doing what she's doing.

And that, as we've seen, seems consistent with our broader explanatory habits—with the observation that much of what we say when we're explaining what we've done is confabulation: stories we've made up (though quite sincerely) for ourselves and in response to others. In short—to overstate the point only slightly—because people don't really know why they do what they do, they give explanations of their own behavior that are about as reliable as anyone else's, and in many circumstances actually less so.[14]

The Situationist Challenge

I am not, for the moment, going to worry about whether all these psychological claims are true or whether we can give an account of the results that better comports with our common sense about why people, ourselves included, do what they do. The question I want to ask is: Why should ethical theory care about these claims at all?

Suppose I give you change because (in part) I just got a whiff of my favorite perfume. Of course, if I had a settled policy of never giving change, even that pleasant aroma wouldn't help. So there are other things about me—the sorts of things we would normally assess morally—that are clearly relevant to what I have done. But let's suppose that, other things being equal, if I hadn't had the whiff, I'd have ignored your plaintive plea to stop and change your dollar for the parking meter.[15] I had, in these circumstances, an inclination to do what, according to the virtue theorist, a kind or helpful or thoughtful person—a virtuous person—would do; and I acted on that inclination. A typical virtue theorist will think I have done the right thing because it is the kind thing (and there are no countervailing moral demands on me). But, on the situationist account, I don't act out of the virtue of kindness, and therefore this act doesn't accrue to my ethical credit. Well now, do I deserve praise in this circumstance or not? Have I or haven't I made my life better by doing a good thing?

A situationist might well say that, as a prudential matter, we should, in fact, praise someone who does what is right or good—what a virtuous person would do—whether or not she did it out of a virtuous disposition. After all, psychological theory also suggests that praise, which is a form of reward, is likely to reinforce the behavior. (What behavior? Presumably not helpfulness, but being helpful when you're in a good mood.) For we tend to think that helping people in these circumstances, whatever the reason, is a good thing.[16] But the virtue ethicist cannot be content that one acts *as if* virtue ethics is true. And we can all agree that the more evidence there is that a person's conduct is responsive to a morally irrelevant feature of the situation, the less praiseworthy it is.

If these psychological claims are right, very often when we credit people with compassion, as a character trait, we're wrong. They're just in a good mood. And if hardly anyone is virtuous in the way that virtue ethics conceives of it, isn't the doctrine's appeal eroded?[17] Given that we are so sensitive to circumstances and so unaware of the fact, isn't it going to be wondrously difficult to develop compassion, say, as a character trait? We just can't keep track of all the cues and variables that may prove critical to our compassionate responses: the presence or absence of the smell of baking is surely just one among thousands of contextual factors that will have their way with us.

How, if this is so, can I make myself disposed to do or to feel the right thing? I have no voluntary control on how aromas affect me. I cannot be sure that I will have a free dime show up whenever it would be a fine thing to be helpful.

There are some philosophers—among them the afore-mentioned John Doris (author of *Lack of Character*) and, even more strenuously, my colleague Gilbert Harman—who take the social-science literature about character and conduct to pose a serious and perhaps lethal challenge to the virtue ethi-cist's worldview. Talk all you like about virtuous dispositions, the challenge goes: we're just not built that way. Owen Flana-gan, who has long worked at the crossroads of psychology and moral theory, once proposed this maxim: "Make sure when constructing a moral theory or projecting a moral ideal that the character, decision processing, and behavior described are pos-sible, or are perceived to be possible, for creatures like us."[18] Plainly, there are costs for those who fail to clear this hurdle.

For one thing, our virtue theorist faces an epistemological difficulty if there are no actually virtuous people. As in all spheres of thought, so in moral deliberation: we sometimes need to think not only about what the right answer is but also about how we discover what the right answers are. Hursthouse, remember, claims that:

1. The right thing to do is what a virtuous agent would do in the circumstances.
2. A virtuous person is one who has and exercises the virtues.

3. A virtue is a character trait that a person needs in order to have *eudaimonia,* in order to live a good life.

No interesting version of virtue ethics holds that doing the right thing is all that matters; we should want to be the kind of person who does the right thing for the right reasons. Still, Hursthouse and others insist that virtue ethics isn't *entirely* "agent-centered," rather than "act-centered"; it can also specify what the right thing to do is—namely, what a virtuous person would do. How are we to follow that advice? If we were fully virtuous, we would find ourselves disposed to think and act and feel the right things. But we are not. If we knew someone who was virtuous, we could see what she would do, I suppose. But, given the depressing situationist reality, maybe no actual human being really is (fully) virtuous. And even if a few people did get to be virtuous against all the odds, we would have to have some way of identifying them, before we could see what they would do. So we would need, first, to know what a good life looks like and then we would need, second, to be able to tell, presumably by reflecting on actual and imaginary cases, whether having a certain disposition is required for a life to be good; and required not in some instrumental way—as nourishment is required for any life at all—but intrinsically.

If experimental psychology shows that people cannot have the sorts of character traits that the virtue theorist has identified as required for *eudaimonia,* there are only two possibilities: she has identified the wrong character traits or we cannot have worthwhile lives. Virtue theory now faces a dilemma.

The problem for the idea that we have gotten the wrong virtues is a problem of method. For virtue theory of the sort inspired by Anscombe, we must discover what the virtues are by reflection on concepts. We can, in principle, reflect on which of the stable dispositions that psychology suggests might be possible—being helpful when we are in a good mood, say—are constitutive of a worthwhile life; or which—being unhelpful when we aren't buoyed up by pleasant aromas—detract from a life's value. But to concede *that* is to accept that we'll need to do the experimental moral psychology before we can ask the right normative questions. On this horn of the dilemma, virtue theory will find itself required to take up with the very empirical psychology it so often disdains.

On the other horn of the dilemma, the prospect that we cannot have worthwhile lives makes normative ethics motivationally irrelevant. What is the point of *doing* what a virtuous person would do if I can't *be* virtuous? Once more, whether I can be virtuous is obviously an empirical question. Once more, then, psychology seems clearly apropos.

Still, we should not overstate the threat that situationism poses. The situationist account doesn't, for example, undermine the claim that it would be better if we *were* compassionate people, with a persistent, multi-track disposition to acts of kindness. Philosophical accounts of the character ideal of compassion, the conception of it as a virtue, need make no special assumptions about how easy or widespread this deep disposition is. Acquiring virtue, Aristotle already knew, is hard; it is something that takes many years, and most people don't make it. These experiments might confirm the suspicion that compassionate men and women are rare, in part because becoming compassionate is difficult. But difficult is not the same as impossible; and perhaps we can ascend the gradient of these virtues only through aspiring to the full-fledged ideal. Nor would the ideal be defeated by a situationist who busily set about showing that people whom we take to exemplify compassion—the Buddha, Christ, Mother Teresa—were creatures of environments that were particularly rich in the conditions that (according to situationists) elicit kindly acts.[19]

Finally, we could easily imagine a person who, on the virtue ethicists' view, was in some measure compassionate, and who actually welcomed the psychologists' research. Reading about these experiments will only remind her that she will often be tempted to avoid doing what she ought to do. So these results may help her realize the virtue of compassion. Each time she sees someone who needs help when she's hurrying to a meeting, she'll remember those Princeton seminarians and tell herself that, after all, she's not in *that* much of a hurry—that the others can wait. The research, for her, provides a sort of perceptual correction akin to the legend you see burned onto your car's rear-view mirror: *objects may be closer than they appear.* Thanks for the tip, she says. To think that these psychological claims by themselves undermine the normative idea that compassion is a virtue is just a mistake.

We might also notice what the situationist research *doesn't* show. It doesn't tell us anything about those seminarians (a healthy 10 percent) who were helpful even when rushing to an appointment; perhaps that subpopulation really did have a stable tendency to be helpful—or, for all we know, to be heedless of the time and careless about appointments. (Nor can we yet say how the seminarians would have compared with, say, members of the local Ayn Rand Society.) There could, consistent with the evidence, be a sprinkling of saints among us. Some will dispute whether the dispositions interrogated by social psychology can be identified with the normative conception of character traits elaborated by the classical virtue theorists.[20] And, of course, the situationist hypothesis is only that, in explaining behavior, we're inclined to overestimate disposition and underestimate situation. It doesn't claim that dispositions don't exist; it hardly could, since one stable disposition it reports is the tendency to commit the Fundamental Attribution Error.

None of these caveats wholly blunts the situationist point that the virtues, as the virtue ethicists conceive them, seem exceedingly hard to develop—a circumstance that must leave most of us bereft of *eudaimonia*. But virtue ethics is hardly alone in assigning a role to elusive ideals. Our models of rationality are also shot through with such norms. In the previous chapter, I mentioned the nineteenth-century hope that, as one formula had it, logic might be reduced to a "physics of thought." What succeeded that project was an approach captured in another formula, according to which logic is, in effect, an "ethics of thought."[21] It tells us not how we do reason but how we ought to reason. And it points toward one way of responding to the question we have posed to the virtue ethicist: How might we human beings take seriously an ideal that human beings must fall so far short of attaining?

Model Heuristics

We can draw inspiration, that is, from the sphere of deductive and inductive reasoning, where we also have ideals we fall far short of attaining, but where, by contrast, we understand (not perfectly but a great deal better) how to connect an unattainable ideal with actual practice. For example, in thinking about what consequences to draw from our beliefs, we can be guided by the idea that a good argument—in the sense of a good piece of reasoning—will take us from true beliefs to other true beliefs, or from probable beliefs to other beliefs that are probable. Formal logic and mathematical probability theory define standards here. But they are very difficult to conform to in practice. Someone whose reasoning conformed to the standards of formal logic would presumably never have inconsistent beliefs; would never, that is, have a set of beliefs that, taken together, entailed a contradiction. What could be more illogical, after all, than believing a set of things that cannot, as a matter of logical necessity, all be true? But to meet that standard, one would have to be able to see instantaneously (as philosophers have sometimes supposed God might do) all the logical consequences of any set of propositions; in effect, you would have to do all the necessary reasoning instantaneously and without error. You do not need the word of an experimental psychologist to suppose that that is a standard no one meets.

Now, in real life reasonable people will not hold most of their beliefs with the level of conviction that we call certainty. Most of us, most of the time, will allow that most of what we believe about the world could turn out to be wrong. So our actual reasoning is not from certainties to certainties but from the probable to the probable. Philosophers and economists have a way of measuring the strength of our beliefs. It's called "assigning subjective probabilities." Frank Ramsey showed how it could be done, and there are pretty convincing arguments that someone who understands the laws of logic should prefer to have subjective probabilities that conform to the mathematics of probability. If you have a subjective probability of .75 that it's raining, for example, you should have a subjective probability of .25 that it isn't raining, since the probability of a proposition and its negation ought to add up to 1.[22]

The same tradition has a way of measuring the strengths of our preferences: by assigning what are called "utilities" to descriptions of states of the world. And, once again, convincing arguments show that, for example, if you prefer state A to state B and state B to state C, you should prefer A to C, as well: preference, as we say, should be transitive. But, alas, actually keeping your preferences transitive is going to require reasoning abilities none of us has.

Philosophers call the rational pursuit of ends, given our knowledge of the available means, "means-end rationality." (Social scientists usually just call it plain "rationality.") This can be understood as requiring us, once we have rationally organized subjective probabilities and preferences, to pursue our ends by maximizing our expected utilities. We consider all the acts that we might undertake and multiply, for each act, the probability of all the possible mutually exclusive outcomes by their utilities, adding them up to get the expected utility of that act. Then we choose the act that has the highest expected util-

ity.[23] But now, to the practical impossibility of keeping our subjective probabilities and our preferences in order, we have
added the practical impossibility of doing the millions of calculations necessary to compute all the necessary expected utilities.

So how should we actually decide what follows from our
beliefs? How should we organize our preferences? Or decide
what to do? Well, if we can't pursue what pure reason, conceived in the way I have just sketched, requires, we might try
developing rules—for shaping our beliefs and their strengths
and organizing our preferences and making our decisions—
that have the following property: *given the way we are and the
way the world around us is, if we follow these rules, there is a good
chance that we will do or think or prefer what we would do or think
or prefer if we did have all the logical capacities in the world and all
the time we needed to exercise them.* We imperfect creatures
should follow rules that we can actually live by and that will
lead us to do as often as possible what someone who was rationally perfect would do.

A rule that has this property is nowadays called a "heuristic": it is, in a phrase of Gerd Gigerenzer, a German psychologist who is an enthusiast for such rules, a "fast and frugal" way
of getting an answer.[24] It needs to be fast, because we have
limited time, and it needs to be frugal—that is, relatively
undemanding on our capacities for getting and handling information—because we have limited cognitive capacities.

In assessing a heuristic, we need to bear at least four points
in mind.

First, we need to be clear what question the rule aims to answer. In the cases I was considering just now, these were: What

should I believe, given what I already believe? How should I organize my preferences? And: What should I do, given my beliefs and preferences?

Second, we need a standard—which might be given by probability theory and deductive logic and the theory of rational choice—by which we can identify, from a theoretical perspective, what the right answer is. In this case, the strengths of your beliefs should conform to the laws of probability; if Q follows logically from P, then you should believe Q if you believe P; you should maximize expected utility.

Third, in real cases we won't have the time or the capacity to apply this standard. And so we need to think both about what our actual capacities are and about what the contexts in which we'll apply the heuristic are like, because that will determine what counts as frugal. Suppose, for example, that you live in a region where both purple and nonpurple mushrooms are plentiful. Almost all poisonous mushrooms in your region are purple; and those few poisonous mushrooms that are not purple are only mildly poisonous. If the task is to decide which mushrooms to eat, and the standard is that you shouldn't get poisoned, here's an attractive heuristic:

Check if it's purple. If it isn't, eat it.

Notice that the frugality of this rule depends on what you are like, as well as on what the world is like: if you're color blind and you can't distinguish purple from brown, it's not a frugal heuristic at all. (Applying this rule also requires a tiny bit of elementary reasoning—enough to get, by the principle of *modus ponens*, from "It's not purple" to "Eat it.")

Fourth, a good heuristic not only must guide you right much of the time, but also, when it does go wrong, must not go wrong too disastrously. In choosing heuristics, you'll have to decide what risks you're willing to take to get an answer to the question you set yourself. And that's going to depend, in part, on how important it is to you to answer the question.

Even when these conditions are all met, there are likely to be many heuristics that one could consider. Perhaps—to expand upon my mushroom scenario—all the poisonous non-purple mushrooms in your area also have green spots. Adding an extra level to the rule:

> *Check if it's purple. If it isn't, check if it has green spots. If it doesn't, eat it.*

might be worthwhile, because it increases accuracy—defined by your rate of avoiding poisonous mushrooms—while only slightly decreasing speed and only slightly increasing the resources you need to mobilize. (Two color assessments, not one; an extra step of reasoning.)

So, to look for a heuristic, we need a task, a standard, and an understanding of our environment and our own resources; and we then need to ask, about each rule we consider, whether we are capable of applying it in the time available for the task, how often it will lead us astray, what the costs are of being wrong, and how important it is to get the answer right. Given these answers, we must then decide which heuristic best meets our needs: perhaps by maximizing the expected benefits of its application.

Moral Heuristics

We can now return to the problem posed for virtue theory by the allegation that its idealizations are remote from our human capacities. Let's try out the obvious solution suggested by the model I just discussed. If we're not capable of being virtuous—of reliably doing the right thing for the right reason—can we, *faute de mieux,* adopt "moral heuristics" that will help steer us right?[25] To do so, as we saw, we will need to identify a task, a standard, an assessment of our own resources and circumstances, and so on.

Well, in the domain of ethics, as Aristotle defined it, the task is, very broadly, to decide how to live our lives; but when virtue theorists apply themselves to moral issues, the task seems—a tad less broadly—to figure out what to do in the circumstances we face. As for our standard, let's stipulate (for the moment) that, as our virtue ethicists say, the right thing to do is what a virtuous person would do.[26] We're supposing that our capacities don't include globalist virtues and that it's very difficult to develop them. But we have many capacities—sensitivity to human suffering, a raft of emotions, such as empathy and sympathy, and feelings of compassion—that could be enlisted toward making us live lives more like the lives we would lead if we *could* develop the full-fledged virtue of compassion. Furthermore, there are many features of our environment that we might mobilize to help us in this way. The virtuous person tells the truth, doesn't steal, keeps promises. People around us are disposed to respond to those who disobey such moral norms with resentment and criticism; we ourselves are disposed to respond to their assessments with embarrassment and shame. We are equipped with a psychology apt for friendship and with the desire to be well thought of by our friends. These facts about us and about our environment, banal and familiar as they are, seem to be exactly the sorts of things that might guide us in constructing rules for proceeding, even if we cannot do what the virtuous person would do simply by making ourselves virtuous.

I have no idea how to organize all the psychological knowledge in the world (let alone all the anthropological and sociological information as well), in order to pick rules of life for us imperfect creatures that will maximize the likelihood of our doing what a perfectly virtuous person would do. But perhaps I don't need to. Perhaps our evolutionary histories have already "designed" some heuristics for us; perhaps, that is, our judgments are already guided by implicit moral heuristics. And indeed, there are naturalistic, if conjectural, accounts of what such moral heuristics might look like—notably, one sketched by the legal scholar and political theorist Cass Sunstein. As in much of the literature on cognitive heuristics, his focus is on how moral heuristics may lead us astray. He notices, for example, that people are so averse to being injured from products designed to increase safety that they'll disable an airbag even when doing so doubles their chance of dying in a crash. Here, the underlying heuristic might be: *avoid betrayals of trust*. Usually, it steers you right; here, it steers you wrong. That's the way with heuristics. For remember, the idea of a heuristic is to pick a way of deciding what to think or feel or do that we imperfect creatures can actually use—a way that tracks imperfectly, if usually well enough, what one really ought to think or feel or do.

As a law professor, Sunstein has long been interested in how juries make their decisions, and another striking example comes from the literature on this topic. Every car, we know, could be made safer: every car assembled represents a trade-off of safety against other factors (production costs, mileage, and so on). Now suppose that a manufacturer actually goes to the trouble of commissioning a cost-benefit study, and decides against taking some precaution that would, it calculates, cost a hundred million dollars and save only four lives. Suppose that another manufacturer sells a car with a similar risk profile—but never bothers to make the calculation. There's reason to think that a jury will take a far dimmer view of the first company than of the second. That looks like a perverse outcome, but it might follow from a heuristic such as: *don't knowingly cause human death*.[27] To talk about moral heuristics is to acknowledge that our intuitions will sometimes lead us astray, sometimes even in seemingly extra-moral ways (as when, outraged by betrayals of trust, I disable my airbag).

Unlike cognitive heuristics, of course, moral ones don't let you simply do the math and compare outcomes. We can't sic a food inspector on the mushrooms of morality. That's why I began by positing that we'd take our standard from the virtue ethicist: do what is honest, don't do what is dishonest; do what is charitable, don't do what is uncharitable; and so forth. Embrace the virtues, shun the vices.

By now, though, you may be wondering whether the virtues aren't just moral heuristics dressed up as character traits: loyalty is a virtue, and "betrayal of trust"—disloyalty—looks like a corresponding vice. Perhaps the car company that did the risk analysis has triggered a heuristic that corresponds to Hurst-housean vices like "cold," "calculating," "brutal," and "grasping."

That's an avenue one might explore, except that it just defers a difficulty: you're left having to find some further standard that the heuristic was trying to approximate. One obvious possibility here is that the best act is one that maximizes the satisfaction of human desires, or some such goal—the utilitarian tradition. Another possibility is that virtues are valuable because they lead us to follow universalizable rules of conduct—the deontological tradition. But both traditions face a gantlet of objections, and the revival of virtue ethics, as we've seen, was meant to provide an alternative to them, not serve them as a handmaiden.[28] In short: if a virtue rule is a heuristic, it must be a fast and frugal way to follow, more or less, some other standard. If it isn't a heuristic, we need some other heuristics to guide us, since the standard it proposes is one we imperfect creatures cannot attain.

There is a deeper problem here. For faithful Aristotelians, this whole approach, in which we seek moral heuristics that will guide us imperfect creatures to do what a virtuous person would do, is bound to look very peculiar. Virtue ethics wants us to aim at *becoming* a good person, not just at maximizing the chance that we will do what a good person would do. The strategy for developing moral heuristics that I have explored is preempted by the very conception of virtue that our virtue ethicist endorses. By contrast, there's no gap between the possession of means-ends rationality and the pursuit of strategies designed to maximize rational outcomes. In this sense, rational is as rational does.

For cognitive heuristics are, so to speak, twice dipped in

means-end rationality. First, the right outcome is defined by what someone equipped with ideal means-end rationality, someone possessed of infinite cognitive resources, would do. Second, we then apply means-end rationality to determine how people with limited cognitive resources can maximize their chances of doing what's right according to the first test. When we try to concoct a heuristic of virtue, we must start, analogously, by defining the right outcome as what someone ideally virtuous would do. Since we're not ideally virtuous, the heuristics model now introduces means-end rationality to maximize our chance of doing what's right by the first test. The trouble is, of course, that virtue ethics requires that we aim at the good for reasons that aren't reducible to means-end rationality. With the cognitive heuristic, what matters is the outcome: but if virtue ethics tells you that the outcome isn't the only thing that matters, then you cannot assess heuristics by means-end rationality—by looking at the probability that they will produce certain outcomes.[29] Here, we might distinguish, as Christine Korsgaard does, between *actions* and mere *acts*, where an action is an act done for the sake of some end. A utilitarian could be concerned with the act alone, concerned that the agent does the right (utility-maximizing) thing, regardless of motivation; but for Aristotle and Kant—both of whom distinguished between acting in accordance with duty and acting from duty—the unit of moral concern is something more fully specified.[30]

To be sure, the fact that virtues are meant to be constitutive of a life of *eudaimonia*—so that they are traits necessary to make our lives worthwhile—is consistent with the view that a virtuous person's life will have good effects as well. Perhaps a life of virtue will be an enjoyable life: as I mentioned earlier, Aristotle certainly thought that a fully virtuous person would take pleasure in the exercise of virtue. But the value of the virtues doesn't come from the good results of virtuous acts or from the enjoyment that virtue produces. It is intrinsic, not instrumental. A virtuous life is good, because of what a virtuous person *is*, not just because of what she *does*.

We can distinguish, then, between *having a virtue* and *being disposed to do the virtuous act over a wide range of circumstances*. We can distinguish between, on the one hand, being an honest person, someone who has that virtue as the virtue ethicist conceives of it, and, on the other, being someone who, across a wide range of circumstances, behaves honestly. Suppose honesty matters in my life because it promotes reliability and thereby helps me support the flourishing of others. If that were so, I might explore some alternative possibilities by which I might refrain from deceiving others. Perhaps someone has developed a Bad Liar pill, which will impair my capacity for successful deception; or perhaps our town has collectively decided to add the drug to the water supply, as a moral counterpart to fluoridation. Equivalently, we could try to heighten our ability to detect deception. (This is just a thought experiment: I recognize that, under these circumstances, society would come unraveled as soon as one confronted a question like "What do you think of my tie?" or "Does this dress make me look fat?") Either strategy amounts to a similar trade-in: a scenario in which I strive to be honest in all situations is exchanged for a scenario in which I can usually be relied upon not to deceive others. Plainly, it is a mistake to deny the instrumental significance of honesty; but our moral common sense recoils at the idea that honesty matters only because of this instrumental significance. Denying that significance courts moral narcissism; but reducing honesty's importance to that instrumental significance threatens to replace the ethical subject with the object of social engineering. In all events, my aim is not to fine-tune the dictum that an action is right if it's what a virtuous person would do. Rather, my hope is to illustrate how alien that dictum is to what made the eudaimonist tradition appealing in the first place.

Sartor Resartus

There's an old story about a fellow who, having been measured for a suit by a singularly inept tailor, arrives to try on the custom-made garment. Though the customer is a man of regular proportions, the suit is a disaster. For one thing, the customer points out, the left sleeve is five inches longer than the right sleeve. The tailor dismisses the complaint: "Just stick out your left arm—*really* stretch it out, like you're reaching for a fly ball—and, you'll see, the sleeve will fit fine." But, the customer protests, what about the trousers? The cuff of the left leg is trailing on the ground. "Bend your left leg, and walk on your toes," the tailor coaches, "and that'll take up the slack." Yes, but the back of the jacket droops like a potato sack. "Not if you round your shoulders and hunch your spine," the tailor persists. Defeated, the customer shuffles out of the shop in his new suit, his body bizarrely contorted according to the tailor's instructions. A few minutes later, he's accosted in the street by a posh gentleman, who asks for the name of his tailor. "You want the name of *my* tailor?" the first man asks, incredulous. "Whatever for?" The other man coughs a little, sheepishly, before explaining: "Because anyone who can fit a man like you must be a wizard."

We disserve virtue ethics—you will have anticipated my point—when we twist and turn it so that it will measure up to the tasks performed by those traditions Anscombe caustically surveyed in "Modern Moral Philosophy." It was to defend the claim that virtue ethics is a "rival" to deontology and consequentialism that Hursthouse derived from it a decision procedure for right action. In her view, "such a specification can be regarded as generating a number of moral rules or principles. . . . Each virtue generates an instruction—'Do what is honest,' 'Do what is charitable'; and each vice a prohibition—'Do not act unjustly, do what is dishonest, uncharitable.'"[31] The trouble isn't that this is bad advice. The trouble is that virtue ethics became distorted when it was repurposed for the narrower conception of morality (that "peculiar institution," in Bernard Williams' mordant description) that is the subject of mainstream moral philosophy. Virtue ethics isn't best considered a rival to deontological or consequential approaches at all. What are our duties to others?—Kant's question, by convention—underlies the deontological approach. How should one live one's life?—Aristotle's question—underlies the eudaimonist approach. Once an account of excellence is reduced to a cluster of duties and a procedure for fulfilling them, once aretaic appraisal is reduced to deontic appraisal, virtue ethics rather loses its point. And its way.

I am not saying that the focus on character and motivation

in virtue ethics is always right. The goodness or badness of an act isn't really reducible to an assessment of the virtues or vices of the person who performs it. When you see someone kicking a dog in order to hurt it, Thomas Hurka has pointed out, you condemn this as a vicious act, whether or not you've determined it arises from a stable disposition to perform such acts. Likewise, it would be silly for a military review board to deny a soldier a medal for bravery on the grounds that the brave act was out of character.[32] Virtue ethics can be reprocessed in ways that eliminate the worries of empirical moral psychology, but only at the cost of what's valuable about it. Judith Jarvis Thomson, for example, has developed a version of virtue ethics that speaks solely in terms of virtuous acts—or the prohibition of vicious acts—and dispenses with character altogether: it's a morality of doing, not being. Though it would solve the problem I've been discussing, this is a proposal I'm inclined to resist.[33] It preserves what's perhaps least appealing about the character-based approach—the fusty indeterminacy of those lists of predicates—while jettisoning its distinctive contribution: the recognition that what we *are* matters for human flourishing as well as what we *do*.

Still, if virtue ethics grasps something important—that being and doing both matter to human life—it does not follow that we can use it to adjudicate those conflicts between persons that are one focus of moral life. The vocabulary of virtue ethics has sometimes called to mind what Kant, in the tradition of natural lawyers such as Hugo Grotius and Samuel von Pufendorf, referred to as "imperfect duties" (being praiseworthy rather than obligatory). But their company shows why we might not want to enlist virtue ethics as a yardstick for settling moral disagreements. Grotius' goal was to settle disputes, among sects, among merchants, and it's in this context, Jerome Schneewind has argued persuasively, that virtue talk shows its limitations: "Since virtue theory must treat disagreements with the virtuous agent as showing a flaw of character, it discourages parties to a moral dispute from according even prima facie respect to differing points of view." Rather than listening to your case, I shall be inspecting, and impugning, your character.[34] Yet too many virtue theorists have been ready to sacrifice an appealing ethical account for a not-so-appealing moral one. When you see a vision of human excellence limping out of the clothier's shop as a rather ill-shaped program of obligation, you might pause before lauding the tailor.

There's a historical reason, as well, to be suspicious of the claim that virtue ethics is straightforwardly a "rival" to deontology and consequentialism. While modern virtue theorists have often seen a convergence between Kant and Aristotle, and urged a joining of forces between Kantians and virtue ethicists, they scarcely mention the most important nineteenth-century theorist of virtue and character ethics, and never under that description.

I refer to someone whose concerns were far more Aristotelian than those of our neo-Aristotelians, someone deeply engaged by the subjects of *eudaimonia* and the cultivation of *arête* (rendered in his bywords "well-being" and "self-development"). I refer to someone who, in an era when a New Testament–derived conception of the virtues had eclipsed the Aristotelian one (the virtues of meekness and humility being remote from the ideal of *megalopsychia,* greatness of soul), railed against the notion that "whatever is not duty is sin" and the exaltation of a "pinched and hidebound type of human character." I refer, of course, to John Stuart Mill. For surely *On Liberty* is as much a meditation on virtue ethics—enshrined in the character ideal of individuality—as it is a political tract. Hence the insistence that individuality, which he took to resonate with "a Greek ideal of self-development," was an element of well-being, or *eudaimonia.* "There is," Mill urged, "a different type of human excellence from the Calvinistic; a conception of humanity as having its nature bestowed on it for other purposes than merely to be abnegated":

> "Pagan self-assertion" is one of the elements of human worth, as well as "Christian self-denial." There is a Greek ideal of self-development, which the Platonic and Christian ideal of self-government blends with, but does not supersede. It is not by wearing down into uniformity all that is individual in themselves, but by cultivating it and calling it forth, within the limits imposed by the rights and interests of others, that human beings become a noble and beautiful object of contemplation; and as the works partake the character of those who do them, by the same process human life also becomes rich, diversified, and animating.[35]

In this account of individuality, the cultivation of virtue or excellence isn't merely conducive to, it is a constituent of, *eudaimonia.* (That virtue ethicists such as Philippa Foot could accuse

Mill of neglecting *arête* when it was a central theme in his work is more evidence for the Renanian art of forgetting.) "It really is of importance," Mill insisted, "not only what men do, but also what manner of men they are that do it."[36] Only a misguided theoretical parsimony would make us choose between considerations of character and considerations of consequence.

The Situation of Ethics

It's not just the elements of ethical theory that are heterogeneous; the virtues are various, too. We shouldn't assume that every virtue functions in pretty much the same way. Some virtues (continence) have to do with our management of our selves; some (kindness), with our management of our relations with others. Nobody should be tempted by the notion that all that matters is nobility of sentiment, lest we find ourselves keeping company with Mr. Pecksniff.

> When Mr. Pecksniff and the two young ladies got into the heavy coach at the end of the lane, they found it empty, which was a great comfort; particularly as the outside was quite full and the passengers looked very frosty. For as Mr. Pecksniff justly observed—when he and his daughters had burrowed their feet deep in the straw, wrapped themselves to the chin, and pulled up both windows—it is always satisfactory to feel, in keen weather, that many other people are not as warm as you are. And this, he said, was quite natural, and a very beautiful arrangement; not confined to coaches, but extending itself

into many social ramifications. "For" (he observed), "if every one were warm and well-fed, we should lose the satisfaction of admiring the fortitude with which certain conditions of men bear cold and hunger. And if we were no better off then anybody else, what would become of our sense of gratitude; which," said Mr. Pecksniff with tears in his eyes, as he shook his fist at a beggar who wanted to get up behind, "is one of the holiest feelings of our common nature."[37]

Nor can we specify the relative importance of the various virtues outside particular contexts. For Aristotle, the virtues aren't presented in some ranked order, but are taken to be uncodifiable. The good seems to be plural: there's no such thing as goodness in itself. Things are good when they are good for human beings, and there is a plenitude of ways of being good. To be good, as Judith Jarvis Thomson has usefully insisted, is always to be *good in a way*.[38] We can parse these various ways of being good, see the virtues as admirable in distinctive ways and for distinctive reasons.

Justice, for instance, which requires giving others their due, seems important not so much for the life of the just person as for the life of those around her. Their lives will go better if she is just; for then she will give each of them their due. It contributes to my *eudaimonia* because it is good to be someone who helps others achieve theirs. A similar story goes for compassion, which entails a similar responsiveness to the needs and interests of others. But here we need to grasp that, while the beginning of the defense of these "other-regarding" virtues is, indeed, in what they lead us to do for others, we are also the kind of creatures whose flourishing depends, precisely, on how we are *regarded*. It follows that a good life will require us to live with people who not only treat us well but also think of us with kindness and compassion even when there is not much for them to do. Here, too, then, the virtues have the double face of being and doing. And one can tell such stories for each of the virtues. Even if I'm persuaded by situationist moral psychology (if from nothing else) that I cannot be a prudent or just or courageous or compassionate person through and through, as our virtue ethicist wants me to aim to be, I can see the point of being prudent or just or courageous or compassionate; and, at least sometimes, that fact can get me to behave accordingly—which is part of what makes for a good life. What I am contributes to (or detracts from) my *eudaimonia* intrinsically; but it can contribute to *eudaimonia* through conduct as well. Excellences—and they could be intellectual as well as moral—involve performance, not just mere potential: character, in a manner of speaking, isn't just in the head.

Why Virtue Matters

The starting point for my story is ethical: we begin by acknowledging, in the homeliest terms, that many things contribute to making a life good. Some of them have to do with our bodily natures and needs. Some have to do with the needs of the spirit: for love, for beauty, for truth, for significance. And many have to do with needs we share with others: they make our lives better by making us better lovers, brothers, or daughters, better friends, better citizens; or by making us willing to act to help others achieve their interests and their ends. And all of us have legitimate aims that lovers and spouses, brothers and sisters, children and parents, friends and fellow citizens, can help us meet.

Some of these considerations, as we saw, favor being a person of a certain kind—thinking and feeling a certain way—because that is valuable. Others favor doing something because the act is good for us or for someone else. Still others favor certain feelings because of what they make us do. Again, if we think of ethics in the way I have been suggesting, we will conclude neither that all that matters is the kind of person we are nor that all that matters is what we do. And, it seems to me, the understanding of virtue required by a viable ethics is not the globalist one: so we can accept what is true in situationism. Individual moments of compassion and moments of honesty make our lives better, even if we are not compassionate or honest through and through.

Indeed, one way in which the facts of moral psychology matter for the prospects for virtue ethics is in helping us identify what is valuable in virtue ethics. The facts matter, first, because, as I say, we cannot be obligated to be a kind of creature that we have realized we cannot become. Second, once we think about why the virtues might matter—and, as we shall see, there is much to learn here from outside philosophy—we will recall Aristotle's insistence that virtue requires knowledge; for perhaps one thing it requires knowledge about is our own psychology.

Finally, empirical moral psychology can help us think about

how to manage our lives, how to become better people. Situationism rightly directs us to focus on institutions, on creating circumstances that are conducive to virtue. Virtue theorists have sometimes directed us toward an excessively inward model of self-development; situationism returns us to the world in which our selves take shape. It cautions us about shortcuts like "character education," an enthusiasm of some virtue ethicists, who have been inspired by Aristotle's talk of developing *arête* while ignoring his unfashionable discussions of external goods, like wealth. In this, they seize on just the wrong thing. They would do better to try to increase our capacities and resources; to try to promulgate the circumstances in which our excellences can be elicited—the conditions in which we can flourish. And though, as I say, virtue ethics should not be hammered into a moral calculus, one aspect of flourishing is certainly moral. Here, at least, I'm in full agreement with my colleague Gil Harman when he says that if we want to improve human welfare, we may do better to "put less emphasis on moral education and on building character and more emphasis on trying to arrange social institutions so that human beings are not placed in situations in which they will act badly."[39]

Alas, it takes little imagination to conjure up such situations. Recall, say, the Rwandan genocide in 1994, when many thousands of Hutus took machetes to their Tutsi neighbors. If you and I had been planted on this earth as Hutus at that time and place, we too would probably have been participants. Unfortunately, such examples can be endlessly multiplied. Attending to the particular situations that give rise to such episodes—the ecology and economy of Rwanda at the time, for instance, where most of the population was living barely above subsistence—is sometimes, erroneously, taken as exculpatory, just as nonmoral explanations of moral progress are, erroneously, taken to be corrosive of their moral stature. So let me venture that there is, perhaps, a socio-historical counterpart to the Fundamental Attribution Error: it is to overrate the importance of culture or ideology, and underrate the importance of circumstance, of what used to be called "material conditions." But there has been plausible work—by scholars such as Russell Hardin, Donald Horowitz, and David Laitin—about the situations in which intergroup bloodshed tends to arise, and such work may provide guidance about how we might avoid these outcomes.[40] The conjunction of virtue ethics and situationism urges us to make it easier both to avoid *doing* what murderers *do* and to avoid *being* what murderers *are*. We can admire moral heroism while deploring the circumstances in which it can arise. It's good to feel compassion; it's better to have no cause to.

Much of this chapter has been given over to a line of argument that takes off from experimental moral psychology: the case against a globalist conception of character. In the next chapter, I want to take up a different way in which psychology challenges moral theory: not by undermining particular claims but by challenging its methods. Again, this will be an encounter, not a conquest. Our ethical theories must acknowledge the empirical facts about our mutable ways—they must recognize the serious man in the playful man, the patient man in the angry man—but they aren't reducible to them. We can't be content with knowing what kind of people we are; it matters, too, what kind of people we hope to be.

3

The Case against Intuition

"I am afraid," replied Elinor, "that the pleasantness of an
employment does not always evince its propriety."

"On the contrary, nothing can be a stronger proof of
it, Elinor; for if there had been any real impropriety in
what I did, I should have been sensible of it at the time,
for we always know when we are acting wrong, and with
such a conviction I could have had no pleasure."

—JANE AUSTEN, *Sense and Sensibility*

The Evidence of Self-Evidence

Astronomers have stars; geologists have rocks. But what do
moral theorists have to work with? For centuries, they typically
claimed to proceed from truths that were self-evident—or,
more modestly, from our moral intuitions. Moral theories
would explain, and be constrained by, these intuitions—that's
the way with theories—and so moral theorists had to have a
story about what kind of intuitions counted. Thomas Reid,
founder of the so-called Common Sense school (a sort of
ordinary-language philosophy *avant la lettre*), urged that we

"take for granted, as first principles, things wherein we find an universal agreement, among the learned and the unlearned, in the different nations and ages of the world. A consent of ages and nations of the learned and vulgar, ought, at least, to have great authority, unless we can show some prejudice as universal as that consent is, which might be the cause of it. Truth is one, but error is infinite." At the same time, he held that "attentive reflection" was itself "a kind of intuition."[1] It had great authority, too, and would help chasten intuitions of the first kind.

His successors were often more fastidious when it came to listening to the unlettered. William Whewell, in his 1846 *Lectures on Systematic Morality*, insisted that he was proceeding from self-evident principles—but then grappled with the question of to whom they were self-evident. We could have no coherence in our views, he argued, if we submitted them to "a *promiscuous Jury* from the mass of mankind." Rather, self-evidence would be tested by "a Jury of men as men," thoughtful and wholesome specimens: "They are men as well as the first twelve you might take at Temple Bar, or at Timbuctoo," by which he meant that they are "true men; or at least men who have laboured and toiled, under favourable circumstances, to be true to their humanity." Whewell believed men such as these "pronounce on my side;—that they decide such fundamental Principles as mine to be true and universal Principles of Morality." In his view, "*Vox populi feri* is not *vox veritatis*. It would be more suitable to say *Vox humani generis vox veritatis*."[2]

Nor did Henry Sidgwick, half a century later, stray far when he called for philosophers to study, "with reverent and patient care," what he dubbed "the Morality of Common Sense," by which he did *not* mean the moral judgments of the common run of man (it would be "wasted labor" to systematize the morality of the worldly, debased as it was by "their sordid interests and vulgar ambitions"). The Morality of Common Sense referred, rather, "to the moral judgments—and especially the spontaneous unreflected judgments on particular cases, which are sometimes called moral intuitions—of those persons, to be found in all walks and stations of life, whose earnest and predominant aim is to do their duty." The moral philosopher was to be "aided and controlled by them in his theoretical construction of the Science of Right."[3]

The basic picture here—moral theory as the perfection of elevated intuition—is anything but foreign to modern moral philosophy. In the past century, though, the endeavor has taken on an increasingly scientific tinge. Sir David Ross, in *The Right and the Good* (1930), proposed that "the moral convictions of thoughtful and well-educated people are the data of ethics just as sense-perceptions are the data of a natural science." Not that such data must always be taken at face value: "Just as some of the latter have to be rejected as illusory, so have some of the former," he allowed, but "only when they are in conflict with convictions which stand better the test of reflection."[4] In the 1950s, John Rawls formalized the method of his predecessors in what became (after some further elaboration) his celebrated notion of "reflective equilibrium"—directing us to adjust our principles to our intuitions, and our intuitions to our principles, until, through mutual calibration, consonance was achieved—and in doing so, he too made explicit reference to such scientific theorizing.[5] And the model of moral philosophy as a sort of intuition refinery has maintained its allure. The philosopher Frank Jackson, writing a century after Sidgwick, takes the task of "moral functionalism" to be to construct "a coherent theory out of folk morality, respecting as much as possible those parts that we find most appealing, to form mature folk morality"—the latter being what folk morality becomes when exposed to "debate and critical reflection." Folk morality may be a complicated and untidy thing, but, Jackson maintains (and Reid, Whewell, Sidgwick, Ross, and Rawls would have concurred) "we must start from somewhere in current folk morality, otherwise we start from somewhere *unintuitive*, and that can hardly be a good place to start from."[6]

Not surprisingly, our moral theories have clashing ambitions: if their plausibility comes from their ability to accommodate our intuitions, their power comes from their ability to challenge still other intuitions. A theory may be applauded for being revisionary, for showing us the error of our quondam judgments—or rejected precisely because it defies common sense. A theory may be commended for revealing the deep coherence of our existing convictions—or castigated for its flaccid indulgence of our wayward prejudices. In one direction, we complain of normative systems that seem impossibly unmoored from human judgment, bicycles built for octopods. "To ask us to give up at the bidding of a theory our actual apprehension of what is right and what is wrong," Sir David Ross wrote, "seems like asking people to repudiate their actual experience of beauty, at the bidding of a theory which says, 'only that which satisfies such and such conditions can be beautiful'"—a request that, he maintains, "is nothing less than absurd."[7] In the other direction, though, we get the bugbear of moral conservatism, propping up the disreputable old theories that our intuitions enrobe. It is the charge James Mill (quoting Alexander Pope) made against Edmund Burke: that in his philosophy "whatever is, is right." Such accusations, on either side of the ledger, often have more than a whiff of the ad hoc. On what basis do we settle them? Here we confront what I'll call the "intuition problem."

A quick pair of examples. For many, it is a point in Jeremy Bentham's favor that, in contemplating the principle of utility, he got right the big issues that his contemporaries got wrong: he was able to challenge the prevailing moral intuitions of his day about slavery, the subjection of women, homosexuality, and so forth. We can laud the triumph of sterling principle over the debased currency of moral common sense. Other moral thinkers, skeptical of the radical impartialism that utilitarianism seems to demand, have, by way of rebuttal, held up to scorn a notorious passage by William Godwin, Bentham's rough contemporary and fellow utilitarian. It's a passage in which Godwin imagines having to choose whom to rescue from a fire: either Archbishop Fénelon, who had much to contribute to the general welfare, or someone without the archbishop's moral distinction—perhaps Godwin's brother, his benefactor, his father. According to Godwin, justice requires that we rescue the archbishop and let our father perish in the flames.[8] Ethicists, in his day as in ours, have shaken their heads in disbelief: Who would want to sign onto a doctrine that had this deeply unappealing result? Here, as so often, it is common sense, not principle, that is taken as dispositive.[9] What guides us here? In the realm of meta-ethics, it would seem, we have clashing intuitions about intuitions.

Reflective equilibrium remains the usual way that philosophers think about the vexed status of intuition in normative ethics. What has made this notion so durable is not that it has solved the difficulties it means to address but that the difficulties themselves have proved so durable—one of philosophy's many *Jarndyce v. Jarndyce*–style impasses. Indeed, one could be forgiven for thinking that reflective equilibrium is really another name for the problem, rather than a solution to it. It's worth recalling that in its earliest, 1951 formulation, Rawls's "decision procedure" was for moral judgments in particular cases. This modest, midcentury notion may have had certain advantages, but in the 1970s and after, the notion was revised and expanded into a strategy not just for arriving at judgments in particular cases but for moral theory more generally; the list of things to be brought into equilibrium was broadened to include background theories and beliefs. As you might fear, the procedure for reaching equilibrium is less than determinate.

Suppose we have a theory, T_1, from which we can derive all our moral intuitions (so far) except intuition INT. (This is the simplest case. In general, of course, there'll be a class of intuitions that don't fit with our current best ethical theory.) Suppose we construct a different theory, T_2, that differs from our existing theory only as much as is necessary to accommodate INT. We cannot now reject INT because it isn't derivable from a theory: it can be derived from T_2. To reject INT on the basis that it can't be derived from T_1, we should need to have a reason for preferring T_1 to T_2 in the first place. There might be pragmatic reasons: T_1 might be simpler. (And, given that ethics is practical, simplicity might be a genuine theoretical virtue here.) But theoretical simplicity is both hard to measure and also, often, a function of what terms you're willing to take as basic, so it may be hard to apply this criterion. A more external kind of practical virtue in a theory might be that others in our own society endorse it (which would further incline us toward conservatism about ethics). At any rate, in the absence of a reason for preferring one theory to another, independently of the intuitions it supports, the contest is between INT and the other intuitions that we must abandon if we accept T_2. The point is that the standard reflective-equilibrium approach is going to help us deal with conflicting intuitions only if we have some independent ideas about the shape of ethical theory as well. It looks as though, as with our nonnormative beliefs construed in a realist way, saving the phenomena—our appraisals, our perceptual judgments—is not enough.[10]

Suppose T_1 were some version of utilitarianism. Rawls discussed the objection that it might sometimes be welfare-maximizing to punish someone known to be innocent, a practice he dubbed "telishment"; he supposed that our intuitive revulsion toward telishment—our strongly held conviction that it's wrong to punish the innocent—counted against utilitarianism. So we could abandon utilitarianism UT_1 for UT_2 (modified utilitarianism), which says that one should maximize utility except where it entails the judicial punishment of innocent people. The utilitarian may want us to bite the bullet and reject the intuition in the name of coherence. But why would we do this, given that we can take the path of modified utilitarianism instead? In seeking reflective equilibrium between theory and intuition here, how to choose between rejecting INT and rejecting utilitarianism? Down the road, of course, other intuitions may lead us to abandon this new theory, too. But before we go any further, it is hard to apply reflective equilibrium as a procedure without already knowing whether to regard UT_2 as inferior to utilitarianism (because, say, it looks unacceptably ad hoc, as many people would agree in this case; the more familiar repair is to subject UT_1 to the constraint that nobody's rights are violated). If what matters is fitting together all the bits—as Rawls's coherentist picture suggests—then we need a better theory than we've been offered for what a coherent theory should look like.[11]

Other philosophers, meanwhile, complain about what they regard as the method's conservatism. Indeed, while Rawls's own "theory of justice" is usually criticized for its counterintuitive implications, his method of reflective equilibrium is often denounced as overly deferential to our intuitions. By subjecting our intuitions to an internal test of coherence, critics say, the method may simply give our old prejudices a haircut and a shave. Where would we be if philosophy had been compelled to respect what used to pass as common sense—the conviction that morality required religion, say, or that slavery was part of the natural order?[12] They notice that Rawls's own work is stippled with appeals to shared intuitions—to what "there is a broad measure of agreement" about, what "it seems reasonable to suppose," what "we are confident" about—and they ask: What do you mean "we," Kemo Sabe?

There's certainly reason to wonder whether "obvious" is a relation masquerading as a predicate (so that we ought to ask always, "Obvious to whom?"). A great Cambridge mathematician, so the story goes, once stood before his class and filled the chalkboard with a vast and intricate equation. Underlining the result, he declared, "As you can see, it's obvious." Suddenly, though, he was seized by doubt, and, with furrowed brow, crept from the classroom. When he returned five minutes later, he was in fine spirits, his worries banished. "Why, yes, indeed," he assured his students, "it *is* obvious."[13]

The intuition problem, I should say, isn't peculiar to moral philosophy, but it's hardest to avoid there, as you find when you consider the alternative credos offered by the anti-intuition camp. David Papineau, for instance, proposes that, rather than giving quarter to common sense, "All claims should be assessed on their merits, against the tribunals of observation and reason"; but when the claims are moral ones, we can't be optimistic that our observations and reasons could be cleansed of our intuitions. Richard Brandt, for his part, exhorts us to "step outside of our own tradition somehow, see it from outside"—and that little word "somehow" betrays an understandable worry about the ease with which we can do so.[14]

The suspicion that our common sense may be littered with perishable and parochial prejudice is, of course, an ancient and enduring one, stretching from Herodotus to the pioneers of modern cultural anthropology. Utilitarian reformers who sought to combat entrenched moral intuitions found encouragement in Helvetius' *De l'esprit,* and its argument that self-interest, including self-interest in the form of class interest, was the hidden wellspring behind talk of virtue and duty (presaging what Engels called "false consciousness"). Over the past decade or two, there has been a renewed assault on the status of moral intuitions, and from another direction. Even as the scientific paradigm has urged moral theorists to treat intuitions as data, a wave of empirically based research into human decision making has depicted many of those intuitions to be—in ways that seem universal, and perhaps incorrigible—unreliable and incoherent.

The Prospects for Common Sense

Consider the following experiment, which will be familiar to many of you. We divide our subjects into two groups. The task, we tell them, is to choose between two policy options as we prepare for an impending outbreak of the Asian Flu. If we do nothing, 600 people can be expected to die. Group 1 gets to choose between policies A and B, which we describe as follows. Policy A will save the lives of 200 people who would otherwise have died. Policy B has a one-third chance of saving 600 people and a two-thirds chance of saving nobody. So Group 1 has these options:

A	B
200 people are saved	One-third chance of saving 600
	Two-thirds chance of saving nobody

Group 2 also gets a couple of options, policy C and policy D, described as follows:

C	D
400 people die	One-third chance nobody dies
	Two-thirds chance that 600 will die

You will notice at once that, granted the background assumption that 600 people will die if we do nothing, A and C are the same policy. It takes only a moment longer to see that since, in this context, "600 people are saved" and "nobody dies of flu" are the same and so are "nobody is saved" and "600 people die of flu," B and D are the same policy, too. These, then, are the same options, differently described.

What happened, though, when the choice was actually put to people? The answer, as the psychologists Daniel Kahneman and Amos Tversky showed in a justly famous experiment, was rather surprising.[15] Those who had to choose between A and B generally favored A; people who had to choose between C and D were inclined to favor D. In fact, roughly three-quarters of each group had these opposed preferences.

This is one of a multitude of examples of what are called "framing effects." People's choices often depend on exactly how the options are framed, even when the descriptions are, rationally speaking, equivalent. Now, Kahneman and Tversky, being respectable scientists, didn't just do an experiment; they offered an explanation of why the experiment comes out this way. They claimed that they could say what it was about the framing that made the difference. Indeed, as is normal, they did the experiment to test the explanation, which they called *prospect theory*. It holds that:

1. People are risk-averse when thinking about gains over what they think of as the background status quo, but

2. they're willing to take risks when they're faced with possible losses with respect to that status quo.

3. They're also more concerned to avoid losses than they are attracted by equivalent gains.

Prospect theory explains these results because when we say we are *saving* 200 people, we take the death of 600 people as the baseline. So we think of the 200 people saved as a gain, even though 400 people are still dying. Since we're risk-averse about gains, we prefer A to B, because B risks that gain of 200. On the other hand, if we think of 400 people *dying*, we're taking the baseline to be nobody dying. Now the 400 people dying are a loss. And since we're willing to take risks to avoid losses, we'll prefer D to C; because now we see C as offering the possibility that no one will die. If you get people to focus on the worst case—that 600 people still die, despite our best efforts—they'll pick the guarantee that we save at least 200. If you get them to focus on the best case—nobody's dying—they'll aim for it, even though it's the less likely outcome.

Now, I don't know what you would have expected people to say here or what you would have said yourself. But, as we saw, a large slice of moral philosophy has consisted in thinking about such cases, forming an intuition about the right answer, and then trying to discover principles that will explain why it's the right answer. (People can, of course, have intuitions about principles as well as about cases, but, except where I say so explicitly, I'm going to use the word "intuition"—as Sidgwick suggested—to refer to responses to cases, or, more precisely, classes of cases.)

One challenge to our methods in moral philosophy posed here is simply this: it looks as though our intuitive judgments about what's right to do are determined in part by things that cannot possibly be relevant. Given that the policy choices are exactly the same whichever way you describe them, people are responding here to something that cannot matter. What's nice about the Asian Flu experiment, in other words, is that it makes its point whichever policy you think is right; it doesn't require that we reason from moral premises in order to get its conclusion. When our intuitions are guided by irrelevant factors, they *can't* be reliable guides.

As it happens, many philosophers, like traditional economists, think we should pick options on the basis of their expected costs and benefits, and so would rank A, B, C, and D equally.[16] (You calculate the expected value of an option by multiplying the value of each of the mutually exclusive possible outcomes by its probability and adding up all those products.) For A and C, the expected loss of life is (1×200) people, since to say that a policy will save 200 people is to say, in effect, that it will save 200 people with probability 1; for B and D the expected loss of life is ($\frac{1}{3} \times 600$) – ($\frac{2}{3} \times 0$), which is 200 again. So from that point of view, preferring any of these options to any other is *irrational* because the policy of assessing options by their expected values is the policy with the greatest probability of maximizing your benefits over the long haul. Here, then, the judgment about what's reasonable is based not on an intuition, but on an argument.[17] But an argument of that sort, too, directs us to revisit the status we accord to intuitions about scenarios like this one.

And once you start to look, you can find the influence of baseline considerations everywhere. Take a little experiment that Thomas Schelling once conducted with his students, to try to draw out their intuitions of justice. He asked them what they thought about a particular tax policy that gave a bigger child deduction—that paid a larger bonus—to rich parents than it gave to their poor counterparts. As you'd guess, students didn't think that policy was fair. Then Schelling redescribed the situation. Suppose the tax code has, as a default, a couple with children, and imposes a surcharge, a penalty, for the childless. Should that surcharge be larger for the poor than for the rich? The students all reversed their position, even though the two scenarios specified the very same distribution.[18]

As with the Asian Flu case, our intuitions hang on what we counted as a loss and what as a gain. There are other ways of manipulating our moral choices that don't involve anything like the gain/loss distinction, and seem even less respectable. In a recent experiment conducted by Thalia Wheatley and Jonathan Haidt at the University of Virginia, people were taught under hypnosis to feel disgust—a brief sense of "a sickening in your stomach"—when they came across an emotionally neutral word such as "take" or "often." Then they were presented with different scenarios. One was about a person acting in morally troubling ways (a hypocritical bribe-taking congressman); another was about someone whose actions were quite morally untroubling (a student-council representative who was in charge of scheduling discussions about academic issues, and who tried to choose topics that would appeal to both professors and students). The scenarios came in two versions that were almost identical, except that one version contained the cue word. The researchers found that when their subjects were responding to the versions that had the cue word, they judged moral infractions much more harshly: the congressman who will "take" bribes from the tobacco lobby was judged a greater villain than the congressman who is "bribed by" the tobacco lobby. As for Dan, the student-council rep, nobody disapproved of him when he sought to stimulate discussion by trying to pick topics of interest both to students and to professors. What's not to like? But when he "often" picked such topics, a significant number of people couldn't help disapproving. Asked to explain, they'd write down such comments as: "It just seems like he's up to something." One subject fingered him for being a "popularity-seeking snob"; another wrote, "It just seems so weird and disgusting." Even more mordant was the comment: "I don't know why it's wrong, it just is."[19]

It isn't comforting to learn that people's moral judgments can be shaped by a little hypnotic priming, given that the everyday world fills us with all sorts of irrelevant associations that may play a similar role. And though the situationist studies I discussed in the previous chapter chiefly involved conduct—and, in the main, what look like acts of supererogation—rather than expressions of moral judgments or justifications, they, too, surely bolster the aforementioned worries about intuitions.

Kahneman and Tversky themselves suggested that prospect theory provides a better explanation of most people's intuitions about a wide range of cases than do the traditional distinctions made by moral philosophers. Of course, philosophers who think that a choice is right according to some principle do not have to hold that the principle explains our actual responses, not least because it is open to them to say that many of our intuitive responses are wrong. The philosopher is bound to regard the pattern of responses in the Asian Flu case, for example, as irrational; so she will not provide a theory that justifies this pattern of responses at all. Indeed, where many people regularly make the wrong choice, a psychological explanation of why they do so supports the philosopher's claim that they are mistaken, because it relieves us of the worry that they are being guided by some rational principle we have failed to discover.

But this sort of research will, at least at first, provide less comfort than dismay. Since we moral philosophers invoke intuitions about cases all the time, the effect of thinking about Schelling's tax-code case or the Asian Flu case is a bit like the effect that thinking about visual illusions and hallucinations has on our confidence in our visual judgments. Descartes pointed out that we often make mistakes about what's really there, as when we're dreaming. And his question was: If you know you make mistakes sometimes, why aren't you worried that you might be making them all the time? Similarly, those studies in the psychology of decision making leave us nervously aware that, at least sometimes, our intuitions are deeply unreliable. What's even more nervous-making is that psychologists have offered what we might call *undermining* explanations for judgments that many moral philosophers have taken to be *correct*, at least in part because they comport with those philosophers' intuitions.

Trolleyology

To approach the problem, consider another line of recent experimental work that starts by observing a troubling conflict between the moral intuitions on which philosophers rely—a conflict that some psychologists suggest should lead us to question the intuitions many moral theories are intended to justify and support. The argument starts from a long-established discussion in philosophy about a range of "trolley problems," which derive originally from scenarios dreamed up by Philippa Foot and elaborated by Judith Jarvis Thomson, among (eventually) many others.[20] Consider a pair of them.

In one scenario, there's a runaway trolley hurtling down the tracks, and it's on course to kill five people who are, unavoidably, in its path. You can save those five people, but only by hitting a switch that will put the trolley onto a side track, where it will kill one person. Should you do it? Philosophers generally say yes. And research conducted in recent years shows that the intuition is widely shared. When polled, most people—80 or 90 percent of us—will say yes.

In a second scenario, the trolley, once again, is hurtling toward the five people. This time you're on a footbridge over the tracks, next to a 300-pound man. The only way you can save those five people is by pushing the 300-pound man off the bridge and onto the tracks. His body mass will stop the runaway trolley, but he'll be killed in the process. Should you do it? Most of us, theorists and civilians alike, say no.[21]

Those responses are, in themselves, neither surprising nor troubling. Though the body count is the same whether you hit the switch or sacrifice the 300-pound man, there are plausibly relevant differences between the cases. When Philippa Foot introduced the trolley scenario, she was exploring a traditional moral idea: the doctrine of double effect, according to which there's a significant difference between doing something that has a bad outcome as a foreseen but unintended consequence and intentionally doing that bad thing, even if the overall outcome is the same.[22] This is relevant to traditional Catholic views about abortion, for example, according to which if a fetus dies in the course of saving a mother's life (because, say, you have to remove her cancerous uterus), the doctor is blameless for the death. Similarly, in wartime, civilian casualties, where unavoidable, are usually seen as a permissible side-effect of military activities, but the deliberate killing of civilians in order, say, to put pressure on an enemy government, is a war crime—even if the net effect of that pressure is to force an end to the war and reduce overall fatalities.

The doctrine of double effect seems relevant here, at least at first glance, since in the footbridge example you are stopping the trolley *by* killing someone: the death of the large stranger isn't an unintended by-product of your stopping the trolley—it's the *means* by which you do it. In the original trolley case, by contrast, the man on the track dies as a foreseen but unintended consequence of your diverting the lethal machine.[23] That's a possible reason, a justification, for our differing intuitions in the two cases. Some philosophers, especially those of deontological inclinations, see an illustration here of the distinction between bringing-about and allowing-to-happen, or between aiding and not harming.[24] Still other philosophers . . . well, countless trolley-related arguments and elaborations have been published in the past quarter-century; by now, the philosophical commentary on these cases makes the Talmud look like *Cliffs Notes*, and is surely massive enough to stop any runaway trolley in its tracks.

A solution to the problem of why it sometimes is and sometimes isn't permissible to end one life to save more than one would start by classifying the trolley problem and the footbridge dilemma as *different* in some important way. To justify the different responses, this important difference would have to be one that *warrants* the different responses—that makes sense of treating the cases differently. One challenge to this approach comes from the psychologists, who are able to classify the two cases differently and thus explain our differential response, but who do so in a way that does not seem to warrant the differential treatment. That was what Kahneman and Tversky did for the Asian Flu case. Prospect theory shows why the different frames lead to different responses, but it wasn't supposed to show that different frames *justify* different responses; indeed, it helped undermine that claim.

As you will already have guessed, some philosophers have detected the shadow of prospect theory over those trolley tracks. Robert Nozick, for one, wondered whether "the relation of the bringing about / allowing to happen" didn't "seem suspiciously like that of the gain/loss distinction." After all, in the real world, we can never be sure what the consequences will be farther down the line. As a result, however the scenario is described, we're likely to treat any action as taking a risk to secure some outcome. Perhaps, then, when we're deciding what to do with the man on the footbridge, his being alive is the back-ground status quo, the baseline, which we seek to preserve be-cause we're risk-averse, even when the net gain is four lives. And perhaps in the original trolley case, by contrast, the five people alive right now are the baseline, so we risk diverting the trolley to avoid the loss; we'll take risks to avoid losses. Of course, if I can get you to see a different baseline—namely, what will happen if you don't intervene—then intervening to reduce the death toll is taking a risk in order to produce a gain. Since you're risk-averse, you should be inclined to leave well alone. And some people do respond to the original trolley problem in that way.[25]

Consider, too, the possible role of "order effects." Research has shown that the order in which moral options are presented to us can affect which option we choose. In the bystander-at-the-switch version of the trolley problem, we are always told first about the five people whose lives are imperiled; we learn about the one person on the side track as a subsequent compli-cation. Having resolved to do whatever you can to stop the train from its destructive course—and having learned about the switch, and the side track—you have already formed a strong resolve: you look to be confirmed in your decision (as confirma-tion bias might suggest) and view countervailing considera-tions with a grain of skepticism.

These thoughts are disruptive, of course, because the ques-tion is what it's right to do, and it's worrying that we can be shifted one way or another on this by a redescribing of the same situation.

A Scanner Darkly

An even more disruptive proposal has been made by the experimental moral psychologist Joshua Greene and his colleagues, who conclude that the difference in our responses to the trolley scenario and the footbridge scenario has to do with the emotional traction of the latter: "The thought of pushing someone to his death is, we propose, more emotionally salient than the thought of hitting a switch that will cause a trolley to produce similar consequences, and it is this emotional response that accounts for people's tendency to treat these cases differently."[26]

How did they confirm this hypothesis? By using functional magnetic resonance imaging (f MRI), which allows you to see which parts of a person's brain are most active at any time. Independent coders divided up various scenarios into moral and nonmoral ones, and then into personal or impersonal ones. The switch-throwing scenario was classified as a "moral-impersonal" scenario; the footbridge example was classified as a "moral-personal" scenario, being, as Greene says, "up close and personal." Then Greene and his colleagues showed that when people were faced with the footbridge dilemma, the parts of the brain that "lit up"—the medial frontal gyrus, the posterior cingulate gyrus, and the angular gyrus—were regions associated with emotion. On the other hand, Greene and his team went on, "areas associated with working memory have been found to become less active during emotional processing as compared to periods of cognitive processing." And, indeed, the right middle frontal gyrus and the bilateral parietal lobe—both of which are associated with working memory—were "significantly less active in the moral-personal condition than" when subjects were thinking about "moral-impersonal" choices, like the trolley problem, or about choices that were not moral at all.[27]

Even those people who *were* in fact willing to kill the stranger on the footbridge confirmed Greene's fundamental claim. Because it looks as though they *overrode* their emotional instinctual response. People who decided that they should push the stranger off the bridge took significantly longer to respond than those who decided not to. They had the emotion-laden response, it seemed, and then they reasoned their way out of it.

Now, so far all we have is a psychological explanation. It may or may not impress you, depending on your confidence in our current grasp of functional neuroanatomy, but let's take the analysis at face value.[28] Confronted with the footbridge dilemma, what *is* the right thing to do? It's true—we didn't need scanners to tell us this—that, given the way our brains work, most people will find it distressing to push a stranger over a bridge, even for a very good reason. But is that a good enough reason not to do it? We have a conflict here between what our intuition tells us—don't kill an innocent stranger—and a powerful reflective thought: Isn't it better if only one person dies? Being told that our "intuition" involves the engagement of a different part of our brain from the part that has the reflective idea might just make it easier to side with that reflective judgment (which, let's grant, is sponsored by another set of intuitions). After all, as I said, philosophers have been engaged for a long time in seeking to find reasons that justify responding one way to the trolley case and another to the footbridge case.

It is fair to say that they have not come up with an answer that satisfies most people who have thought about the matter.

I mentioned just now that the distinction between using someone to stop the trolley in the footbridge case and killing him as an unintended side-effect might be helpful. But now consider another oft-discussed modification of the trolley case: the "loop scenario." This time, when you throw the switch, the trolley goes onto a loop, which has the heavy stranger on it, but then comes back onto the track with the five people on it. What saves their lives now is the fact that the stranger weighs enough to stop the trolley. Once more, it seems, you're saving them *by* killing him, as in the footbridge case. His death is the means by which you save them, not an unintended side-effect. But many people think that switch-throwing in this case is just as permissible as the switch-throwing in the first trolley case I described.[29] Being deluged with trolley problems is one of the professional hazards of modern moral philosophy.

Greene's psychological explanation raises the possibility that (as he thinks) there's just no good moral reason for our making this distinction. Our brains are so constituted that most of us will go one way in one scenario and another in the other: so we've been told *what makes us* respond as we do. We have (at least) two ways of deciding what to do. Sometimes one kicks in, sometimes the other. Which one kicks in is decided by whether or not the killing in question is "up close and personal"; and while that makes a difference to how we will *feel*, it doesn't have any real moral significance. In the absence of a compelling rational explanation, it's possible to conclude that that's all there is to it. As Greene has written in a discussion of other conflicting intuitions:

Consider that our ancestors did not evolve in an environment in which total strangers on opposite sides of the world could save each other's lives by making relatively modest material sacrifices. Consider also that our ancestors did evolve in an environment in which individuals standing face-to-face could save each other's lives, sometimes only through considerable personal sacrifice. Given all of this, it makes sense that we would have evolved altruistic instincts that direct us to help others in dire need, but mostly when the ones in need are presented in an "up-close-and-personal" way.

. . . Maybe there is "some good reason" for this pair of attitudes, but the evolutionary account given above suggests otherwise.[30]

How should a moral philosopher respond?

Moral Emergencies

We might begin by noticing something special about the trolley problem and the footbridge problem. They are both what I will call *moral emergencies*. They are cases, that is, where

1. you, the agent in the story, have to decide what to do in a very short period of time;
2. there is a clear and simple set of options;
3. something of great moral significance—in this case, the death of five innocent people—is at stake; and
4. no one else is as well placed as you are to intervene.

Those four features—limited decision-time, clear choices, high stakes, and optimum placement—together make these situations very different from most of the decisions that face us.

First of all, it's in part the high stakes that allow us to narrow the range of options to consider. An unstated but obvious presupposition of these scenarios is that anything else we could be doing has much lower stakes, which is why we can ignore it. To make this clear, just add to each scenario the further stipulation that, for example, you see the trolley while rushing to defuse a nuclear bomb that only you can defuse, a bomb that will kill hundreds of thousands if you stop to deal with the trolley. Now, plainly, you must neither throw the switch nor push the 300-pound man. You must keep on your way.

Second, the fact that you, the agent in the story, have to decide fast means that you don't have time to get more information. Suppose the five people were old and suicidal; they'd gathered on the tracks in order to end their lives—they were expecting the trolley—and would be displeased to find their plans foiled. Suppose the other person—the man on the line, the stranger on the bridge—is about to find a cure for Alzheimer's disease. It's a convention of such scenarios that you've been told all you need to know. (Or perhaps it's just an application of Paul Grice's maxim of quantity: make your contribution as informative as is required for the purpose of the discussion, but not more so.)

Third, the fact that you are the person on the spot means that you bear a responsibility you wouldn't have if there were others closer or better equipped to act. So it looks as if the choice is yours. You can't just say, "It's none of my business."

The fact that the footbridge and the trolley problems are moral emergencies suggests that they are exactly the kinds of situations in which we will be guided, as Joshua Greene might put it, by the medial frontal, posterior cingulate, and angular gyri rather than the parietal lobe. The person at the footbridge, the bystander at the switch, has little time for reflection, information gathering and processing, deliberation. Adrenaline will be pulsing through her veins. It will be hard, in Hamlet's happy phrasing, for one's "native hue of resolution" to be "sicklied o'er with the pale cast of thought." In such circumstances, there is much to be said for an instinctive reluctance to push strangers over bridges, even if it might be, all things considered, in these horrific circumstances, the best thing to do.

That response looks, in short, as though it meets the conditions I set out in the last chapter for being a good heuristic. Suppose that, in fact, one ought to push the heavy stranger off the footbridge. Even so, there might be reasons for wanting to be the kind of person who couldn't do it. Holding onto revulsion against killing people "up close and personal" is one way to make sure we won't easily be tempted to kill people when it suits our interests. So we may be glad that our gyri are jangled by the very idea of it. That heuristic will lead us to miss the chance to save those five strangers on the trolley-track. But how often does a situation like that arise? As fast and frugal policies go, this one is very much more likely to lead us in the right direction.

Evolutionary psychologists have offered similar explanations for the prospect theory that was offered in explanation of the results in the Asian Flu case. For most of history, humans lived in conditions of subsistence, close to starvation, where the risk of loss was the risk, in effect, of dying. While gains above subsistence are nice, they're not worth taking that risk for. So creatures that do what prospect theory requires seem more likely to survive. (It would take us a long way afield to discuss how good an explanation this is.) Suppose acting according to prospect theory usually leads a person to do what is, so far as the normative philosopher judges, the right thing, even if for the wrong reasons. A person could treat the recommendations of prospect theory as a rule of thumb, a heuristic, and, so long as she's a consequentialist (like Greene) and not, say, a virtue theorist, that heuristic might suit her just fine. She may, of course, want to persuade people that there is a better way of getting to their conclusions, a route that will never lead them astray. But that project will be less urgent if the implicit principle that actually motivates them is, in most normal circumstances, a good enough guide. Notice that appeal to the idea of a heuristic here is not open to the objection I raised in the last chapter. In this instance, the heuristic is one that guides our action according to a presumed standard: it is about what we do, not what we are. We can therefore use the standards of normal means-end rationality to evaluate whether the heuristic does well as a substitute for applying the standard directly. And if there is no currently known way to change our intuitions—if they are a fixed feature of our psychologies—then learning when and how they mislead us will help us to overrule them when we should.

Nor will evolutionary theorists be surprised to learn that we'll overcome our aversion to up-close killing under the right circumstances. Suppose—this is another chestnut of moral philosophy—that you and some fellow spelunkers have allowed a fat man to lead you out of the cave you've been exploring, and he gets stuck, trapping the rest of you inside. Worse still, the cave is flooding, and if you can't get out, you'll all drown, except the fat man. But one of you has a stick of dynamite, and can blast the man out of the mouth of the cave. Can you blow him up to save yourselves? In at least one recent survey, most people said yes.[31] Here, we might suppose, some element of self-defense enters into our judgment: in contrast to the trolley cases, the actor is securing his or her own survival, and, when the stakes are life and death, our moral common sense permits a special concern for oneself.

It is an interesting and unobvious assumption, which hasn't had the attention it deserves, that our responses to imaginary scenarios mirror our responses to real ones. Joshua Greene's account of these cases presupposes, in other words, that our intuition about what to do in the imaginary case is explained by the activation of the very mechanisms that would lead us to act in a real one. Without that assumption, his explanation of why we respond as we do fails. When I think about the footbridge scenario there is, in fact, no 300-pound man around and no one to save. There is no emergency. I'm making a guess about how I'd respond in those circumstances.[32] Greene would say, not implausibly, that the responses activated through the process of imagining yourself to be in that situation look like the ones we expect would be activated if we really were in that situation. And, of course, there are moral accounts of long standing according to which the right thing to do is what a benevolent but fully informed observer would advise you to do: in which case we should perhaps put more stock, morally, in the questionnaire-answerer's counsel than in the switch-thrower's conduct.

Folk Psychology Unplugged

Let me consider one final line of empirical investigation, which shines an equally harsh light on the folk psychology of moral appraisal. Here, the subject of inquiry is the relation between our moral judgments of an act and our ascriptions of responsibility or intent.

In one set of trials, the philosophers Shaun Nichols and Joshua Knobe set out to elicit the intuitions that nonphilosophers had about an old philosophical debate: the relation between determinism and moral appraisal. If we live in a deterministic universe, where all events have causes—are necessitated by the laws of nature and the previous state of the cosmos—can people be held morally responsible for their actions? "Compatibilists," in the philosophical shorthand, think that determinism is, in some sense, compatible with free will (and thus with the moral appraisal of actions); "incompatibilists" think it is not. Nichols and Knobe were able to provoke both compatibilist and incompatibilist intuitions from people—depending on whether the scenarios they presented to them were "affect laden."

Here's how they did it. One group of participants was instructed to consider a universe that was described as being completely deterministic. (Everything that happens *had* to happen.) When asked whether people could be "fully morally responsible for their actions" in such a universe, 86 percent of subjects said no. When they were asked about a particular inhabitant of this universe, Mark, who, as he has done in the past, "arranges to cheat on his taxes," most people denied that he was fully responsible for his actions. So their intuitions about the abstract issue were preserved when they responded to this rather humdrum case. But their intuitions shifted when they were presented with a much more affect-laden scenario: "In Universe A"—a fully deterministic one—"a man named Bill has become attracted to his secretary, and decides that the only way to be with her is to kill his wife and three children. He knows that it is impossible to escape from his house in the event of a fire. Before he leaves on a business trip, he sets up a device in his basement that burns down the house and kills his family."[33] Most subjects given this scenario said they thought that Bill was indeed fully morally responsible.

Nichols and Knobe are inclined to think that people's intuitions about Bill reflect some sort of "performance error," in which case these intuitions shouldn't count in favor of compatibilism (whether or not compatibilism is correct). They wonder whether we're looking at a "moral illusion" analogous to the optical illusion that makes the two lines of the Müller-Lyer diagram look like they're of different length, even when we know they're the same. Nichols and Knobe are also struck by the fact that when you point out the seeming contradiction and ask people to reconcile their warring intuitions, half jump one way, half jump the other. The dissensus among laypeople, they notice, seems awfully similar to the dissensus among philosophers.

Of course, results of this sort don't interpret themselves;

they have to be interpreted. For one thing, it may be overreaching to ascribe the philosophical doctrine of compatibilism to the Bill blamers. Especially if a "performance error" is involved, they may not be asserting the compatibility of determinism and free will; they may be so outraged that they've put the stipulated background assumption *way* in the background. We can also fuss about details: for instance, the word "decides," in the Bill scenario, has a distinctly volitional hue. The vignette situates Bill (but not Mark) in a web of interpersonal relationships, the sort of context that, P. F. Strawson thought, was bound to elicit "participant reactive attitudes," like reproach, approbation, gratitude, and other responses that suggest an ascription of moral agency.[34] Indeed, to call the Bill scenario "affect-laden"—as if "affect" were some fungible substance, like blood or bile—is to underdescribe it. The scenario elicits a particular kind of affect: moral repugnance. One can imagine other affect-laden scenarios that involve no moral judgment (e.g., a man who suffers a series of gruesome calamities, for which nobody is to blame) and that mightn't trigger a suspension of the incompatibilist intuition.

Nor would the results have come as a surprise to Gilbert Ryle. "We discuss whether someone's action was voluntary or not only when the action seems to have been his fault," he ventured more than half a century ago. It was a *déformation professionelle* of philosophers, he thought, to describe as "voluntary" acts that were commendable or satisfactory. In his view, "the tangle of largely spurious problems, known as the problem of the Freedom of the Will, partly derives from this unconsciously

stretched use of 'voluntary' and these consequential misappli-
cations of different senses of 'could' and 'could have helped.'"[35]

We know, too, how easily an engaging story can defeat our
allegiance to this or that dictum. Should cars parked in front of
fire hydrants, such as one belonging to Bob the accountant, be
towed? Sure. Now tell me a story about Joanna, a good woman
who's having a bad day, with details about her hopes and
dreams, her kindness to an ailing friend, her preoccupation
with a troubled child. I don't want *her* car to be towed. In the
abstract, we're opposed to theft. But any competent screen-
writer could concoct a story about a cool, big-hearted car thief,
shadowed by a Javert-like detective as he prepares to pull off
one last heist—and get you to switch sides, at least until the
credits roll. In the abstract, people often hold that it's inappro-
priate to respond to machines with reactive attitudes like reproach or approbation; but the *Star Wars* robots C-3PO and
R2D2 handily sweep aside those theoretical commitments.[36] If
there's a discordant element in the story, in short, I just might
read past it.

Still, none of these considerations undermines the basic
idea that strong disapproval may swamp our previous theoretical commitments about, say, causality. Indeed, in another study,
Joshua Knobe showed how people's intuitions about whether
an act was intentional seemed to depend on their appraisal of
that act. This time, he devised a pair of scenarios that didn't require any science-fiction stipulations or, indeed, much imagination. In one of them, the chairman of a company is asked to
approve a new program that will increase profits and also help
the environment. "I don't care at all about helping the environ-

ment," the chairman replies. "I just want to make as much profit as I can. Let's start the new program." So the program is launched and the environment is helped. A second version is identical—except that the program will *hurt* the environment. Once again, the chairman is indifferent to the environment, and the program is launched in order to increase profits, with the expected results.

When Knobe presented these scenarios to subjects in a controlled experiment, he found that when the program helped the environment, only 23 percent agreed that the chairman had "helped the environment intentionally." When the program harmed the environment, though, 82 percent agreed that the chairman had "harmed the environment intentionally." And the pattern recurred when various other scenarios were tested. In the "harm" scenarios, people will assent to the statement that the chairman harmed the environment in order to increase profits; but in the "help" scenarios, they generally won't agree that he helped the environment in order to increase profits. So while you might have supposed that whether you find an act blameworthy depends on whether you have concluded that the act was intended, Knobe's research suggests that something like the reverse is true.

In general, Knobe argues, our intuitions about intentional actions "tend to track the psychological features that are most relevant to praise and blame judgments," and different features become relevant "depending on whether the action itself is good or bad." His analysis here doesn't fault folk psychology for being distorted by moral considerations; the idea, rather, is that such considerations "are playing a helpful role in people's underlying competence itself." (He has come to praise folk psychology, not to bury it.) Once we revisit the question of what folk psychology is *for*, we might see that its tasks include the apportioning of praise and blame. Knobe's findings are, as he recognizes, congruent with Strawson's arguments about reactive attitudes—in particular, the hovering thought that such attitudes might be the basis of our judgments about responsibility, rather than vice versa.[37]

Inspecting these help/harm studies, as with the compatibilism studies, philosophers will want to poke and prod, of course. Perhaps most people wouldn't describe an action's unsought side-effect as either intentional or unintentional without the forced choice of a questionnaire. Perhaps there's something wonky about our use of that English adverb "intentionally," such that the study could not be reproduced in Korean. In Knobe's analysis, the word "behavior" is used to refer not to the chairman's decision to launch the program, but to the chairman's harming or hurting the environment. Perhaps that term is question-begging: philosophers might disagree about whether to designate downstream consequences of an agent's decision, even if foreseen, as an agent's "behavior." For the subjects of the experiment, the question has similar framing effects. That is, the question "Did the agent ϕ intentionally?" foregrounds the proposition that "the agent ϕ'd," and (arguably) produces its own salience distortions.

Knobe has ventured that "the process leading up to people's intentional-action intuitions is a kind of heuristic," constructed so that it normally accords with our ascriptions of praise and blame.[38] But perhaps those very ascriptions of praise and blame flow from a heuristic of another kind. The intuitions elicited by those scenarios about the mercenary chairman look to be socially beneficial: people rarely need to be encouraged to promote their self-interest, whereas they often need to be discouraged from promoting their self-interest at the expense of others. In a manner congenial to consequentialist accounts of moral responsibility, this practical asymmetry corresponds to the asymmetry in our intentional-action intuitions. (For similar reasons, perhaps, we penalize firms for negative externalities but generally don't reward them for positive ones.) If these considerations help explain our judgments, we would expect praise for the sought-after positive effects of courageous, self-sacrificing acts, even if success was the result of sheer fortuity (and, *mutatis mutandis*, blame for sought-after but fortuitous negative effects), which is just what Knobe has found in other studies.[39]

There are other reasons to suspect that the basic results will prove pretty robust. For one thing, the intuitions Knobe describes are intaglioed on common law, not to mention our civil and criminal codes. We regularly hold people culpable for the unsought consequences of their behavior. We have a rich legal vocabulary—"depraved indifference," "reckless disregard," "murder in the second degree," "involuntary manslaughter"—for such violations. They establish agent ownership, in effect, of harms that are not even foreseen but merely foreseeable, and they accord with a broad moral consensus that holds people responsible for such side-effects of what they do. All these features of the law reflect intuitions about moral responsibility that can be elicited with questionnaires and scenarios.

When you take a closer look at folk theories of moral responsibility, in fact, they start to resemble a patchwork quilt: that is, there *are* patterns . . . many different ones. Here's a criterion that researchers have identified, on the basis of various scenario-based experiments: although—as the vignettes about the mercenary chairman showed—we'll hold someone responsible for the foreseen-but-unsought side-effects of an action when those effects are bad, we'll credit the person with good consequences only when the person was aiming for them. Here's another criterion, operative in other situations: you bear greater responsibility for an accident that happens in the course of your doing something discreditable than you do for an accident that happens in the course of your doing something commendable. And yet another: you bear greater responsibility for an accident that has severe consequences than you do for an accident with mild ones. Reviewing the research literature, Knobe and Doris identify an assumption, which they call "invariance," that underlies previous work on moral responsibility. It's the idea that "people should apply the *same* criteria in *all* their responsibility judgments." The evidence, they argue, shows that people in fact apply different criteria in different sorts of cases. Then they throw down the gauntlet: "This discovery in empirical psychology leaves us with a stark choice in moral philosophy. One option would be to hold on to the goal of fitting with people's ordinary judgments and thereby abandon the assumption of invariance. The other would be to hold on to the assumption of invariance and thereby abandon the goal of fitting with people's ordinary judgments. But it seems that one cannot have it both ways."[40]

So long as the patterns identified are countable and compassable, we might suppose that one invariance could be replaced with, say, five invariances. We shouldn't be surprised, though, to find many situations that aren't tightly cabined by one or another ideal type but lend themselves to multiple descriptions. Such variegation would also be predicted by an account of moral epistemology that arises from work that cognitive psychologists have done on neural networks and the nature of categorization. Ever since Eleanor Rosch's work in the early 1970s, it has been a common thought that people categorize objects, situations, and concepts not on the basis of abstract definitions, but by reference to prototypes. We immediately categorize an apple as a fruit; it takes us longer to decide that an olive is one, too. For Paul Churchland, then, moral disagreements should be seen not as disputes about "rules" so much as disputes about which prototypes best accord with a given situation. (Is a fetus more like a tiny person or more like a growth?)[41] On a prototype model, we shouldn't expect invariance, because our perceptions, in a range of situations, will be subject to Necker-cube-style ambiguity, typicality effects, and fuzzy boundaries, so there will be a competition among (or an overlay of) several plausible prototypes. You don't need that apparatus to explain why people may have a variety of moral responses to events, though. The numerous allies of moral or value pluralism often suppose that the judgments people make will depend on what's perspicuous in a particular situation, that we have no fixed algorithm for deciding among our normative concerns. Either way, if it's simply a fact about us that our folk moral psychology is deeply heterogeneous—not to mention riddled with moral mirages—then the convergence and coherence promised by enthusiasts for reflective equilibrium are bound to be all the more elusive.

Seeing Reason

Human beings are inclined to believe that a tethered ball that circles around a pole will, once cut loose, retain a curved trajectory. That's a deep feature of our "folk physics," and it's completely wrong. Knowing that we're prone to this misapprehension—the way we're prone to the Müller-Lyer illusion—can help us overcome it. The mechanisms of the eye are usually reliable in guiding us to correct beliefs about the visible world. But there are, of course, illusions that are consistently produced in specifiable circumstances. Once we know this, we can learn to avoid reliance on our eyes in such circumstances, even though we cannot change the built-in mechanisms of the visual system. I don't slow down to avoid the illusory puddles of water that appear on the highway before me in the heat of summer. I can't stop "seeing" them. I *can* learn that they aren't there. Does research into the vagaries of our folk moral psychology enable us to do something similar?

Understanding where our intuitions come from can surely help us to think about which ones we should trust. Other psychological research will suggest that some of our intuitions will survive, even in circumstances where they have misled us. Here the analogy with the scientific study of our cognitive processes is, as I've said, quite natural. Just as an awareness of optical illusions helps us avoid being misled by them, cognitive psychologists have shown that all of us—including professional statisticians—are bad at taking account of probabilistic information. But this very discovery comes with the knowledge that there are ways around the problem: learning to do statistical calculations rather than following our hunches, or, perhaps, recasting the probabilities as frequencies, about which our intuitions seem more reliable. The proposal that—to put it very crudely—it's our feelings that guide us to the intuition about the footbridge case, while our reason guides us in the original trolley problem is the sort of thing we might want to consider in deciding whether that intuition is right. So is the fact that even if killing the stranger is, in these bizarre circumstances, the best thing to do, I have good reason—based in our current best understanding of human psychology—not to try to make myself the kind of person who would do it.

Again, we might, as various theorists have suggested, treat our intuitions in clusters of cases as the output of a heuristic. But that, of course, entails that some other, better guide determines whether the heuristic has steered us right or wrong. To identify a heuristic, remember, we need a standard. And here's where the analogy with folk physics falters: professional physicists can happily build models of the universe that involve structures—such as Calabi-Yau manifolds and Gromov-Witten invariants—that are utterly remote from our capacity to imagine them, in any meaningful sense. By contrast, moral psychology, however reflective, can't be dissociated from our moral sentiments, because it's basic to how we make sense of one another and ourselves; in a deliberately awkward formulation by Bernard

Williams, moral thought and experience "must primarily involve grasping the world in such a way that one can, as a particular human being, live in it."[42] Could it be that your moral intuitions themselves, fallible though they are, provide a standard for judgment? Moral agents often think so, which is why, in the footbridge cases, philosophers have generally spurned the "obvious" way out of the problem—which is to maximize lives saved by killing the stranger—and struggled to find some other way. Do we have a way to settle the matter? The analogy with color perception might be helpful here. Suppose someone were to propose, as a heuristic, this "blue rule":

If something looks blue and you have no special knowledge about your eyes or the lighting, you should believe that it's blue.

I think it is natural to respond that this isn't just a heuristic. If this isn't the right way to tell whether something is blue, either there's no such thing as looking blue or there's no such thing as being blue. Yes, following this rule can lead you astray; but only if there is something odd about the circumstances that you didn't know about. If it turned out that red things sometimes looked blue when your eyes and the lighting were normal, you'd have reason to conclude that there was something incoherent about the way we understand color. Color is, as Bishop Berkeley used to say, one of the proper objects of vision. It's part of what vision is for; and, from the point of view of a perceiver, the blue rule is the only way of proceeding that makes any sense.

Now consider this rule:

If something seems intuitively wrong (or right) and you have no special knowledge that suggests your moral intuition is distorted, you shouldn't (or should) do it.

This, someone might argue analogously, isn't a heuristic either; from the point of view of the agent, the rule is a constitutive element of the very idea of wrongness. Now, I could have couched the rule in terms of belief: if something seems wrong, you should believe you shouldn't do it. But our interest here is practical: we want to consider what qualifies as a reason to φ, a reason not to believe but to do something. The analogy I want to explore is between certain kinds of reasons for perceptual belief and certain kinds of reasons for action, not between reasons for perceptual beliefs and reasons for normative beliefs.[43]

To see how far we can get with the comparison between the perceptual and the ethical, let's consider the general schema the two cases share. In each, there is a response—belief about a color in the first, action in the second—that you ought to make when a certain condition obtains, provided there is no further reason that you should not respond in that way. Philosophers say you have a "pro tanto" reason to φ, when you are aware of a state of affairs, S, that is a reason for φ-ing, even if there are other further states of affairs awareness of which would mean you ought not to φ. If you have a pro tanto reason to φ and you're aware of no other relevant considerations, you ought to φ.[44] So we can say, in this convenient shorthand, that a thing's looking blue is a pro tanto reason to believe that it is blue: you ought to believe something is blue, that is, if you are aware that it looks blue. And that's so, even if, were further evidence to come along—that a wicked scientist put blue contact lenses in your eyes overnight, say—the new evidence might rationally require you to believe that it wasn't blue.

Similarly, perhaps the fact that something seems wrong is a pro tanto reason not to do it: you ought not to push the heavy stranger off the bridge if it seems to you wrong to do so. And, once more, that would be true even though there are circumstances in which further reasons might require or permit you to do it.[45] The proposal is, then, that our moral intuitions give us pro tanto reasons to act (or not to act), just as our senses give us pro tanto reasons for belief.

The obvious problem with this proposal is that, as we've seen again and again, our moral intuitions may be unreliable. Remember that comment offered by the experimental subject who was asked to think about Dan, the student-council rep: "I don't know why it's wrong; it just is." How are we to decide which among our intuitions provide valid pro tanto reasons? Does the mere fact that it strikes me that I don't feel like doing something—reaching out to Joe, who has fallen into a sewage tank, say—give me a pro tanto reason not to help him? Perhaps the fact that I'm disgusted is a pro tanto reason not to stick my hand out; one that is defeated by the fact that Joe needs help (which gives me a pro tanto reason to reach out to him, in the context, that is not defeated, let us suppose, by any other reasons). How can I distinguish between a pro tanto reason and the mere fact that I do or don't feel like doing something? In the case of perception, we can distinguish the visual properties of things and say that it is our visual awareness of these that gives us pro tanto reasons for (visual) perceptual judgment. And we can identify the visual properties by identifying our eyes as the organs that detect them. But we can't identify the reason-for-action-giving properties of situations by pointing to any organ—and, indeed, moral psychologists are inclined to doubt that there are any such organs. They don't think we have what the Enlightenment philosophers called a "moral sense."

What we do have are many, many responses that give us pro tanto guidance as to how we should feel and act. Let's call these responses "evaluations." One sort of evaluation is an emotion: fear is a pro tanto reason for avoiding something. More precisely, when I fear that P, I have a pro tanto reason to take action to prevent it coming about that P. (Fear of objects is grounded in the belief that some state of affairs whose coming about we fear is likely in their presence.) Reasonable fears are therefore grounded in judgments that our interests will be set back if we don't try to prevent them, because the fact that something will set back our interests is a pro tanto reason for us to prevent it. Yet we have not only fears, but also phobias. Phobias arguably don't give us reason to do anything . . . except to try to get rid of them. And so, when we must distinguish the cases where we should and should not take notice of our feelings, we will want to take account of the empirical research at hand. By illuminating odd features of our evaluations, showing where judgments about cases of a certain form diverge from our other, considered judgments, that research can be a useful adjunct to our intuitions, especially if we consider "attentive reflection," as Thomas Reid urged, to be a form of intuition, too.

Explanations and Reasons

All this sounds soothingly hygienic and prudent. But we are bound to be left with a lingering sense of unease. In a sense, all this talk of *mistakes*—of loss/gain anomalies, help/harm asymmetries, priming effects, performance errors, and so forth—has been a distraction from a larger threat. Learning that our intuitions are imperfect has, at least, one comforting implication: to be told that we sometimes get things wrong implies that we can, in principle, get them right. The lingering unease I mentioned has a different source: the dissonance between viewing moral sentiments as, in some measure, constitutive of a moral judgment and viewing them as a device that nature has bequeathed us for social regulation.

Four decades ago, Strawson noted that human attitudes had become objects of study in the disciplines of history and anthropology but also—and, he thought, of greater significance—in psychology. The humanists could tell us what aspects of our intuitions were specific to our time and place; but the psychologists, more corrosively, could make us distrust habits of mind that were universal and enduring. Strawson had, in part, a sociological point to make: "The prestige of these theoretical studies," he feared, "is apt to make us forget that in philosophy, though it also is a theoretical study, we have to take account of the facts in all their bearings; we are not to suppose that we are required, or permitted, as philosophers, to regard ourselves, as human beings, as detached from the attitudes which, as scientists, we study with detachment."[46]

But the more fundamental concern has to do with the task of

moral theory. We cannot content ourselves with the claim that a given bundle of attitudes solves a social coordination problem—that it is, from some objective point of view, *adaptive*. That's a possible standard for a heuristic, but (at least without further elaboration) it's not moral in nature. The claim that someone, on prudential grounds, should be punished does not entail that he or she is blame*worthy*. As Hume put it, when a man reproaches another morally, he "must choose a point of view, common to him with others; he must move some universal principle of the human frame, and touch a string to which all mankind have an accord and symphony."[47] Moral thought aspires to a register that is universal without being impersonal. It can't be just an esoteric guidebook for a supreme legislator; it has to be intelligible to us ordinary persons. That's why an explanation cannot replace a reason, why a causal account cannot supplant a moral justification. In ordinary life, you'll notice, we invoke psychological explanations only when we're seeking exemptions from moral agency. ("I'm sorry I said that—I haven't been sleeping well lately.") To introduce them into a conversation about justification must seem, in effect, to change the subject.

The vast majority of our decisions, to be sure, are made unreflectively, almost on autopilot; an outfielder can catch a ball without the help of Euler's Method for solving differential equations, and most of the time you can make expert moral decisions without engaging in conscious axiology. Indeed, you'd better, or you'll never get anything done. We needn't worry that, in actual appraisals, we generally start with a verdict, and work backward from there. Tellingly, while most people agree, in the footbridge scenario, that it would be wrong to topple the

300-pound man, they do not agree about *why* it is wrong: in experiments, the justifications that subjects offer are all over the map. Given that morality is practical, we should expect it to involve (in Ryle's venerable distinction) "knowing how," not just "knowing that"—tacit skills in contrast to the possession of propositional content, or the apprehension of truths. Yet the outfielder's intuitions about where the ball will fall do track with the actual movements of the ball. Many philosophers (especially those inclined toward moral realism, which may hold that moral predicates have causal power) will look for *some* link between the explanation and the justification for a decision. And even philosophers who are satisfied with good-enough-for-government-work heuristics, as a default procedure, will insist that people be able to provide reasons when reasons are called for.

"To say that a judgment is due to causes is to imply that it is not based on reasons," Ross wrote, "and so far as this is the case we have no ground for believing it to be true; it will be a mere accident if it is true."[48] This was meant to be a perspectival point, so to speak, not a logical one. As self-conscious moral agents, we can sometimes reflect on ourselves as natural creatures, part of a causal system, as well as reason-responsive ones. Our moral world is both caused and created, and its breezes carry the voices of both explanations and reasons.

In moving from the psychologist's concern with naturalistic explanation to the philosopher's concern with reasons, we move from the issue of what sort of dispositions it might be good for us to have to the issue of what sorts of sentiments might count as moral justifications. These aren't just clashing accounts; they are—in ways I'll explore further in the next chapter—two perspectives. One is that of a sort of cosmic engineer, crafting our natures; the other is that of the moral agent thus crafted. And only a misguided monism would force both perspectives into one. In ethics as in optics, we need stereoscopy to see the world in all its dimensions. The claim that, all things considered, it's good to have certain sentiments, dispositions, and attitudes can be separated from the claim that these sentiments, dispositions, and attitudes are (at least in part) internally constitutive of normativity—of the content of moral propositions. But we needn't choose between them. The first claim defends a disposition by, say, its efficacy in securing some good or ensemble of goods. The second claim holds that some good derives, in a specific sense, from the disposition. The claims are different, but not rivalrous: they do not have to compete in the same explanatory space.

We can, after all, hive off the evolutionary question of why we have some of the evaluations that we have from the question of what, given that we do have these evaluations, we ought to do. Appeals to fitness might explain the evolution of our reactive attitudes; by itself, that fact takes nothing away from the authority of those reactive attitudes—nor, indeed, does it undermine our higher-level moral appraisals of our first-order moral appraisals. And so we can begin to dispel the unease I mentioned a little earlier. Nature taught our ancestors to walk; we can teach ourselves to dance.

This story can be made compelling only if we say more about how our picture of ourselves as natural creatures, the subjects of psychology and the social sciences, can fit with a view of the world in which our intuitions are not just feelings, emotions bubbling up from our neurons and our glands, but also responses to normative demands. We need to explore the relationship between the perspective of the cosmic engineer and the perspective of the agent she engineers; and—a project I'll discuss further in the next chapter—we need to be able to live with both perspectives.

The Varieties of Moral Experience

There is really no more ground for supposing that all our demands can be accounted for by one universal underlying kind of motive than there is ground for supposing that all physical phenomena are cases of a single law. The elementary forces in ethics are probably as plural as those of physics are. The various ideals have no common character apart from the fact that they are ideals.

—WILLIAM JAMES, "The Moral Philosopher and the Moral Life"

The Beginnings of Ethics

There's a tale—no doubt, like many such splendid tales, apocryphal—of a writer who wakes in the middle of the night convinced that she has made a wonderful dreamtime discovery. Rapidly she writes it down; equally swiftly she falls back to sleep. In the morning, recalling her nighttime adventure, she turns with excitement to read these words on the paper by her bed.

Hogamus higamus
Man is polygamous.

Higamus hogamus
Woman's monogamous.

You can see why people have sometimes ascribed this verse to Gertrude Stein, more often to Dorothy Parker; it's rather odd, though, that it has also been attributed to William James.

The idea pithily expressed in these nine words can be found expounded more wordily in many recent discussions of evolutionary psychology. (According to the parental-investment model, the sex that tends to have the greater investment in each offspring—in gestation, lactation, nurturance, and so on—will be the more discriminating in mating choice.) But how does it relate to ethics? Well, moral traditions teach that spouses should be faithful to each other, but, anthropologically speaking, they seldom take male sexual infidelity as seriously as female, and they often permit men to have more than one spouse, while almost always denying that option to women. Now, perhaps evolutionary circumstances, having to do with inclusive fitness, make these traditions and patterns of sentiment natural. Yet when others of us contemplate such traditions—as when, for instance, a village court in northern Nigeria calls for the stoning of the woman, and only the woman, involved in an adulterous liaison—our revulsion and outrage also feel quite . . . natural. The dictum of "doing what comes naturally," we can agree, provides no guidance by itself.

In Chapter 3, I promised a picture of ourselves as creatures enmeshed in causal systems large and small—the subjects of psychology and the social sciences—that could fit together with a view of the world in which our intuitions are not just emotions bubbling up from our brains but also responses to normative demands. Kant gave these perspectives names. We are bound to acknowledge, he said, that we are natural beings, governed by causal laws. From this standpoint, we belong to what he called the world of the senses, the *Sinnenwelt*. But it's not a standpoint we can adopt when we ourselves act as agents: "All men think of themselves as having a free will," Kant noted. You can't think of your own actions as things that just happen. Accordingly, "for *purposes of action* the footpath of freedom is the only one on which we can make use of reason in our conduct." Here we situate ourselves in what he dubbed the world of the understanding, the *Verstandeswelt*.[1]

In this chapter, I'm going to explore a social-science typology of moral emotions, and consider whether we can map them from one realm to the other. As we'll see, they seem to sponsor various strains in our traditions of philosophical ethics. The social-science claims arrive, it's true, with a certain reductionist torque. I'll try to persuade you—it is my counterspin—that we can couple these realms without reducing one to the other. First, though, a few words of caution.

Higamus-hogamus explanations—and, more generally, evolutionary arguments—take the standpoint of the *Sinnenwelt*. Like all Darwinian theory, evolutionary psychology aims to explain how the characteristics of organisms arose by natural selection in their ancestors' environments; what's distinctive is a focus on the adaptation of *behavior*. Most such explanations show only how natural selection of genes *could have* produced a certain observed pattern of behavior; but that was already quite clever, since, as Darwin's critics pointed out almost immediately, it was hard to see how many forms of moral behavior could have evolved by natural selection. Why would organisms be disposed to behave altruistically toward unrelated members of their species? What could explain the evolution of the disposition to make and care about friends?

Explanations of how these forms of "prosocial" behavior might have arisen by natural selection are often extremely ingenious and interesting. But, historically, arguments that root patterns of social life in biology have sometimes been enlisted to rationalize an inequitable status quo. So it's reasonable to regard evolutionary hypotheses with skepticism until they are tested against evidence from anthropology and history about the full range of human variability.[2] And even assuming that a pattern of behavior is shaped by a genetically based mechanism, if it is nevertheless undesirable, we can try to identify what circumstances trigger the mechanism and make sure they rarely arise. Oscar Wilde once remarked that he could resist anything except temptation. (And if he said it once, we can be sure he said it many times. Like evolution, Oscar didn't believe in waste.) Even if there are deep behavioral tendencies in our nature that have evolutionary explanations, they will not be engaged in every possible environment. The more we learn about how the feelings that shape our acts *are* triggered, the more we can adjust the environment to make sure they *aren't*. What is equally important, many tendencies of our nature evolved to produce behavior we *can* endorse. Discovering what triggers these tendencies can allow us to make desirable behavior more frequent, too. In each case—as we dared to hope in the preceding two chapters—psychology can serve ethics.

But, as we'll also see, the mere fact that human beings have some deeply entrenched mechanism or other—a passion for fairness, a yearning for glory—leaves undetermined how it will be expressed, what forms it will take. For us human beings, there is no clear dividing line between nature and culture. If, by the nature of a creature, you mean the ways it can behave—its behavioral possibilities—then human nature is always already cultural twice over. First, it is the historical result of earlier social practices, which shaped our environments, creating selection pressures that stabilized genetically inscribed behavioral dispositions. Second, human behavioral possibilities are, in part, the result of what concepts are available to people; the concepts available to you being, of course, a central dimension of culture. It's only because of an institutional and conceptual background that one can be, say, a Republican or a Democrat, a Catholic or a Muslim . . . or, for that matter, a professional critic or philosopher. Without that background, both *being* a Catholic, Republican philosopher and *acting as one* would be literally inconceivable.

This fact is the result of a deeper truth about the relation between culture and human possibility. All human action is conceptually shaped, because when we act intentionally, there is *something that we think we are doing.* Acts are carried out under a conception. To pay you by check, I need to grasp at least these concepts: signature, banking, money. Concepts acquired from our cultures are essential prerequisites for most of the interesting things we do.[3]

What matters for our ethical lives is which psychological mechanisms we have, more than any evolutionary story about where they came from; they are what help determine our behavioral possibilities, our individual natures. And the cultural context (including, not least, the identities it provides) matters for the same reason: it helps determine them, too. We shall be following our culturally shaped natures through the rest of this chapter. Our task, as we strobe between those two Kantian standpoints, is to see whether we can gain insight into the profoundly variegated nature of our evaluations. In recent years, psychologists—drawing from the work of primatologists, evolutionary game theorists, anthropologists, and economists—have posited separate mechanisms that produce our various moral sentiments. Let's take a closer look at the picture they present.

The Modularity of Morals

The recent literature in experimental moral psychology suggests that the modes of response underlying our moral sentiments can be grouped into five or six fundamental kinds. Maybe there are more; maybe there are fewer. It's best to take these claims as tentative and provisional. But here I'll take my lead (albeit with some leeway!) from a taxonomy of moral cognition that the psychologist Jonathan Haidt and his collaborators have elaborated.[4] The taxonomy distinguishes responses that relate to (the avoidance or alleviation of) harm; to fairness and reciprocity; to hierarchy and respect; to purity and pollution; to ingroup/outgroup boundaries; and to awe and elevation. The proposal is that distinct clusters of intuitions flow from each kind of response, and—even more conjecturally—

that they may correspond to subsystems within our minds. The proposal acknowledges, though, that these responses may overlap, collaborate or conflict, in the actual texture of our moral experiences.

It's usual nowadays to call the hypothesized functional subsystems of the mind "modules"—terminology made standard by the philosopher Jerry Fodor. Modules are specialized (responding to a particular *domain* of stimuli), fast, automatic, and informationally encapsulated (not much affected, that is, by information from other parts of the mind). Thus, our visual-processing system takes light impinging on the retina as its domain, quickly and automatically translates retinal events into an image of the world, and is (with interesting exceptions) pretty much unaffected by what we believe. You can't, say, make something that you know is white look white, just because you're aware that there's a red light shining on it. Your visual processing system isn't designed to adjust to that information. The cognitive scientist Dan Sperber calls the inputs that a module evolved to respond to its "proper domain." By contrast, the "actual domain" of the module includes everything that sets it off on its fast, automatic, informationally encapsulated path.[5]

But while talk of modules is a fixture of cognitive science, there's a lot of debate over how to define them, and how real they are. For starters, how many are there—a whole lot or just a few? The anthropologist Alan Fiske, for instance, has famously argued that all interpersonal relations can be sorted into precisely four categories: sharing, ranking, matching, or pricing. Why just four? Because they correspond to four social modules, and it would be cognitively taxing, he thinks, to have too many of those. Theoretical parsimony is thus founded on the assumption of neuropsychological parsimony.[6] But other people think that we're massively modular. Dan Sperber, for one, wants us to lower the bar for what counts as modular, and he finds modules, or at least "somewhat modular" processing systems, almost everywhere he looks. Let me suggest that we sidestep the disputes over what, precisely, qualifies as a "module," and use the term permissively, without implying grand claims about the neural architecture of our moral psychology. (For my immediate purposes, the term also has, in its favor, the fact that it's shorter than "fundamental kind of response.")

Now, modules are meant, as I say, to be automatic—the psychologists invoke them to make sense of abilities and intuitions, and, in the realm of morality, take them to produce "flashes" of approbation or disapprobation. From the perspective of the psychologists, then, it may be perverse that I'll be relating these hypothesized modules to positions in our explicit moral reasoning. These psychological modules were meant to obviate appeals to moral reasoning; once conditioned by local concepts and habits, those "flashes" are regarded as pretty much constitutive of morality. That's not my view, but, for the moment, I can defend my approach with an uncontroversial observation. Because people are, among other things, reason-exchanging creatures, we should surely expect the modules that guide our evaluations and actions to have influenced some of the duties, obligations, and values that people have discussed explicitly. And, of course, the way we arrived at these modules was by working back from the things people do and say.

COMPASSION

The first and most obvious moral module—which is also to say the first class of evaluative responses—relates to the prospect or spectacle of human suffering. The philosopher Shaun Nichols has explored these responses in terms of what he calls the "Concern Mechanism." It takes, as input, representations of distress, and produces, as output, sentiments that (among other things) can motivate altruism. Even babies and toddlers, who are too young to be much good at thinking about the inner lives of other people, evince concern in response to signs of distress. In one study, for example, a nineteen-month-old child, seeing her mother hurt her foot, scooted over to the mother, said "hurt foot," and rubbed the afflicted extremity. Conversely, psychopaths, who are often very good indeed at figuring out what other people are thinking (and manipulating them), show abnormally low levels of response to the suffering of other people.[7] One inference is that the Concern Mechanism is part of what makes normal people much less likely than psychopaths to cause harm.

It might also explain why people everywhere seem able to distinguish between violations involving harm or suffering and violations of convention. In one study, young schoolchildren who knew that chewing gum in class was against the rules were told that, at another school, the teacher didn't have a rule against gum chewing. The kids agreed that it wasn't wrong to chew gum at that other school. When they were told that the teacher at the other school didn't have a rule against hitting, however, the kids held that hitting at that other school would still be wrong. Nichols also tells us about a study involving Amish teenagers which suggests, as he says, that such moral assessments are even taken to be independent from God's authority. What if God had made no rule against working on Sunday? A hundred percent of the Amish teens said that it would be fine to work on Sunday. What if God had made no rule about hitting? Most of them felt that hitting would still be wrong.[8]

Faced with a suffering person, then, our natural response is an emotion—compassion, let's call it—that gives us a pro tanto reason to express sympathy and offer aid. Compassion of this sort is not inevitable, needless to say, but when it fails, it's often because it's trumped by a distinction between an ingroup and an outgroup (more on that later) or because the suffering is otherwise seen as merited. It is the character of pro tanto reasons, remember, that they can be overridden. (As we'll see, both the psychological mechanisms that generate the psychological distinction between ingroup and outgroup members and the instinct to punish norm breakers are themselves universal, too, though culture fixes what classifications of people as insiders and outsiders are possible and shapes what norms we recognize, and so determines what we will be disposed to punish.)

Our capacity for compassion has also, as we should expect, shaped our explicit traditions of moral deliberation. Philosophers may alight on the discussions of sympathy toward our fellows in Lord Shaftesbury or Francis Hutcheson (who held that our *sensus communis* shaped us to be "uneasy at their misery"), and then in David Hume or Adam Smith (for whom "our fellow-feeling for the misery of others" resulted, as Smith put it at the start of *The Theory of Moral Sentiments,* from our imaginatively "changing places in fancy with the sufferer"), because many eighteenth-century theorists were preoccupied with the subject of sympathy, fellow-feeling. But this is not to slight the deliberations over the previous millennium or so, nor its salience in the scriptures held holy by various creeds. In the nineteenth century, Arthur Schopenhauer took compassion (which, he thought, "displayed a truly wonderful effectiveness at all times, among all nations, in all situations of life") to be the basis of morality, issuing in duties of justice and philanthropy.[9] We'll also find it enshrined in what Ross calls the duty of nonmaleficence—that is, the obligation not to harm others; and in what others have commended as the virtue of kindness. But the moral theories that give pride of place to the relief or avoidance of suffering and harm tend to be consequentialist. A central tenet of John Stuart Mill's moral theory is what is called the "harm principle," which says that the only justification for abridging someone's freedom is "to prevent harm to others." Although this was meant to be counsel to legislators, the sort of utilitarianism Mill espoused, inasmuch as it aims to maximize well-being, must require us as individuals to try to minimize— or, at any rate, reduce—suffering.

RECIPROCITY

The responsibility to relieve or prevent suffering isn't the only thing that moral agents care about, of course. So here's a second candidate for moral modularity. It relates to issues of *fairness or reciprocity,* and, in contexts where a norm of fairness is broken, it can produce feelings of guilt and shame (if you're the perpetrator), gratitude (if you're a beneficiary), or resentment (if you're a victim). The voice of resentment speaks the loudest. "That's not fair!" is one of the commonest moral complaints voiced by children at age four and older. How did that feature of our psychologies arise? In *Utilitarianism*, Mill argues that the desire to punish is an essential element of what he called "the sentiment of justice." In his view, "It would always give us pleasure, and chime in with our feelings of fitness, that acts which we deem unjust should be punished." This is true, he thinks, even when the acts aren't unfair to *us*. Mill assumes that the desire to hurt those who break the rules is not natural. And so he gives a rather complicated story about why we experience this sentiment: one that involves sympathy, an instinct for self-defense, and a recognition that it's in our individual interest to do what serves our collective interests—all of which, by contrast, he does take to be natural.[10]

It turns out, though, that Mill's assumption was mistaken. People everywhere seem to have a natural tendency to punish antisocial behavior of this sort, a tendency you can demonstrate quite easily. The easiest way is just to offer them a chance to play what's called an ultimatum game.

Here's an example: There are two players and they're given a pot of $100 to divide. Player A gets to offer a share to player B and, if B accepts, they get what A has decided. If B rejects the offer, no one gets anything. A and B don't ever meet and know nothing about each other except that they're playing the game. Classical game theory predicts that A will propose a split in which B gets the smallest possible amount—one cent—because he's a rational maximizer of his own interests who assigns no value to giving money to anonymous strangers. And B should accept: after all, one cent is better than nothing. Cross-culturally, however, A almost always offers B a significant amount—often a 50-50 split—and B almost always rejects an offer that's too much below that 50-50 split, which he regards as somehow cheating. (This happens even among economics students trained to think that it's always irrational to turn money down.) B, in other words, is willing to turn down money to punish a stranger who does what she thinks is unfair; and A, knowing this, and not wanting to go away with nothing, makes sure to make B an offer she's not going to refuse.[11] That's the case even when the two players know they're never going to play the game together again.

The behavioral economists Ernst Fehr and Simon Gächter, who have done many such experiments, point out that throughout the human past, "crucial human activities . . . constituted a public good"—that is, everyone benefited from such activities whether or not they contributed to them. Each person had, as a result, no direct incentive to cooperate, since they'd get the benefits anyway. (Someone who doesn't do their fair share in maintaining a public good is a "free rider.") A disposition to punish defectors from cooperation solves that difficulty, as Fehr and Gächter explain:

> Everybody in the group will be better off if free riding is deterred, but nobody has an incentive to punish the free riders. Thus, the punishment of free riders constitutes a second-order public good. The problem of second-order

public goods can be solved if enough humans have a tendency for altruistic punishment, that is, if they are motivated to punish free riders even though it's costly and yields no material benefits for the punishers.[12]

The cross-cultural results of ultimatum games suggest we are, indeed, so motivated.

In 2003, Gächter reported an interesting variation on this theme; it involved ultimatum games run with people from Belarus and Russia, who, it emerged, punished those who were unusually generous as well as those who were stingy.[13] There are, it turns out, societies in which someone who offers too much in an ultimatum game will be punished, in effect, for being uppity or condescending ("I don't need your charity!"). Conversely, in ultimatum games conducted in a remote society where gift-giving was culturally central, overly generous offers were declined because, it seems, the player just didn't want to feel under an obligation ("I couldn't possibly accept this"). Such evidence should remind us, if we need reminding, that even if the psychological mechanisms here are general, their expression will depend a good deal on cultural context. Still, throughout countless iterations of such bargaining games, researchers find that people reliably get mad at cheaters, and cheaters know it. If—to put matters with caricatural simplicity—the Concern Mechanism is triggered by suffering and produces compassion, this second module is triggered by unfairness and produces, in the first instance, resentment. Here your response is not to an injury incurred by another but to what you conceive as an injury incurred by yourself.

What traditions in moral thought might derive from a module attuned to fairness and reciprocity, and, especially, to their violations? There's no shortage of them. Some evolutionary game theorists would tell us that resentment is, in effect, more prosocial than compassion. Intuitions about fairness can lead to egalitarian impulses. They can underwrite what Ross called the duty of justice, by which he meant the obligation to prevent, or correct, a mismatch between someone's happiness and what we take to be their merit (the robber must not live high while his victim starves); the duty of gratitude, by which he meant our obligation to repay others for their past favors to us (although a burdensome sense of indebtedness is not what we would normally call "gratitude"); and the duty of reparation, the obligation to compensate others for past wrongs which rests "on a previous wrongful act." Justice is sometimes counted among the virtues; and Rawls's celebrated account of "justice as fairness" makes the value of fairness central to political morality.[14] Indeed, ideals of fairness and reciprocity underwrite all contract-based systems of morality, from Thomas Hobbes to David Gauthier, which start with our hypothetical assent to hypothetical bargains. Finally, intuitions about fairness are universalist in this special sense: there is something that I deserve not in virtue of *who* I am but, so to speak, simply *because* I am. The core concern of morality is what we owe to others, and we cannot parse that idea without concepts of fairness and reciprocity. Those concepts could further entrain the thought that you should act as you would have me act—that there are rules that are binding on all of us—and are thus consonant with the Kantian idea of the categorical imperative, the maxim you could will to be universal law. However different the moral lexicons we've just surveyed may be (we've managed to invoke aretaic, deontological, and contractarian traditions), is it inconceivable that they share a taproot?

Hierarchy

A third module has to do with *social hierarchy,* and implicates attitudes such as respect and contempt. The evaluations it yields reflect the way that we, like our primate ancestors and cousins, have emotions attuned to status in social groups. Culture fixes the concepts—master, slave; corporal, private—and the hierarchies—class, military rank—that determine status. But status-sensitivity comes with the human territory. I won't try to represent the vast primatological, anthropological, and sociological literature on the subject. Here, the only unobvious idea, to us moderns, is that hierarchy might engage specifically *moral* emotions.

Our ancestors would have had little trouble with the notion, we can be sure. For consider the venerable idea of honor. Expressive assaults on your personal status—dignitary affronts—were things they killed over. In a 1610 treatise on dueling, John Seldon, a scholar and friend of Francis Bacon's, listed "the *lye* given, *fame* impeached, *body* wronged, or *courtesy* taxed" as chivalric breaches that would justly provoke *seul à seul* combat among those of gentle birth; four years later, Francis Bacon, in a speech denouncing the practice, ventured that "men of birth and quality will leave the practice, when it begins to be vilified, and come so low as to barber-surgeons and butchers, and such base mechanical persons."[15] But those of lower status, too, had their codes for the violent restoration of honor. In our folk moralities, especially where the "culture of honor" is strong, being "disrespected" famously remains a fighting offense. Now, that's a sociological, not a normative, observation—but it does help us see the genealogical connections between elements in the modern lexicon of liberalism and those in a feudal lexicon we imagine we have renounced.

Perhaps you think you can dispense with *honor*. What about *duty?* The concept of duty, too, was originally anchored in a hierarchical social order. When speakers of Middle English and Anglo-Norman referred to *dueté,* they often had in mind those actions that were incumbent upon one in virtue of one's position, what one owed to others in the hierarchy: hence, in the fourteenth century, John Gower refers to "la dueté des Roys" to love and serve God, maintain holy church, and protect the laws.[16] And, of course, the classical and medieval concept of *dignitas* was, by stipulation, the possession of an elite. So I'm inclined to endorse a point both Michael Walzer and Peter Singer have made: that, historically, progress has come not so much from the alteration of principles or evaluative concepts as from the expansion of the class of their beneficiaries.

The democratization of dignity seems to have been propelled by two vectors. First, there were disputes about the sources of dignity: Was it necessarily the inheritance of noble birth or could it be acquired by achievement? In a poem entitled "Of True Nobility," Horace, the son of a freed slave, laments the Roman tendency to suppose that low birth might make someone base, and endorses the view that "it's no matter who your parents are, so long as you are worthy"—so long, that is, as you have the characteristics of a freeborn person. Second, because predicates derived from hierarchy are relational and ordinal, it's internal to the logic of dignity that someone who, in one context, might be taken to be without dignity could nonetheless have more dignity than someone (or something) even less dignified. It was precisely when Cicero (in *De Officiis*, I.30.106) was comparing human beings to animals—the latter, he thought, care for nothing but bodily pleasure—that he made reference to what was "dignam hominis"; worthy not of philosophers or senators but of humanity *tout court*.[17]

But though the effort to expand the ranks of those worthy of dignity or respect is ancient, it was the success of that effort (incomplete but substantial) in the seventeenth and eighteenth centuries that marks the origins of our moral modernity. Edmund Burke's famous insistence that "the occupation of a hairdresser or of a working tallow-chandler cannot be a matter of honor to any person" already had a beleaguered air. At the same time (as I've remarked elsewhere), in democratizing a sentiment that the feudal order conferred only upon those of gentle birth, European liberalism presupposes some aspect of that feudal conception of dignity. (You can chart similar developments in other cultures: the Asante concept of *animuonyam*, "respect," was, as an old proverb tells us, something to which no slave was entitled; yet once reconfigured as the property of all persons, it could be enlisted in the support of human-rights talk.) So there is a forgotten radicalism in the now-commonplace view that all human beings have an inviolable dignity; or that all persons must be respected.[18] Also, a forgotten conservatism.

As topsy-turvy as it sounds, then, a great deal of egalitarian rhetoric speaks the language of hierarchy. Even the concept of the "dignitary affront" has been worked hard, in the past decade, by legal scholars who want to ensure equal respect for women and minorities in the expressive realm. However paradoxical— and however remote from the psychologist's schema—it may seem, moral universalism plainly speaks the language of status. Kant's insistence that "you treat humanity, whether in your own person or in that of another, always as an end and never as a means only," his insistence upon the "unconditional and incomparable worth" of all persons, recruits for all humanity the respect that a monarch might have considered his due. (In familiar religious cadences, too, you'll find something of this: if we are all "children of God," we must enjoy a close relationship indeed to the King of Kings.) Many contemporary moral accounts are, in this way, dignitarian. Consider the version of contractualism ably defended by Thomas Scanlon, according to which an act is wrong if disallowed by principles "that no one could reasonably reject."[19] Here morality as such is balanced upon the plinth of our respect for the autonomy of all other persons, so long as they are reasonable. Each moral agent is, in some sense, a sovereign among sovereigns.

PURITY

A fourth module yields perceptions of *purity and pollution*, and is anchored in our capacity for disgust. People everywhere make evaluations that draw on this module, a module whose proper domain, in Dan Sperber's term, is dangerous food. Disgust is engaged by many sexual acts that are taboo, as well as by physical contact with people of low caste or a disfavored race: that's its actual domain. (Here, we'd have to say, it interacts with intuitions about hierarchy and outgroups.) Feelings of disgust clearly also depend on the concepts, norms, and institutions with which we are endowed by our societies. Developmental psychologists have explored the contagion-like concept of "cooties" that stirs many children at eight years of age and older; and every tribe, we know, has its own taboos.

In the moral realm, this module is implicated in the idea of *abomination;* and helps to underwrite, for instance, the Holiness Code of Leviticus, with its strictures against eating animals that have died of natural causes, intercourse with a menstruating woman, incest and bestiality, making "any cuttings in your flesh," and so forth. Many of these violations are to be remedied by ritual forms of cleansing; others (e.g., when a man lies with a man "as with a woman") by death. Ideals of modesty and chastity seem to have the same wellspring. But, again, these are just descriptive observations. Should such intuitions have purchase in our reflective moral accounts?

Many philosophers would say no, and Haidt himself has argued that the moral views espoused by liberals (unlike those held by conservatives) tend to eschew the promptings of the purity module. In an interesting round of studies, he and a couple of colleagues crafted a set of stories involving what he calls "harmless taboo violations," and presented them to a few hundred people in an interview setting. In one scenario, a family whose pet dog is killed by a car decides to eat the remains. In another, a man has sex with a chicken carcass that he then cooks for his dinner. The researchers found that subjects who were college students and of high socioeconomic status tended to regard the acts as disgusting but not morally impermissible, whereas subjects of a lower social and educational status (mainly blacks from Philadelphia and Porto Alegre, Brazil) overwhelmingly declared the acts to be morally wrong. What's more, Haidt says, members of the second group justified their condemnation by simple reference to disgust, disrespect, or a violated norm ("Because you're not supposed to do that with a chicken!").[20] Haidt, not surprisingly, isn't very impressed with such justifications; he thinks people have the intuition and then, working backward from this verdict, reach for the closest excuse at hand. Perhaps, though, the reason Haidt discounts their justification is simply that he has the contrary intuition— namely, that the taboo violation *isn't* a moral offense—and he is working backward from *that* verdict. As Bernard Williams once observed, "You can't kill that, it's a child" is a better reason than any reason we can point to for why it's a reason.[21] If "You can't have sex with that, it's a dead chicken" is (as I rather suspect) a bad reason, we'll want to be able to say why.

Nor should we be too quick to assume that our own moral reasoning is, or should be, disengaged from such responses. In one of Williams' best-known scenarios, Jim, a harmless botanist, has wandered into a South American town where Pedro, a militia captain, had been planning to shoot twenty Indian hostages. But now Pedro has another idea: if his distinguished visitor will shoot just one of them himself, Pedro will spare the others. Williams himself thought, and many philosophers have concurred, that our aversion to the act could be a legitimate ethical consideration against doing it, "a consideration involving the idea, as we might first and very simply put it, that each of us is specially responsible for what *he* does, rather than for what other people do." Tellingly, the subject of this and similar arguments has been designated the problem of "dirty hands."[22] Your intuition that Jim has reason for reluctance—and, if he accedes to Pedro's request, for regret—may relate to the value of integrity (as Williams supposes), but it may also arise from some tacit notion of moral *taint*. Can you be sure this notion plays no role in the footbridge scenarios? Suppose, in response to such a scenario, you shudder as your imagination conjures five pedestrians on a steeply banked track, screaming in terror as the trolley hurdles toward them; your Concern Mechanism is engaged. You might even think that the fat man ought to be killed in order to save them—but not by you. There is something abominable, you feel, in having a direct hand in a person's death; it would forever taint the perpetrator, and, like Jim, you have reason to feel special responsibility for what you do.

Outsiders and Saints

In more recent work, Haidt and his colleagues have introduced additional modules. A fifth—seemingly an odd man out—has to do with the ingroup/outgroup distinction. We know that human beings are "kind-minded," that the development of social identities—however multiple, mutable, and context sensitive—is a deep and constitutive feature of our natures. Yet can this feature really play any role in our reflective moral accounts?

Consider the philosophical literature on partiality (which is what philosophers call playing favorites with people to whom you have a special connection, including yourself). Surely any adequate ethical theory must accommodate the idea of "special responsibilities," duties or obligations that we have in virtue of our "thick" relations—those of love and friendship, for instance, but of shared citizenship, too. Josiah Royce maintained that a meaningful life had to be parsed in terms of loyalties to (worthwhile) causes and to the communities that served them: "loyalty to loyalty" was his ideal.[23] And, obviously, various forms of solidarity are behind some extraordinary forms of supererogation.

Just as obviously, the ingroup/outgroup distinction can license extraordinary acts of cruelty. But there has occasionally been some uncertainty about what's meant by an "outgroup." On the one hand, there's the simple attenuation of sympathy with social distance; as Hume remarked, our sympathy declines as we move outward from family member, to fellow villager, to fellow national, to the stranger across the world. Here, the endpoint is indifference. Although Deuteronomy 14:21 enjoins against eating anything that "dieth of itself"—very good advice, that—it also says: "thou shalt give it unto the stranger that is in thy gates, that he may eat it; or thou mayest sell it unto an alien." And social scientists have done studies to confirm that victims who are familiar and resemble us are more likely to arouse our empathy.[24]

But indifference of this sort is distinct from the emotions that typically arise along the ingroup/outgroup boundary. One of those emotions is, as Haidt says, extraordinary sensitivity to treason, betrayal, perfidy, disloyalty. Another is the reverence that people have toward a member of their group who strove for its collective elevation. (Thus Benedict Arnold; thus Nathan Hale, both names still reverberant.) Sometimes, as with treason or heresy, outgroup status is acquired: traditional religious communities may engage in "shunning." Sometimes, as with various despised ethnic minorities, one is born into it. In "outgroup" conflicts, properly understood, familiarity is what helps to breed contempt; intimacy is linked to antagonism. These are Cain-and-Abel conflicts, where one group defines itself in opposition to another. Here the endpoint is eliminationist enmity. At their worst, they can lead to genocidal massacres. How? The familiar answer is: By persuading us that members of some outgroup aren't really human at all. That's not quite right: it doesn't explain the immense cruelty—the abominable cruelty, I'm tempted to say—that are their characteristic feature. The persecutors may liken the objects of their enmity to cockroaches or germs, but they acknowledge their victims' humanity in the very act of humiliating, stigmatizing, reviling, and torturing them. Such treatment—and the voluble justifications the persecutors invariably offer for such treatment—is reserved for creatures we recognize to have intentions and desires and projects.[25]

Even when people are at their worst, of course, there will be a few who resist joining the marauding mob—who are kind when their fellows are cruel, charitable when others are callous. As we contemplate their moral heroism, we are moved in a special way. And so a final module that Haidt has added to the repertory of moral modules is meant to encompass such "positive" emotions as admiration and awe; and a feeling he calls "elevation." When we think about saints—secular or otherwise—we may experience these emotions: we think especially of those who imperiled themselves for the welfare of others. But we can be moved in this way by the behavior of groups, too, and Haidt exemplifies this module in a description by a Massachusetts Unitarian named David Whitford of his response to his congregation's decision to welcome gay members: "when all hands went up and the resolution passed unanimously, I cried for the love expressed by our congregation in that act. That was a tear of celebration, a tear of receptiveness to what is good in the world, a tear that says it's okay, relax, let down your guard, there are good people in the world, there is good in people, love is real, it's in our nature."[26] Elevation can literally move us to tears.

In the traditions of our moral thought, elevation comports well with virtue ethics, and its preoccupation with the supererogatory, or, at least, what other moral traditions would consider supererogatory. Awe involves two contrary sentiments: on the one hand, it draws upon our suspicion that we would ourselves fall short; on the other, it inspires the ardor for emulation. Virtue ethicists frequently direct our attention to moral exemplars—the Gandhis, the Raoul Wallenbergs, the Mother Teresas. It's a secular version of a popular religious refrain: What would Jesus do?

Multiplex Morality

Now, you will already have started to wonder how modular these hypothetical modules really are. If you cheat me—or treat me without dignity—am I not harmed? In Shakespeare's

Richard II, Thomas Mowbray says, "Mine honour is my life; both grow in one: / Take honour from me, and my life is done." We have already remarked on the fact that people of low caste are regularly represented as being impure or polluted (a condition that blends considerations of hierarchy with their outgroup status). Is ingroup solidarity free of a sense of reciprocity? What about the resurgence of interest in "stigmatic" punishments among legal scholars: when we punish someone in this way (for example, by requiring the drunk driver to advertise his status on his bumper), is the stigma best understood on the pollution model ("cooties") or on the hierarchy model (dishonor; the "white feather") or on the outgroup model (as with "shunning")? Is gratitude—if it is to be more than a felt obligation to discharge a debt—reducible to reciprocity or does it not borrow from elevation, buoyed by the sense that we have been helped by an act of supererogatory kindness? Is the awe that we experience when contemplating the venerated moral saint entirely different from the awe that commoners once experienced in the presence of royalty? ("Nothing has a greater tendency to give us an esteem for any person, than his power and riches," Hume observed. Might this tendency be recruited by the mechanisms of moral admiration?)

Our interrogation could continue indefinitely. So we should be clear that these conjectured modules interact in countless ways, and we shouldn't pretend that they "cut nature at the joints"; tomorrow, someone might come up with a different and more persuasive taxonomy. The best case to be made for such modules is just this: when we try to reduce one of these categories to another (or another set of these categories), there always seems to be some residue left. And the same holds on the level of moral theory: parsimonious theories that aim to reduce everything to a reckoning of harm and fairness, say, just don't account for the full range of our moral intuitions, including reflection-resistant ones.

Yet talk of modules also presents temptations that are best resisted. The idea of cognitive modularity was originally inspired by Noam Chomsky's work toward a universal generative grammar, and some people have come to think that, just as a universal grammar seems to underlie our linguistic competence, so too a universal moral grammar might underlie our moral competence. In a couple of places in *A Theory of Justice*, Rawls, emboldened by Chomsky's incandescent example, floated this idea. Our "ability to recognize well-formed sentences" requires "theoretical constructions that far outrun the ad hoc precepts of our explicit grammatical knowledge," he noted, and "a similar situation presumably holds in moral philosophy." Lately, some theorists, encouraged by the model of modularity, have tried to go further with the linguistic analogy—much further than Rawls did.[27] Now, there's a sense in which Rawls's point is obviously true of nearly anything you do—riding a bike, playing in or refereeing a basketball game, combing your hair, or, to take an instance of Gilbert Ryle's, angling. If you tried to reduce those capacities to rules (which, for physical activities, would include protocols for responding to complex proprioceptive signals), you'd immediately see that those rules could never be conscious and explicit: that's the nature of know-how, of skills, of having a *capacity*. Imagine the challenge of getting a machine to see the way you see, resolving a field of light of varying intensities and frequencies into a sofa, a table, a Persian carpet, and so forth.

But when we venture beyond this truism, the analogy with modern linguistics—the analogy, that is, between the good and the grammatical—soon falters. Within communities, moral clashes occur frequently (as our taxonomy of morals would suggest), whereas speakers of a sociolect seldom disagree about whether a sentence is well formed. You just don't hear Estonians quarreling over subject-verb-object word order (and not just because Estonian word order is not terribly important!). Though linguistics explains *diversity*, it doesn't explain *disagreement*. Linguistics is descriptive: the linguist's theory is meant to accord with the observable facts of performance: a competent speaker's intuitions about language use are presumptively conclusive. Ethicists, by contrast, typically have not only normative concerns but revisionary ones: they do want to change our performance. What's more, moral philosophers are typically concerned with the issue of justification—how our judgments could be defended (or criticized), not just how we happen to arrive at them, and they have various opinions about the link between the two. The possibility of that distinction simply doesn't exist in the model of "linguistic competence," where our internal processes and structures both generate our sentences *and* determine whether they are well formed. On the other hand, the aspect of language that's crucial to morality—its public and communicative role—is a fairly marginal concern in Chomskyan linguistics. The dream of a generative grammar for morality is probably a nonstarter.

Finally, as I warned, my interest in the conjectured taxonomy of morals is at odds with the psychologists' rationale for offering it. Haidt calls himself a "social intuitionist." He thinks that our moral judgments are usually determined by reflexive intuitions. These intuitive flashes are the building blocks that make it easy for children to develop certain (culturally specific, socially regulated) virtues and virtue concepts. He also thinks that our moral judgments may have no real relation to the explicit reasons that we will, if prodded, offer for those judgments. So Haidt isn't any old intuitionist: many intuitionists hold that your intuitions have given you some kind of moral knowledge. Aristotle and Hutcheson and Whewell and Ross and Moore and countless other ethicists have thought something like this. But Haidt's experiments are meant to erode that assumption. Yes, sometimes we give plausible-sounding reasons for our disapproval of some act. But there are classes of situations where well-educated subjects are bound to feel a flash of disapproval *for no good moral reason,* and they offer reasons in those cases, too. And the researchers give having "no good moral reason" an empirical gloss: they mean being able to come up only with reasons that you will abandon when challenged. When Haidt and his collaborators point out that someone's reasons make no sense—perhaps because they appeal to inferences that were ruled out by the scenario—these subjects experience what he calls "moral dumbfounding." They're pretty much at a loss for words.

The force of these studies is to make us doubt that there's any deep relation between our moral judgments and the explicit rationales we offer for them. The social intuitionist acknowledges that explicit reflection can sometimes shape your views, but thinks that's anomalous. In this scheme, there really aren't any "moral reasons" in the sense that moral philosophers typically use the phrase. There are ways of spreading and shifting norms; and one of them might be the sort of explicit arguments that so many philosophers are in love with. But these arguments don't succeed because they're right. They seem right because they succeed.

Well, up to a point, Lord Copper. As we saw, if you're in the explanations business, reasons look like a distraction; if you're in the reasons business, explanations look like a distraction. Where the explainer goes wrong is in mistaking the force of the causal story. Haidt, writing with Fredrik Björklund, offers a sort of plebiscitary account of justification: "A well-formed moral system is one that is endorsed by the great majority of its members, even those who appear, from the outside, to be its victims." And where's the evidence for that? Certainly this justification doesn't meet the publicity constraint: Does anybody really think a moral system is just merely because it has been accepted by most members of a society?[28] Here, the social intuitionist offers us something contrary to our intuitions, because he thinks that, having devised a psychological account of morality, there's nothing else to be said. But as Aldous Huxley once put it, "Man is a double being and can take, now the god's-eye view of things, now the brute's-eye view."[29] There are contributions to be made from either perspective . . . and contributions to be made by maintaining both.

Double Vision

During the heyday of operant conditioning in the mid-1960s, the science-fiction writer Harry Harrison published a story entitled "I Always Do What Teddy Says." It is set far in the future, in a world where nobody has committed murder for centuries. Its developmental psychologists long ago determined that our moral capacities are shaped in our early, most plastic stages, and they helped to design an automated teddy bear that every child receives at birth, as a constant companion. These teddies, we learn, "teach diction and life history and morals and group adjustment and vocabulary and grammar and all the other things that enable men to live together as social animals." The teddy's conversation is simple but effective: "No, no, Davy. Mum wouldn't let you do that. . . . Fork in left, knife in right." This civilization is proudly aware that, owing to such nurture, its citizens can think about murder without being capable of doing it.

But now Davy, our protagonist, is David, an eighteen-year-old, and he is summoned by his father and his father's fellow dissidents (academics denied tenure, naturally). The head of state for the past twenty-three years, leader of the "Panstentialist movement," is bad, as all the dissidents agree. His death would be a good thing. So surely it would be a good thing if someone were to bring about his death. Though David follows their reasoning, he's puzzled: Who in this world would be capable of such an act? Just one, as it happens. Patiently awaiting this day, the conspirators tampered with David's teddy bear when he was still an infant. They explain to David that he is the one man alive who is capable of doing what must be done, and hand him a refurbished antique implement known as a gun. Soon after the jolting revelation, the young man rushes upstairs, and retrieves Teddy from a high shelf:

> The little furry animal sat in the middle of the large bed and rolled its eyes and wagged its stubby arms.
>
> "Teddy," he said, "I'm going to pull up flowers from the flowerbed."
>
> "No, Davy . . . pulling up flowers is naughty. Don't pull up the flowers." The little voice squeaked and the arms waved.
>
> "Teddy, I'm going to break a window."
>
> "No, Davy . . . breaking windows is naughty . . . don't break any windows . . ."
>
> "Teddy, I'm going to kill a man."
>
> Silence, just silence.

Teddy is a machine, and there is something machine-like in the absolute inability of adults in this world to defy its normative strictures. But, as it turns out, David's ability to engage in moral reasoning is unimpaired. While he lacks an intuitive aversion to killing, he retains a theoretical opposition to it. He swiftly concludes that, although the head of state rules with a heavy hand, the old man will not rule forever—and the worse prospect would be a world into which guns and violence had reappeared. Laying out his reasons, he turns against the conspirators, and, finally, against his old plaything. "Oh Teddy," he says, weeping, "you should have told me."[30]

Harrison's fable is something of a period piece, but no less suggestive for that. The author maintains a double vision, stipulating that, even in a world where the mechanisms of psychological control of motivation have been perfected, human beings remain moral actors—which is to say, they remain recognizably human. They can still talk about what makes something the right decision or the wrong one. They can urge the importance of one consideration over another. And, of course, the same holds in our own less-perfected world.

In the footbridge problem described in Chapter 3, we faced a choice between, on the one hand, following our moral intuitions—which is the natural standpoint of the agent—and, on the other, overruling them, because we came to suspect that our brains deliver these intuitions to us in response to the wrong question: How physically close is the person I'd have to kill? The cosmic engineer may have made us that way for a good purpose. But no responsible person thinks that the distance between a permissible and an impermissible homicide could be measured by a hundred yards of track. As we saw, we *could* understand our natural revulsion against killing as a heuristic (so to speak, an intuition implanted in us by a mass-produced teddy, whose designer had overall social welfare in mind). But, as we also saw, we could invoke the heuristic for our own purposes only if we had another account of why it was, or wasn't, justified. The outsider's perspective—the perspective of the *Sinnenwelt*—does not answer this moral question for us.

Suppose, though, we take the perspective of Kant's *Verstandeswelt* and make the obvious connection between what I called an "evaluation" and the more familiar idea of a "value."

Values guide our acts, our thoughts, and our feelings. These are our *responses* to values. Because you recognize the value of great art, you go to museums and to concerts and read books. Your aesthetic responses give you pro tanto reasons to seek out art and music and literature. Because you see the value of courtesy, you try to understand the conventions of whatever society you live in, so that you can avoid giving offense. You act as you do because you respond to the values that guide you: that is what it is to be guided by evaluations. Kindness leads you to admire some gentle souls, and leaves you irritated by other, thoughtless ones. Your response to this value, the evaluations it generates, gives you pro tanto reasons for these responses. You *ought*, absent other considerations, to admire the kindly person; you *ought*, too, to resent unkindness. And (as Anscombe might remind us) that *ought* is just the ordinary *ought*, not some mysterious moral *ought*. It's the same as the *ought* in "You ought to think it's blue, because it looks blue."

When you think of kindness as a universal value, you want everybody to want to be kind. And since you want them to agree with you, you also want *them* to want everybody to want everybody to be kind. Many contemporary people will say it's the fact that you want these things that makes it true you value kindness, because many modern people think that values are things we made up, projections of our preferences (in this instance, preferences drummed up by our Concern Mechanism). But from the standpoint of the *Verstandeswelt*, we can only think of it the other way around. You prefer that people should be kind *because you recognize the value of kindness*. You want people to agree with you because then they will be kind and encourage kindness in yet other people by expressing their admiration or their gratitude; if you can get people to recognize the value of kindness they will do what kindness demands. You want them to be kind because the lives of kind people are *eo ipso* worthier than the lives of the unkind. You will think of your regard for kindness not as a mere personal preference but as the acknowledgment of a universal truth; you will agree with William Wordsworth when he wrote, in "The Old Cumberland Beggar," that people

> Long for some moments in a weary life
> When they can know and feel that they have been,
> Themselves, the fathers and the dealers-out
> Of some small blessings; have been kind to such
> As needed kindness, for this single cause,
> That we have all of us one human heart.

The same goes for every value that we think is universal: our taking it to be universal reflects a judgment that everyone has a good reason to do or to think or to feel certain things, and so, also, all of us have reason to encourage these acts and thoughts and feelings in others.[31]

From the perspective of the *Verstandeswelt,* each of us naturally responds to the world not just with cool judgments about how it is, but also with emotions that ground the way we act. My colleague Mark Johnston has written of the way in which a feeling can have what he calls the "authority of affect," by which, as he says, he means to refer not "to its sheer effectiveness as a source of desire or action, but rather to the fact that the presence of the affect can make the desire or action especially intelligible to the agent himself. It can make the desire or act seem apt or fitting in a way that silences any demand for justification."[32] These feelings—the resistance we feel to pushing the heavy stranger off the bridge—present themselves to us in what I'm calling "evaluations." But if we *should*, in fact, push the stranger off the footbridge, then this feeling is not an evaluation but a misevaluation. Just as, in perception, there are illusions, so there are illusions in our processes of evaluation. Here, too, we need a way to distinguish real reasons from apparent ones. Let's call an intuition that *seems* to provide a pro tanto reason for action or feeling a "subjective evaluation." Some subjective evaluations are genuine evaluations, providing real reasons. Some are mistaken. Deciding which is which—which subjective evaluations are responses to values, to the things that really matter—is a fundamental normative challenge.[33]

The Language of Morality

Fortunately, it's not a challenge we have to take up alone. Because our natures are cultivated (albeit by parents and peers, rather than by furry and officious automata) and our values are shared, we go astray when we think of a moral vocabulary as the possession of a solitary individual. Concepts of kindness or cruelty enshrine both a pattern of acts and feelings *and* a consensus about their value. The language of values is, after all, *language*. And modern philosophical reflection on language shows that language is, first and foremost, a public thing, something we use together. (A key insight of Allan Gibbard's modern classic *Wise Choices, Apt Feelings* is that there's a constitutive relation between the possession and the expression of norms.) An evaluative vocabulary is first a tool we use to talk to one another, not an instrument for talking to ourselves.

And evaluative language is *thick:* even little words often come trailing a big complex of beliefs and values and attitudes. Try explaining "rude" to a Martian while you stand on one leg. That's why virtue ethicists often sound as if they're courting tautology. It's bad to be vile and beastly; good to be noble and courageous. These propositions don't seem terribly informative because the norms, the evaluations, are already entrained by these words. When you describe Aristotle's "golden mean" theory, you'll similarly find yourself on the border of tautology: to be too cautious, too incautious—those conditions are bad by definition, and even predicates that don't contain the word "too" typically contain the too-ness. When Searle and Foot made their arguments, back in the 1960s, for how you could get an "ought" from an "is," they were demonstrating how norms and values are built right into our words.[34]

I've said that moral justification is a social and expressive verbal practice; and our language itself embodies a rich repertory of norms and values. We use values not only to think for ourselves but also to guide one another. In particular, our *language* of values—not just the concepts but our actual mobilization of them in speech—is one of the central ways we coordinate our lives. We appeal to values when we are trying to get things done *together*. And we talk value-talk all the time. As the Germans say, "Tue Gutes und rede darüber": "Do good things and talk about it."

Indeed, we talk about values even when we are not deciding what to do in real life. We are constantly evaluating acts and feelings in conversations about fictional narratives, whether in literature or the movies or on television. Why, you might ask, should we care how other people think and feel about stories? Why do we talk about them in this language of value? One answer is just that it's part of being human. People tell stories and discuss them in every culture, and we know they have done so back as far as the record goes. The *Iliad* and the *Odyssey*, the *Epic of Gilgamesh*, the *Tale of Genji*, the Ananse stories I grew up with in Asante, weren't just read or recited; they were discussed, appraised, referred to in everyday life. We wouldn't recognize a community as human if it had no stories, if its people had no narrative imagination. From the standpoint of the *Verstandeswelt*, we recognize exchanging stories as one of the things humanly worth doing.

But the answer of the *Sinnenwelt* is that evaluating stories together is one of the central ways we language-users coordinate our responses to the world. And that alignment of responses is, in turn, essential to maintaining the social fabric, the texture of our relationships. Indeed, from the standpoint of the *Sinnenwelt*, it's presumably because natural *and* cultural selection "discovered" the advantages of using narratives in this way that they are so much a part of human nature. Folktales, plays, operas, novels, short stories, telenovelas; biographies, histories, ethnographies; fiction and nonfiction; painting, music, sculpture, and dance: every human civilization has ways of revealing to us values we had not previously recognized or of undermining our commitment to values we had settled into. Armed with these terms, equipped with a common language of value, we can often learn to share those responses that I am calling evaluations.

In short, narratives can sometimes be enlisted in the task of suasion rather than solidarity. Justification, I said, is essentially conversational; and though it makes universal claims, it's seldom a matter of plugging particulars into a pregiven moral algorithm: stories can shift our views. Ethicists sometimes fear that science will alienate or estrange us from our values; yet the exercise of estrangement—of testing our values by trying to distance ourselves from them—is one that humanists have pursued as vigorously as scientists. They explore the conduct and concepts taken for granted in other societies; they satirize their own society by writing—in the tradition of Montesquieu's *Persian Letters*, or Goldsmith's *Citizen of the World*—as if they were a stranger. Like scientists, they redescribe the familiar in unfamiliar terms. These redescriptions, too, are experiments in ethics.

I have no interest in tidying up the messy array of terms— "obligations," "responsibilities," "duties," "rights," "principles," and so on—that we ordinarily enlist in discussing our evaluations. All can be part of the activity of *making salient,* and that activity isn't to be scanted. As the prototype theorists would remind us, a dime can be classified with a dollar and a Euro; or with a pie and a Frisbee. Which feature is salient—which thing is like another—depends on the context. Moral perception is a way of seeing, and seeing is always seeing *as* and seeing *that.* The fact that, in the real world, moral arguments typically are salience arguments is what gives such power to activities like storytelling, but also to simple images. Think of the icon, devised by a Quaker abolition society in the eighteenth century, depicting a shackled slave, kneeling and with hands raised in supplication, with the legend "Am I not a man and a brother?" It was not a moral treatise, but it had an argument to make: see me as someone like yourself.

The historian Martin Gilbert tells of a Polish peasant woman, during the Second World War, who happened to hear a group of villagers propose throwing a little Jewish girl into a well. The woman said, "She's not a dog after all," and Renee Lindenberg's life was saved.[35] The peasant offered no invocation of grand theory, the inherent dignity of man, the iniquity of Nazism, the injustice of religious discrimination, the workings of natural law, the sacredness of life, or the stringency of rights. Just a simple comment about a category. *She's not a dog after all.* What does the language of moral argument sound like? Sometimes, it arrives with the sonorities of John Milton or Frederick Douglass or Elizabeth Cady Stanton or Reinhold Niebuhr; and as part of a campaign to transform a system of social practices, perhaps it must. Sometimes it sounds like the peasant woman, who had the thought that a Jewish girl should be treated better than an unwanted whelp, and who didn't suppose that you could settle questions of justice with a headcount.

There are many, many more things to be said, of course, about how the psychologies shaped by our evolutionary and our cultural histories have made us into creatures living in a dense web of subjective evaluations that propose guidance as to how we should feel and act. We do know that once we reflect, we will sometimes repudiate our evaluations. When should we treat an intuition as a starting point—for example, a reasonable fear? When should we reject its demand that we should feel or act in a certain way—as with a phobia? How can we adjudicate among evaluations when they pull us in different directions? One way to answer such questions, as we've seen, is to draw on the perspective of the *Sinnenwelt* and use anthropological, sociological, historical, and psychological knowledge, which can explain what we are responding to, how easy it would be to stop responding as we do, and what we might be like if we responded differently.

There's nothing disruptive about such an endeavor; there is—as the genealogy I traced in the first chapter might suggest—nothing even especially novel. Our world is already deeply informed by science: the triumphs of science and technology are a part of most people's outlook, and have been for some time. Thomas Hill Green's *Prolegomena to Ethics*, which was composed in the late 1870s and early 1880s, opens with a chapter entitled "The Idea of a Natural Science of Morals." He expresses no surprise "that the evolutionists of our day should claim to have given a wholly new character to ethical enquiries," although he worries that the ostensible discovery that "our assertions of moral obligation are merely the expression of an ineffectual wish to be better off than we are, or are due to the survival of habits originally enforced by physical fear," would lead to the conclusion that "in inciting ourselves or others to do anything because it ought to be done, we are at best making use of a serviceable illusion."

Yet the perspective of the *Sinnenwelt* preceded the current higamus-hogamus epoch. Think of the humoral psychology of

Galenic medicine, preserved in words like "melancholy," "phlegmatic," "choleric." For Aristotle, the "movement of the soul" was no figure of speech: the *anima* really was imagined to have wriggled this way and that in response to different situations. And, of course, religious traditions have long preached about the frailties of our framing: talk of literal "possession" by evil spirits is just one extreme; think, too, of the language Abraham Lincoln used when he hoped we would be touched by "the better Angels of our nature." There are studies showing that very young children distinguish between artifacts and creatures; confronted with an utterly unfamiliar creature and an utterly unfamiliar machine, they ask of machines, but not creatures, "How does it work?" And of creatures, but not machines, "What does it eat?"[36] Yet by the time human beings come of age—this seems true across cultures and centuries—they soon come to view creatures, sometimes and in certain respects, as artifacts: they learn to pose some version of the cognitive scientist's question: How does it work?

The questions we put to the social scientists and physiologists are not normative questions. But their answers are not therefore irrelevant to the normative questions. Much of their research is at an early stage, as sociologists, anthropologists, and, increasingly, economists study our moral psychologies in the laboratory and in the world. One element of the story that we already have is evident, however. The modularity of our moral psychology is only a starting point of our plural commitments, for sociocultural contexts shape the basic psychology in different ways in different places and times. And one of the main ways they do this is by providing us with a vocabulary of evaluation, a language of value, one that is responsive to, but underdetermined by, the complexities of our nature. Even though the fundamental task of ethics is to shape one's own life, that task is pursued with the conceptual resources and through the social institutions of a human world. In my concluding chapter, I'll say more about that fundamental task— and about the practical and disciplinary ends of ethics.

5

The Ends of Ethics

Lucentio: And therefore, Tranio, for the time I study,
Virtue and that part of philosophy
Will I apply that treats of happiness
By virtue specially to be achieved.

—WILLIAM SHAKESPEARE, *The Taming of the Shrew*

If You're Happy and You Know It

Ethics is, in that formulation of Aristotle's, about the ultimate aim or end of human life, the end he called *eudaimonia*. Of course, philosophical ethics has not always shared that vision; nor should philosophers be confident that history has given them a special lien upon the subject of human flourishing. There's a sense, as I suggested in the introduction, that the members of my profession became philosophers in the way that the Vlach, after the union of Wallachia and Moldavia in the mid-nineteenth century, became "Romanians," claiming a glorious ancient pedigree through a nomenclatural coup. The slippery movements of group designations are familiar to all historians, not to mention any sports fan who has watched the Jets, who used to be the Titans, play the Titans, who used to be the Oilers.

Still, our names can express our aspirations. In the pages that follow, then, I want to sidle up to that great end of ethics, see how we might best make sense of it, and offer a final accounting of what "naturalism" means within the realm of human values—and within the project of *eudaimonia*.

So what is that devoutly-to-be-hoped-for thing, anyway? If you think of *eudaimonia* as happiness, and believe, as many modern people claim to do, that happiness is just a matter of satisfying your felt desires, you will think that evaluations are just desires gussied up with fancy talk. The antiquity of this temptation is shown by the antiquity of the rebuttals: through more than two millennia, thinkers have vigorously demonstrated that mere subjective contentment isn't a worthwhile aim. One way to deepen our grasp of *eudaimonia* is to understand why "happiness" is, at least for us today, a terribly misleading translation of that Greek word.

How many times on TV and in the movies have we heard a parent tell a child, "I just want you to be happy"? But what does that mean? Here are a few notions you'll encounter these days. First, happiness is a feeling; you are happy if and only if you think you are happy. For a feeling just is a state of mind, like a pain, that you can't have without being aware that you have it. A more sophisticated thought often follows: whether you are happy or not is to be decided by standards set by you. Together, these claims amount to construing happiness as something deeply subjective: it's a feeling; we all know whether we have it, and each of us sets the standards for our own happiness.[1] Call this the *subjective conception of happiness.*

As philosophers have never tired of pointing out, this isn't really a conception that withstands scrutiny. No loving and thoughtful parents could mean that they just wanted a child to be subjectively happy. Consider the happiness that comes from a successful relationship. If all that matters is how you feel, then if you *feel* it's going well, it *is* going well, and it's of no consequence if your partner is merely feigning affection, so long as the illusion is maintained. But, of course, what matters in relationships requires that our feelings be apt; it requires the truth of at least some of the beliefs that partially constitute those feelings. When Dad tells his daughter he wants her to be happy, he doesn't mean it's fine if her boyfriend goes on *pretending* to love her. It's not just that a boyfriend who doesn't love you is, no doubt, less reliable than one who does. Daddy, especially a soap-opera daddy, could be rich enough to make it worth the boyfriend's while to keep up the act, and his daughter would still be in trouble. People who don't grasp this—who care only whether their beloveds *appear* to love them—are simply not capable of love.

The philosopher Robert Nozick proposed a famous thought experiment along these lines in *Anarchy, State and Utopia.* Imagine there was an "experience machine" that would provide any experience you wanted. "Superduper neuropsychologists could stimulate your brain so that you would think and feel you were writing a great novel, or making a friend, or reading an interesting book," he wrote, even though you'd just be floating in a tank with electrodes plugged into your brain.

Would you plug in?[2] Films like the Wachowski brothers' *The Matrix* or Cameron Crowe's *Vanilla Sky*—or Alejandro Amenábar's marvelous *Abre los Ojos* (Open Your Eyes), on which it was based—exploit the possibility of something like an experience machine to raise exactly the question Nozick asks. And his answer—that what matters is not only how our life feels, but also whether our experiences and achievements are real—is not only right but right in a way that Aristotle would surely have thought obvious. Whatever Aristotle meant by *eudaimonia*, he didn't mean subjective happiness.

To say that feelings aren't the only things that matter is not to go to the other extreme and say that they don't matter at all. No doubt some of the experiences I have in my relationships are part of what is good about them, part of what makes the relationships contribute to my flourishing, to what is good in my life. Loving couples know the feeling of walking hand in hand under the stars, confident in each other's love; lying together at night, conscious of each other's breathing, feeling the warmth of each other's bodies. These experiences are valuable parts of a life in love. Again, though, the experiences must be in some sense apt. The shared life is a good life because two people are really making a life together: if your partner is not a real person but an automaton or an electronic phantasm, you're living in what we appropriately call a fool's paradise. You may think your life is going well, but you're wrong.

What about that thesis that each person sets the standards for his or her own happiness? People find it plausible, I think, because they follow a train of thought that goes like this: "What matters in your life matters because it matters *to you;*

because it is one of your aims. Succeeding in what matters to you is what's important—important in the sense that getting it contributes to your happiness, your *eudaimonia*. Anything you care about matters to you. Ergo, getting what you care about contributes to your happiness." Here is one of the many places where morality matters for ethics, and one of the many ways in which *eudaimonia* is shown to be indissolubly social, because the question of what we owe to others—in the classical formulation, *suum cuique tribuens* ("giving to each his due")—is inherently interpersonal. Suppose, like a character in the fantasies of the Marquis de Sade, I take pleasure in humiliating other people. That I care to humiliate people doesn't mean that if I succeed in doing so my life is going well. You can't set success at sadism as one of the aims of your life and thereby make a life of cruelty a good life. So one reason that you can't set your own standards for happiness is that some standards are morally wrong.

This helps explain why so many thinkers, from Socrates on, have connected happiness with virtue. However many things you have achieved, however much pleasure you have experienced, however many friends you have, however wonderful your relationship with your spouse and however successful your children, if you have achieved all this at the expense of neglecting your moral obligations, your existence is less successful than it would have been had you paid proper attention to what morality demands. As I argued in the second chapter, this connection between morality and ethics is internal: doing what is morally right is one of the constituents of human flourishing. So we don't need to believe in a providential invisible hand, assigning happiness to the saints, to insist on the connection between virtue and happiness, properly understood. A sinner may think he's happy. But insofar as he's a sinner, his life is thereby made less successful, whether he knows it or not. Whatever it is that he wants, the rest of us should want him, truly, to be better than he is.

It's also true that some aims, however genuinely desired, are not significant enough to add to the value of a life. You cannot give a saucer of mud significance in your life simply by announcing you want it; and, indeed, if you find you do want it for no purpose, this is not a reason to go looking for a saucer of mud, but rather a reason to seek clinical help.[3] If the standards were whatever you decided they were, you could make your life a smashing success simply by setting the standards absurdly low. Someone could set as his aim that he should do whatever job came along moderately well and make enough money to have fun from time to time. "I am satisfied," he might say, looking back on his life at the end. "I had fun occasionally, I was a work-to-rule bureaucrat; I avoided the entanglements of love and friendship, which would only have risked my wanting things—like loyalty and reciprocation—that you can't guarantee." And we would say, rightly, that if that is all there was to it, this person, far from having lived well, had wasted his life.

In short, you aren't flourishing just because you're getting what you want. We can grasp the alternative vision, shared by the soulless libertine or lifer—we can imagine a moment when, in Philip Larkin's mordant words, "every life became / a brilliant breaking of the bank, / A quite unlosable game"—but we cannot enter it.[4] What we want has to be *worth* wanting: it has to be consistent with human decency and connected with humanly intelligible values. Aristotle's view was, indeed, that life was a challenge to be faced; that to live well was an achievement.

The Ways of Well-Being

Considerations such as these have persuaded many philosophers to adopt what Derek Parfit once dubbed "objective-list" ethical theories. He suggested that a good life must involve things like "moral goodness, rational activity, the development of one's abilities, having children and being a good parent, knowledge, and the awareness of true beauty" . . . and, in general, the more of these things the merrier, so long as you recognize their worth and desire them for their own sake.[5] Accounts like these move between an objective and a subjective perspective. If they dropped the subjective dimension, they would be an overreaction to the problems that afflict the purely subjective conception. From the fact that we cannot set ourselves just any standards we like, it doesn't follow that we play no role at all in setting our standards. As John Stuart Mill wrote, in *On Liberty,* "If a person possesses any tolerable amount of common sense and experience, his own mode of laying down his existence is the best, not because it is best in itself, but because it is his own mode."[6]

Why might this be true? Here's one reason. People start life with many potentialities. There are so many things they could do; there's so much they could be. Their world contains many options, many values. The arts, athletic achievement, community, friendship, love . . . all of these matter; and there are many different ways of balancing them. Furthermore, there are pairs of

virtues—loyalty and independence, bravery and compassion—
that are difficult, if not impossible, to give full rein in the same
life. Courage and loyalty: these are soldier's virtues. Independence and compassion? Not so much. A parish priest governed
by courage and loyalty might not be the ideal person for a civilian flock to go to with their pastoral problems. That is why in
Le rouge et le noir, Stendhal's great novel of ambition, Julien
Sorel's actual life as a cleric in black is undermined by his sub-
merged ambitions for the martial life of the red tunic. Julien's
problem is that he is a priest whose model is Napoleon.

Because there are so many worthwhile things we could do,
because we cannot give every value equal weight, we will have
choices to make, in shaping our lives, among values and among
paths through the world. Now, talk of "choosing among values" is
a piece of shorthand, and a misleading one, insofar as it suggests
that the activity is purely volitional. From the subjective point of
view, where you're *recognizing* a value, you may have no more
choice in cherishing some ideal, or some person, than you do in
deciding what color the sky will appear to you. Of course, you can
try to bring it about that you come to value something; but there
is no guarantee of success. The novelist Vladimir Nabokov discussed the predicament of being tone deaf while having a beloved
son who was an opera singer. Time and again, he tried to apprehend the *point* of music, and turn a second-order value—the value
he placed on perceiving the value of music—into a first-order
value. Time and again, he failed.

Still, John Stuart Mill enunciates a distinctively modern
idea when he says that each person is in charge of charting her
way through these options. In many societies in the past—as,

sadly, in too many today—people believed women's lives should be arranged by fathers, brothers, or husbands; they thought, as well, that ordinary people's choices should be made for them by social superiors. They believed, in effect, that many adults ought to be treated like children. Those were the traditions that Mill sought to challenge when he maintained that the responsibility for the success of each life lay ultimately in the hands of the person whose life it was. Our role in shaping the very standards by which our lives will rightly be assessed is a matter of negotiating among the many available options.[7]

Mill spoke, in the passage I just cited, of "laying down" one's "own mode of existence," and this has justly been criticized for suggesting an implausible conception of how we make our lives. One problem I've already mentioned: the error of creeping volitionism. (As he knew very well, Mill did not *choose* to fall in love with another man's wife; it just happened.) Nor can we decree what social forms, concepts, and institutions will be available to us. A related problem is that we often fall into things unplanned for, not least because we cannot predict how others will act. You can set out to find a spouse; but to succeed, at least one other person will have to cooperate. This is an instance of a more general point, which Aristotle noticed and insisted upon. Whether your life is successful—this is one of the ways in which reality matters—is not just up to you. As Aristotle said, *eudaimonia* requires "external goods," for "it is impossible, or at least not easy, to play a noble part unless furnished with the necessary equipment." Among such external goods were friends, wealth, political power; and to have the very greatest measure of *eudaimonia*, he supposed, we would be advantaged by "good birth, satisfactory children, and personal beauty."[8]

We can reduce our dependence on some of these external goods by devoting ourselves to aims that do not require or that actively exclude them. The monk who is voluntarily celibate can rightly deny that his childlessness makes him unsuccessful; having children would undermine his vocation. But, as Aristotle's talk of beauty and good birth shows, some things that add to (or detract from) a man's *eudaimonia* begin in childhood, before he has a chance to decide how much place he will make in his life for them. As adults, perhaps, we may have more control over how these shape our life.[9]

What Aristotle meant by good birth—birth into a noble family—may strike you as something that doesn't really add to the value of a person's life at all, save, perhaps, instrumentally, by giving one good connections (or by placing one in situations conducive to virtuous conduct). But Aristotle probably thought that a man's life was better just because he came from a good family, even if he never pulled any strings; even if, at birth, he left his home for a place where his family's status was unknown. No doubt *you* don't believe that. I wonder, though, if some native-born Americans wouldn't think of their Americanness in the same sort of way: a good thing, not just instrumentally (instrumentally, judging by the economic and social indicators, it might be better to be a Swede) but in itself. That thought amounts to taking your nationality as an important element of who you are, an element that defines one of the standards by which your life should be evaluated because you have opted for (or perhaps just slipped into) taking your nationality seriously.

And once you take it seriously, your life's success is the success of an American—which makes your *eudaimonia* dependent in part on the political fate of your nation.[10]

In talking of nationality, I have crept up on one of the central concerns of contemporary ethics: the issue of our social identities. Race, nationality, religion, gender, sexual orientation: all of these may be connected profoundly with your sense of who you are and with your *eudaimonia*. Social identities—as Aristotle, with his talk of noble birth, saw—are among the external goods on which we rely for our success. They are, equally, part of our individual natures.

That phrase "social identity" is fairly recent, its currency dating from the post–World War II era; in the nineteenth century, the relevant issues were sometimes discussed under the rubric "my station and its duties." In 1876, F. H. Bradley—whose excoriations of atomistic accounts of individualism can sound strikingly contemporary—insisted that once we saw ourselves as socially embedded creatures, whose actions were only intelligible in a fretwork of relations with others in our community, we had to take seriously those obligations that arose from our social roles.[11] Of course, there is a good deal of variation in how our social identities figure into our flourishing. My maternal grandfather, whose father was an English peer, was known in his village as the "red squire"; he was—he meant to be—a traitor to his class. Mab Segrest in her book *Memoir of a Race Traitor* recounts her work against racism in her home state of North Carolina in the 1980s.[12] Segrest took up the cudgels against racism, she insists, *as a white person:* her work for North Carolinians against Racist and Religious Violence was meant exactly as a form of betrayal of a competing notion of white identity—one identified with by many members of her family—which sought to maintain white supremacy.

A social identity is only one aspect of ethical identity, to be sure. Our own projects may be irreducibly social; and, in a variety of ways, my *eudaimonia* may be inextricable from someone else's. Another Lydia Davis story, or meta-story, tells a parable along these lines; it's entitled "Happiest Moment," and here it is, once more in its entirety:

> If you ask her what is a favorite story she has written, she will hesitate for a long time and then say it may be this story that she read in a book once: an English language teacher in China asked his Chinese student to say what was the happiest moment in his life. The student hesitated for a long time. At last he smiled with embarrassment and said that his wife had once gone to Beijing and eaten duck there, and she often told him about it, and he would have to say the happiest moment in his life was her trip, and the eating of the duck.[13]

That's the end of a story; and the end, or one of the ends, anyway, of a life.

As I said in Chapter 2, part of what is attractive in the picture of ethical life offered by virtue theory is the notion that we can reasonably care about what we *are*, and in ways that go beyond our gender, race, religion, nationality, and the like. Gentle, humorous, charming people are, no doubt, the product of nature and nurture. But there is a further question of how much someone *cares* about being gentle or humorous or charming. As we noticed in the previous chapter, moral values—in the rump sense of morality—always have a second-order extension; but these scarcely exhaust the universe of values. For some people, being gentle is part of their self-conception. They are pained when they harm others through insensitivity. Being gentle matters to them in ways beyond the morally necessary strictures against harm. Other people pride themselves on their gimlet-eyed ability to detect bunkum; they cultivate a nose for claptrap. (And because they enjoy their especial resistance to the specious and meretricious, they don't mind that not everyone shares their ability.) It's good to be gentle; good to be undupable. But it's not essential to be preoccupied with such traits. Balancing such minor virtues and deciding which of them one identifies with most strongly is an ethical task.[14] It entails a concern for what one is.

Life's challenge is to take the possibilities that your genes and your physical and social environment have given you and make something of them. Aristotle recognized the importance of habituation: of the way in which we can shape our dispositions by deciding to go against what we were initially inclined to do. In the process, some of what our societies have given us—a religious tradition, for example—is going to be thought about and revised. Perhaps we will reflectively appropriate the tradition; perhaps we will reject it altogether. The process through which endorsement or revision happens will usually take place in groups (sometimes very small ones) and in conversation (sometimes with imaginary interlocutors). We find ourselves judging our own subjective evaluations, our first intuitive responses to a situation that faces us, whether in reality or in the imagination. And in deciding whether to try to reshape ourselves into new habits, we hold ourselves up to this standard: Can I live with this evaluation and be the person I am trying to be? You may recall the scene from James Brooks's movie *As Good As It Gets,* where the curmudgeonly writer played by Jack Nicholson says to the Helen Hunt character, "You make me want to be a better man." Making a self is part of making a life. The experience of awe may entrain something of this aspiration: inspired by your example, I wish to be a better person, and apprehend the truths that are perspicuous to you, though not yet to me. Sometimes that means learning new evaluations, perhaps by trying to habituate myself to respond to things differently.

With what results? To answer this question, we may turn to the standpoint of the *Sinnenwelt.* There are facts about our natures that are germane to any reasonable effort to change our ways. (It wasn't irrelevant that the Jack Nicholson character suffered from an obsessive-compulsive disorder.) But we ask this question always, in the end, from the standpoint of the *Verstandeswelt.* In Chapter 3, I mentioned William Godwin's notorious passage about Fénelon and the fire; philosophers in his day and ours, I said, found the prospect of letting one's father burn for the sake of the illustrious stranger so repellent as to call in question the underlying thesis of impartialism. We might, were we his compatriots, have been relieved to learn that a venerable archbishop survived a brush with death, and not overly saddened by news of the death of some obscure dissenting minister in the same mishap. But we would never have made that choice if the choice, and the father, had been ours; and we would wonder what kind of cold-blooded creature could do so.

Surprising as it may seem, this idea wasn't entirely foreign to Godwin. Several years after he published his *Enquiry Concerning Political Justice*, where the notorious passage about Fénelon and the fire appeared, he was roused to defend himself against his critics. He took them to task for, as he wrote, "constantly supposing that, if the father is saved, this will be the effort of passion, but if Fénelon is saved, the act will arise only from cool, phlegmatic, arithmetical calculation." Not so, Godwin maintained: "No great and honourable deed can be achieved, but from passion. If I save the life of Fénelon, unprompted to do so by an ardent love of the wondrous excellence of the man, and a sublime eagerness to achieve and secure the welfare and improvement of millions, I am a monster, unworthy of the appellation of a man, and the society of beings so 'fearfully and wonderfully made,' as men are." And he makes a rather fascinating concession:

> First, I will suppose that I save in preference, the life of the valet, who is my father, and in so doing intrench upon the principle of utility. Few persons even upon that supposition will be disposed severely to blame my conduct. We are accustomed and rightly accustomed, to consider every man in the aggregate as a machine calculated to produce many benefits or many evils, and not to take his actions into our examination in a disjointed and separate manner. If, without pause or hesitation, I proceed to save the life of my father in preference to that of any human

being, every man will respect in me the sentiment of filial affection, will acknowledge that the feeling by which I am governed is a feeling pregnant with a thousand good and commendable actions, and will confess, according to a trite, but expressive, phrase, that at least I have *my heart in the right place*, that I have within me those precious and inestimable materials out of which all virtuous and honourable deeds are made.[15]

"Trite, but expressive," Godwin apologizes. Yet perhaps also indispensable?

As a social reformer, Godwin sought, not without success, to challenge his countrymen's contentment with the status quo (or, anyway, to heighten their discontentment with it) through normative discussion, the urgings of similitude and salience, and, of course, arguments from what he hoped were self-evident axioms. But, as we've just seen, there are other ways in which we adapt our subjective evaluations. Sometimes, as even Godwin recognized, they will not fit with the person we're trying to be. Sometimes, Godwin acknowledged, we had reason to care about what *kind* of person someone was—whether he was worthy of "the appellation of a man"—as well as what deeds that person did. And though Godwin may have tried to square this circle, to eliminate any remainder, we find what we always find in these cases: a square and a circle.

A square and a circle—and many other forms besides. Matters would be tidier if we could at least decree that what we owe to others must always prevail when it conflicts with our individual projects. But we cannot even say that. Sometimes the moral requirement (the promise kept, say) is minor, while the detriment to our dreams is devastating. We ought to keep our promises. But only a fanatic would forbid me to break my promise to dine with you in order to seize a rare opportunity to achieve my dreams. I'm on the verge of completing my concerto grosso for tuba, prepared piano, and viola, and am confident it will win a nationwide competition if I can deliver it before the impending cutoff date for submissions. My apology to you for breaking our dinner date is sincere, but I do not doubt that my decision was the right one. (Nor can I count on your post facto consent, for you may disapprove of the project in question: "When are you going to stop wasting your life on that dodecaphonic hooey?" you grumble.) It's true that one can't have a successful life in which one's own concerns stifle all the legitimate demands of others. But life is complicated and we face many, often conflicting, demands; the needs of other people aren't the only thing that matters. So there will be difficult trade-offs between different values. That's one reason that John Stuart Mill, though dismissed as a monist by some postmodern critics, called for "experiments in living."

Not every experiment is worth trying: there are, he knew, "things which experience has shown not to be useful or suitable to any person's individuality." (The twentieth century gave us a great deal more experience along those lines, alas.) Still, he didn't think that the value of a form of existence could always be determined a priori, in the manner of a geometric proof; even here—especially here—a measure of empiricism was in order, so that "the worth of different modes of life should be proved practically, when any one thinks fit to try them."[16]

The Nature of Naturalism

Mill's proposal will trouble some of those who have taken sides in a debate that dates at least to Socrates' question in the *Euthyphro:* Is an act loved by the gods because it is good or is it good because it is loved by the gods? Endorsing the first has been thought to lead to the recognition of the "autonomy of ethics"; endorsing the second is thought to prefigure "naturalism," in which the goodness of an act is defined in terms of other-than-good things. I should say at once that "naturalism," in ethics, is a frightfully ambiguous term. Most utilitarians may be taken to be naturalists, inasmuch as they try to define the good in terms of human welfare, and inasmuch as human welfare is an empirical phenomenon, such that questions of its maximization refer to natural facts about the world. Ethical properties, on this account, are reducible to natural properties. An account of virtue ethics, inasmuch as it defines the good as the realization of those human capacities identified with *eudaimonia,* would be another candidate. G. E. Moore, who insisted that goodness was undefinable, was the canonical critic of naturalism in this sense. (Like Impressionism, Fauvism, and Cubism, "naturalism" was baptized by its enemies.) Yet there are ethicists who are profoundly hostile to naturalism of this sort, but who also hold that moral facts are, indeed, facts about the world, and that normative sentences may be true or false in the way that nonnormative sentences may be true or false. Some realists of this school call themselves nonnaturalists; some prefer to say they are nonreductive naturalists. Here, I can offer only a disciplinary diagnosis: I suspect that a preoccupation with whether moral sentences are "fact-stating" or "truth-apt" is, in some measure, an artifact of the exaggerated authority that the philosophy of language—my own subdisciplinary alma mater—has enjoyed for much of the postwar era.

Let me here acknowledge, in the spirit of preemption, that extraordinary and inventive work in meta-ethics has, in the past few decades, been devoted to elaborating and defending positions that go by names such as moral "realism" and (predictably) "antirealism"; "cognitivism" and (of course) "noncognitivism"; "internalism" and (inevitably) "externalism"; and we shouldn't neglect the resurgence of moral constructivism. They come in surprising combinations; each position has been wonderfully subtilized and ingeniously defended. Yet it would not be unfair to say that, in each case, we have reached something of an impasse. This is not meant as any kind of dismissal: one would not want to be in the position of the *Edinburgh Review* editor Francis Jeffrey, who began his review of Wordsworth's 9,000-line epic *The Excursion* with the blithe judgment: "This will never do." And yet, on the level of meta-meta-ethics, we ought to proceed with a proper sense of the stakes. Philosophers often suggest that the question of whether or not, when we make moral judgments, we express beliefs about the way the world really *is* morally, is a hugely important question. From the point of view of getting on with your life, though, it's really crucial only if you're a particularly devoted meta-ethicist.

In Robert Musil's novel *Die Verwirrungen des Zöglings Törless* (The Confusions of Young Törless), there is a memorable conversation between Törless and his friend Beineberg about imaginary numbers. Törless objects: "There is no such thing.

Any number, whether it's positive or negative, yields something positive when it's squared. So there can't be a bona fide number that's the square root of something negative." To which line of thought, Beineberg responds, "if one was to be too conscientious, there would be no mathematics." And he reminds his friend that, after all, one can't really grasp the idea of parallel lines meeting infinitely far away. Here is young Törless' reply: "But what's remarkable is precisely that . . . one really can do calculations with such imaginary or otherwise impossible values and end up with a tangible result."[17]

It matters that some sort of objectivity about the normative is a reasonable hypothesis, because an objective picture allows us to see the project of ethics as a shared human endeavor. But even those whose metaphysical consciences will not allow them to take normative truths to be part of the furniture of the world will end up with lives in which they must respond to normative demands. Whatever our metaphysical scruples, we will pretty often get the same "tangible result." My late friend Richard Braithwaite, a philosophical logician, once reformulated Einstein's theory of relativity—straightened out the kinks, as he thought. He was pleased to call the result the Braithwaite-Einstein Theory of Relativity. Curiously, however, the universe itself looked suspiciously the same under the Braithwaite-Einstein theory as it did under the original Einsteinian version. The universes inhabited by the sophisticated realist and antirealist, the sophisticated cognitivist and noncognitivist, are the same universe; and most of what these thinkers want to say about first-order ethics is the same. (And if it isn't, it's almost never because they disagree about the metaphysics.)

What's at issue is the perfectly interesting question of how best to construct a semantics for moral propositions, or how best to understand the causal story of our moral judgments. A theory of bread provides no more nourishment than a theory of stones: this is to the discredit of neither. But as Jesus said, "What man is there of you, whom if his son ask bread, will he give him a stone?" We should try to keep clear, as meta-ethicists have not always done, what the stakes truly are. When we leave this set of problems behind, it will not be because a glorious knock-down argument has settled matters, but because, as regularly happens in the history of the moral sciences, philosophers have grown bored, for the moment, with the debate and so have moved on. And when we leave it—no doubt to return to it again in later decades or centuries—we will still be faced with the challenge of making our lives.

In the meantime, and for my own limited purposes, I shall endeavor to treat without prejudice realists and quasi-realists and anti-realists. That's because there is another vision of naturalism that subtends these positions, and finds allies and antagonists among them all.[18]

That is the vision of naturalism that has wended its way through these pages, and it can be defined negatively: it denies the autonomy of ethics, at least in its stronger forms. It denies that the exploration of value must proceed without reference to the phenomena that scientists study, the causal systems of the material world, the framings of our nature. It denies the claim that—in a recent formulation—considerations proper to science, on the one hand, and considerations of meaning and values, on the other, belong each to a separate, nonoverlapping magisterium.[19] It insists that the relation between moral inquiry and some new empirical discovery should remain an open question. In the name of the moral sciences, it would remove the wedge between "moral" and "science."

It does *not* therefore take the language of the physical realm as the repository of ultimate truths—as the pre-Babel idiom of an epistemological Eden—into which all other descriptions must be translated. There is one world. But that one world admits of more than one description. We would miss the point of Kant's "two standpoints" distinction if we took the *Sinnenwelt* as somehow primary to the *Verstandeswelt,* so that every normative predicate was to be cashed out in psychological, biological, chemical, physical terms. In fact, we would mistake the nature of both realms. On the one hand, science is deeply normative: scientists may (within measure) quarrel about norms of rationality, of permitted inference, but those norms are fundamental to and constitutive of their disciplines. On the other hand, arguments about values are always also arguments about the world.

Those who wish to protect the absolute autonomy of ethics often complain about the lure of "scientism." The complaint is not without content: there are enthusiasts with an exaggerated notion of what science can provide. Yet these critics often want to cabin science out of a similarly exaggerated sense of its power. Milton was of the Devil's party without knowing it, Blake famously charged, and something like this is true of the no-science-please-we're-humanists crowd: they denounce science, as others denounce Satan, from the fervor of belief.

The reciprocal errors of outlandish ambitions and baseless

fears are greatest when we approach the realm of biology, venturing inferences about our mammalian past or our neurological present. If we are designed to be attuned (inter alia) to hierarchy and to purity, we should expect that such naturalistic accounts may be taken to be, well, debasing and sullying. You'll recall that, in Chapter 4, I referred to the unease that can be prompted by all causal stories about normative concerns. What Ryle called the Bogey of Mechanism is curiously persistent. The question, as before, is whether that feeling withstands reflection. For, as Ryle pithily noted, "physicists may one day have found the answer to all physical questions, but not all questions are physical questions."[20]

Consider the contention that the authority of moral judgment cannot survive an evolutionary account of its origins—a contention that can be found among both advocates and enemies of such accounts. With bracing antipodean vigor, the philosopher Richard Joyce has argued that morality is socially useful in all kinds of ways, and that its usefulness depends upon the purported authority and inescapability of moral prescriptions. Yet an examination of its evolutionary origins, he thinks, reveals morality to be no more than a fiction. From these factual claims, a prescription swiftly follows. According to Joyce (plainly one of those who take pride in their gimlet-eyed undupability), we must steel ourselves to abjure the Matrix-like fiction of morality, distancing ourselves from "any theory that would render us epistemic slaves to the baby-bearing capacity of our ancestors." What is to be done? "The only honest and dignified course is to acknowledge what the evidence is and our best theorizing indicates and deal with the practical consequences," he writes. "If uncomfortable truths are out there, we should seek them and face them like intellectual adults."[21] It's hard to miss: the authority and inescapability of ethics have apparently survived its putative debunking. We are urged to see through the myth of morality in language riddled with "oughts," not to mention appeals to virtues such as honesty, dignity, and valor. The testimony here that ethical judgments are indeed inescapable, not just purportedly so, is all the more persuasive coming from a witness for the prosecution.

Notice, too, that plenty of naturalistic stories about ourselves and our concepts just don't occasion this kind of anxiety. Developmental psychologists tell us that infants of three or four months grasp various law-like features of the physical world—say, that objects are permanent, cohesive, and cannot pass through solid surfaces—and they do so, it has been argued, because of "hard-wired" perceptual-cognitive modules, not because of any accumulated empirical warrant. The same holds, it seems, for all manner of geometric intuitions relevant to orientation, and for much else besides. Point to an object, and a toddler will see, as a distinct entity, the thing you're trying to indicate. (The toddler sees the kitten: not the patch of fur three millimeters above its left eye, with which your finger is aligned; not a more approximate area encompassing kitten, grass, and flagstone; not the kitten-glimpsed-through-window concept; and not any of these things construed strictly as part of a singular and nonrecurrent historical moment.) This is what makes learning possible. Do these psychological findings fatally compromise our everyday experience of the world? Do we worry that our perceptions of the physical realm must "render us epistemic slaves to the baby-bearing capacity of our ancestors"? If not, why not? Obviously, the worry is specific to morality: we are to treat it like a Boy in the Bubble, for whom contact with the larger world must prove fatal. But we need not accept the choice between surrendering morality and sacrificing science; we can, as I propose, relinquish the error of holding that ethics is autonomous.

The basic dispute here could very well pass for forty-three, in the dusk with the light behind it; but it's age-old. For Montaigne, in the essay "Of Custom," the scandalous claim was that "the laws of conscience, which we say are born of nature, are born of custom." For many humanists these days, the opposite claim is what's scandalous. Really, though, it's the same scandal. Montaigne, having studied the world's cultures and conversed with a cannibal, knew that one man's meat was another man's person. Yet once we've inquired into the origins of our ways—grasped their contingency and particularity, which he illustrated through a raft of ethnographic anecdotes—what would happen to the authority of custom? Montaigne described two different ways of responding. Some "masters" were convinced that all such inquiry into origins must be renounced, lest custom be unsettled. Others, in a spirit of nihilistic devilry, responded (just as the masters feared) by supposing they could craft their own values, recklessly innovating as the spirit moved them. Once you distanced yourself from blind allegiance to custom, you would discover that many received certitudes "have no support but in the hoary beard and the wrinkles of the usage that goes with them," he wrote. Montaigne was no fan of heedless innovation, which could simply replace one set of errors with another: "Whosoever meddles with choosing and changing," he writes, "usurps the authority to judge, and he must be very sure he sees the weakness of what he is casting out and the goodness of what he is bringing in." At the same time, he had strong reformist tendencies of his own. Was the choice really between violent disenchantment and mindless habit, between reckless invention and oblivious ancestor worship? Montaigne, being Montaigne, saw that there was another way to go. Yes, a person might glimpse that hoary head and shriveled face, and wince; "but when this mask is torn off, and he refers things to truth and reason, he will feel his judgment as it were all upset, and nevertheless restored to a much surer status."[22] There is, then, a third way between recklessness and mindlessness: it's the surer state—not one of certainty, but of *greater* certainty—to which we can aspire through our common human capacities of reason and observation, our shared ability to muddle our way toward the truth. If our parochialisms reflected, as he thought, a feature of our common natures, so could the remedy.

Indeed, why must "naturalism" undermine rather than underwrite moral objectivism? Isaiah Berlin, in the last essay he wrote, slyly ventured that the objectivity of values was related to the objective fact that "men are men and women are women and not dogs or cats or tables or chairs"; since we're human beings, there are only certain values that we can intelligibly pursue.[23] Many of these values will be different; some must be common, or we would cease to be human. When we refer to the *fact* of value pluralism, we're referring to the fact that there is a plural-ity of real values, intelligible and worthwhile ideals. To insist that the authority of those ideals is undermined by their origins in human nature is to deny the humanity of our humanity.

A Show of Hands

The practice of so-called experimental philosophy, as I suggested at the beginning of this book, is really more traditional than what we currently conceive as traditional philosophy. So— a disciplinary caveat—methodologically, too, we should be wary of exaggerated hopes and baseless fears. The arguments with which philosophers concern themselves often have an ancient pedigree, and, I've heard it suggested by a skeptic of experimental philosophy, the history of these arguments could casually be regarded as an n-person experiment. Someone floats a view, last year or a millennium ago, and we find that it gains, or fails to gain, adherents. There's a natural experiment in that, no? And, as we've seen, the evidentiary status of intuition isn't vexed merely in the realm of moral inquiry. A team of philosophers and cognitive psychologists—Edouard Machery, Ron Mallon, Shaun Nichols, and Stephen Stich—once conducted a fascinating study about people's intuitive responses to an argument made in Saul Kripke's *Naming and Necessity*. Suppose, Kripke wrote, that Gödel's theorem was actually the work of a fellow named Schmidt; Gödel somehow got hold of the manuscript and thereafter was wrongly credited with its authorship. When, ignorant of the misattribution, we talk about "Gödel" in this context, the "descriptivist" view of reference (a view favored by Frege and Russell) would say that we're really referring to

Schmidt: we're talking about the author of the theorem, and Schmidt is the creature who answers to that description. "But it seems we are not," Kripke wrote. "We simply are not."[24]

In the "What do you mean 'we,' Kemo Sabe?" spirit, the research team devised scenarios that were analogous to Kripke's thought experiment, and presented them to undergraduates in New Jersey and in Hong Kong. The Americans, it turned out, were more likely to give the "causal-historical" responses that Kripke assumed his readers would share. The Chinese students, by contrast, were mostly descriptivist in their intuition. So how is the truth of a theory of reference to be vouchsafed by such culturally variable intuitions?[25] Good question. But here's the thing: both views, the descriptivist and the causal-historical, have adherents among philosophers; *both* intuitions have their advocates. And the right answer, if there is one, isn't necessarily to be determined by a headcount. Where surveys show people have incompatible intuitions, we should predict that each intuition has some past philosopher who constructed a theory around it. Knobe and Nichols, writing about how people responded to their scenarios about uxoricide and determinism, noticed what happened when their nonphilosophical subjects were pressed to reconcile disparate intuitions about free will and responsibility. The subjects split evenly on the topic, and the split, our theorists remarked, seemed to mirror the philosophical one. The results in the theory-of-reference experiment fit this pattern: it usefully confirms an already existing professional dissensus. But it doesn't exactly uphold Ezra Pound's exhortation, "Make it new."

Recall Joshua Knobe's pair of scenarios about the mercenary chairman. Suppose that, rather than collecting responses from subjects, Knobe had written, in the canonical manner, "It would be natural, in the first case, to say that the chairman had harmed the environment intentionally, whereas . . ." and so forth. From there, he could have proceeded to make his inferences (which are, necessarily, grounded on other intuitions, intuitions that aren't submitted to survey). How much would have been lost?

Well, something—perhaps a sort of epistemic humility, or, anyway, hygiene. It does not detract from the research into situationism to say that its findings would not have altogether surprised Xenophon: and exposing our intuitions about what's "self-evident" to empirical testing is a salutary discipline. Mathematicians, rightly, care not one whit about untutored intuitions as to the truth of the Riemann hypothesis; and Cicero, we know, thought it an embarrassment for a natural philosopher, a *physicus,* to seek for truth in the asseverations of custombound souls.[26] But it's different when we're trying to make sense of a shared moral vocabulary.

Different how? Nobody supposes that perplexities in deontic logic are to be resolved by a show of hands, and experimental philosophers rarely make the mistake of supposing that a dispute will be *settled* by a survey of opinion, save when that opinion is what the dispute is about. Often, their experiments are best regarded as distributed thought experiments, pluralized intuition pumps. The experimentalists are not, thereby, committed to some program of plebiscitarian metaphysics. The contributions of the method are partly negative, chastening some assumptions about what's "obvious"; and partly positive, shining a light on anomalies of our moral folk psychology, and connecting them to philosophical arguments. The experimental results, since they are never self-interpreting, enter into a spiral of interpretation and inference, argument and persuasion.

In themselves, experiments of this sort can't provide answers to the issues they probe—though they can sometimes raise good questions—and this has to do with the nature of ethics, certainly as Aristotle conceived the subject. Anyone looking for decision procedures, a way of ranking values or a set of rules for choosing among them, should be warned that a "naturalized ethics" is never going to get us there. This isn't because of any crevasse between "is" and "ought"; it's because there's no there there. Normative theories, if they are sensible, do not offer algorithms for action.[27]

The Quandary Quandary

What, decisions without decision procedures? That's another feature of Aristotelian ethics that seems incongruous to the way the subject has often been approached in the past century. We love our moral dilemmas—our footbridges and trolley tracks and fat cavers and the rest. How is it that Aristotle failed to share our enthusiasm? A few decades ago, Edmund Pincoffs pointed out the historical novelty of what he called "quandary ethics," and raised hard questions about the disciplinary distortions it had engendered.[28] Quandary ethics, as the name suggests, took the central problem of moral life to be the resolution of quandaries about what to do. One of its favorite methods was to examine stylized scenarios, like the trolley problem, and figure out what we should do and why. While explaining the *why,* you would come up with theories about how to decide what to do quite generally, often some variant of: do your duty, maximize happiness, do what the virtuous person would do. Contemporary ethicists have sometimes thought that they've left such quandary ethics behind, and it's true that they're somewhat less inclined to pose quandaries in order to prove the merits of one system of moral decision making over another; but—as John Wisdom once remarked—every day, in every way, we are getting meta and meta. Philosophers still prize quandaries when their quarry is a meta-ethical issue—say, whether moral judgments are inherently motivating; whether moral statements are truth-apt statements of facts about the world— and, in the course of this book, we've seen how quandaries have been recruited by researchers with a naturalistic interest in the intuitions they provoke.

I am not a foe of quandaries; but, especially when we're trying to come to grips with the larger subject of *eudaimonia,* students of the moral sciences—not least experimental philosophers—should recognize how stark their limitations are. To turn to them for guidance in the arena of ethics is like trying to find your way around at night with a laser pointer.

For one thing, quandary ethics often starts with a mistaken picture—what we might call the *umpire fantasy,* in which the right answer will be the one delivered by a judge or umpire charged with rendering dispassionate appraisals. An umpire, we can at least pretend, is someone who doesn't make the rules but applies them. That's not us: in determining our "own mode" we make at least some of the rules, Mill rightly insisted, as well as following them. Equally misleading is the idea that, like the

umpire, we're outside the game. Because we're not just um-
pires—we're players. We have particular interests and ambitions that we reasonably take into account. Our evaluations are
made *through* our passions, not despite them. Quandary ethics
may ask how we balance morality against prudence. But that
sets the presupposition in favor of others, as if I ought to decide
impartially between my interests and those of the stranger, as if
I should ignore the fact that I have a life and that my life is my
special concern. (The same error arises when people talk as if
"ethics" wins whenever altruism defeats self-interest.) In all
these ways, the judge or umpire is the wrong model.

Let me broaden the point. The agent in quandary ethics is
often, like the scenarios, relentlessly abstract, rendered with all
the sfumato of an Etch-a-Sketch drawing. It's as if everything
that a particular individual holds dear, derives consolation
from, or aspires to—everything that confers her individuality—
cannot much matter. Specificity of that sort is made to seem a
distraction. Recall that wrenching moment from Tolstoy's story
"The Death of Ivan Ilyich," where the dying man ponders a
syllogism he was taught in his youth:

> "Caius is a man, men are mortal, therefore Caius is mor-
> tal," had seemed to him all his life to be true as applied to
> Caius but certainly not as regards himself. That Caius—
> man in the abstract—was mortal, was perfectly correct;
> but he was not Caius, not man in the abstract: he had al-
> ways been a creature quite, quite different from all others.
> He had been little Vanya with a mamma and a papa, and
> Mita and Volodya, with playthings and the coach and the

nurse; and afterwards with Katya and with all the joys and griefs and ecstasies of childhood, boyhood and youth. What did Caius know of the smell of that striped leather ball Vanya had been so fond of? . . . Caius was certainly mortal, and it was right for him to die; but for me, little Vanya, Ivan Ilyich, with all my thoughts and emotions, it's a different matter altogether. It cannot be that I ought to die. That would be too terrible.

That was the way he felt inside himself.[29]

Ivan's reasoning here is presented, explicitly, as a train of illogic; but it also gropes toward a truth. A normative discourse that centers on Caius—on "man in the abstract"—is missing something. That striped leather ball matters. Our project-dependent values, the range of our individual commitments and ideals and aspirations and self-shapings: these matter. Quandary ethics ignores our particularity.

I pointed to a second problem with quandaries when I remarked, in Chapter 3, that all those trolley cases were moral emergencies, where the options are given in the description of the situation. We can call this the *package problem.* In the real world, situations are not bundled together with options. In the real world, the act of framing—the act of describing a situation, and thus of determining that there's a decision to be made—is itself a moral task. It's often *the* moral task. Learning how to recognize what is and isn't an option is part of our ethical development. Part of the point of the stringency of the prohibition against murder, Anscombe once observed, was *"that you are not to be tempted by fear or hope of consequences."*[30] So a proper response to a situation like these would be to look, first, for other options. To understand what's wrong with murder is, in part, to be disinclined to take killing people as an option. If we want to learn about normative life from stories, I suspect the stories that are most helpful are going to be movies and novels and the like, in which characters have to understand and respond to complex situations, not just pick options in an SAT-style multiple-choice problem. In life, the challenge is not so much to figure out how best to play the game; the challenge is to figure out what game you're playing.

Yet another problem with quandary ethics has been its tendency to figure moral judgment as a solitary act. Hobbes says, in *The Elements of Philosophy*, that language serves "by accident to signify and make known to others what we remember ourselves."[31] The picture of moral thought in much modern moral philosophy is Hobbesian: language is for thinking, not for speaking; for me, not for us. So let's call this problem the *Hobbesian howler*. For, as I said, moral language, *as* language, is essentially public. The avowal and endorsement and revision of norms are conversational activities. It can't be unimportant that human beings spend so much of their days talking to other human beings (and yes, on occasion, being talked *at*). For all their references to "justification," quandary theorists have had little to say about justification as an actual, social process. The normative realm is, in ways both broad and deep, about conversation. And conversation is an n-person game.

A final point. In the quandary paradigm that has come to shape "applied ethics," moral discourse has effectively been relegated to instances of conflict, to "problems." A problem arises (what shall we do with the frozen embryos? shall euthanasia be authorized?) and ethicists spring into action. Here, morality has been reduced to something like a clinical intervention: a moral dispensary for the afflicted. The Aristotelian notion of ethics, by contrast, had to do with everyday existence—with the life that you sought to live. (To continue this perhaps ungainly metaphor: wellness, not illness, was its primary concern.) Temperance, continence, kindness, friendship, simply being nice: these are not solutions to conundrums but questions of existence—questions about what kind of people we are and wish to be. Quandary ethics, in short, has too often been about what you should *do*. It may be "practical," in the Mr. Fix-It spirit, but not in a way that acknowledges the intimate relation between social practices and values. One cannot riddle one's way to the good life, and if the term "ethics" conjures a hectoring moralism, a focus on misdeeds, a list of italicized demerits, then something has indeed been lost.

Complications

When I find myself next to a talkative stranger on a plane, I sometimes get asked what I do. If I say I'm a philosopher, the conversation often comes to a pretty grinding halt; when it doesn't, the next question is often: "So, what's your philosophy?" I usually take the easy way out. "My philosophy," I say, "is that everything is more complicated than you thought."

Many people have the opposite philosophy: they are devotees of parsimony, and strive always for theoretical minimalism, the elegant reduction. (These are people for whom the miracle is to turn wine into water.) Faced with the sort of story I have been telling, one might reasonably ask: "Does it all have to be this complicated? What about those good, clean, simple stories out there: virtue ethics, consequentialism, deontology, contractualism? You have felt free to see the merits in appeals to virtues and to consequences and to rules and to reasonable consent, and not felt obliged to give a general decision procedure for how to fit them all together. Some of our evaluations, you said, we will reasonably abandon in the face of criticism from others or our pictures of ourselves. Which ones, when?"

Give me a case, I reply, and we can discuss it. Abstraction here, I think, is a vice. When should you not trust your eyes about the colors of things? There's no interesting general answer to that question, either. But let me add that what recommends the alternative approaches over the one I am commending is mostly just that they appear simpler. And the fact is that once you take them seriously, the simplicity disappears. Take a familiar version of maximizing consequentialism, which assesses the goodness of the situations that will result from various courses of action and picks the act that will produce the best overall situation. But there are uncountably many options we could, in principal, consider; and, in any case, there's really no such thing as the goodness of a situation. To be good, I hope we've been persuaded, is to be good for something, good in some particular way. And there is nothing in general that situations are good for. So, if we're to keep the story simple, - we must decide to maximize something about the situation: like pleasure, which the early utilitarians favored, presumably because they took it to be good for us. But if we pick pleasure, then we have to answer the question that Mill addressed, by distinguishing between higher and lower pleasures: Would you rather be Socrates dissatisfied or a satisfied pig?[32] Pick the avoidance of pain as our goal, instead of pleasure, and we avoid even the satisfactions of the pig. So what should we pick as our maximand? Human flourishing? We can't aim to maximize *that*, because part of what it is for people to flourish is for it to be *them* that make the decisions. So sometimes we can improve their lives only by leaving them alone. And, anyway, if you accept the thought that it matters what kinds of people we are and not just what we do—Mill's nonutilitarian insight in *On Liberty*—then you won't think that maximizing outcomes is ever going to capture everything that matters, because sometimes what we are means, as the deontologist and the virtue theorist can both agree, that we cannot look to the consequences. That, I think, is one lesson of life on the footbridge.

I insist: what recommends these simple stories is that they're simple. Nobody reasonable imagines that pain and pleasure or the satisfaction of preferences, however meaningless or bizarre, is what life's all about. Nobody starts out with the notion that "Can I universalize the maxim of this action?" is the only question worth asking. (Or can be certain that we'll be able to tell what the maxim is.) Nobody really holds the narcissistic view that all that matters is what virtues you have. (Or agrees, quite, on what virtues matter most. The index for Hursthouse's *On Virtue Ethics* contains entries for honesty, control, charity, compassion, and wisdom. None for humor, wit, conviviality, originality, raconteurship, or love.) Nobody has a non-question-begging way of settling disagreement by appeal to the consent principle. From any of these beginnings, things have to get very complicated if you're to end with something plausible. It's like starting with Ockham's razor—just a sharp blade with a handle—and finding you need to add a beard trimmer, a nail clipper, and a whole host of Rube Goldberg accessories, and then continuing to maintain that all you have is still just a razor. People buy the stories initially because they have the theoretician's charm of simplicity. So if we have to make them complicated to get it right, they lose their advantage over the pointedly unparsimonious story I've been telling.

And the messiness of ethics goes down deep. We can't stop just with value pluralism and noises about "uncodifiability," because once you take account of the fact that values come with implicit criteria—distinctive theoretical niches, as it were—you back up into a sort of methodological pluralism. That was one lesson of Chapter 4, where we shuttled between empirical— ethnographic, sociological, psychological—observations and various themes that were perspicuous in our traditions of moral reflection: the varieties of moral experience, it was clear, couldn't be plotted along two dimensions. And so we've explored the idea that the seeming modularity of morals might correspond to ideals and values that we had reason to care about.

In allowing all this complexity, what have we given up? Well, if you were a value pluralist and a methodological monist, say, you could devise a technique for assigning weights to values that could then be summed, even though the values themselves couldn't be. Or rather, you could flutter your fingers and talk about doing it. There was a long period in which moral philosophers would make reassuring references to "criteria of correctness," "ranking procedures," "lexical priority," "deontic rules," and so forth. By now, these references have come to seem like payments on an interest-only mortgage: they service an obligation that we know will never come due.

There's a reason, I think, that all the great treatises in philosophical ethics—the ones that hold our attention and stir our imagination—are so deeply heterogeneous. Think of comprehensive accounts like Aristotle's *Nicomachean Ethics,* Kant's *Groundwork,* Mill's *On Liberty,* Rawls's *A Theory of Justice:* they're invariably a mélange, containing a welter of moral considerations, including those we call aretaic, consequentialist, deontological, and so forth. Rawls's "Aristotelian Principle," Mill's concern for self-development and flourishing, Kant's "imperfect duties"—all these elements are continuous with the classical traditions. Every comprehensive account accommodates, in one idiom or another, notions of character, consequences, duties, maxims, reasonableness, fairness, consent. Their expositors may try to purge and purify the vision, but, as when a bad mechanic takes apart and reassembles a motor, they always leave the floor cluttered with the parts they couldn't fit in. In the sense that Marx, recoiling at the caricatural claims of some of his disciples, insisted he wasn't a Marxist, we should admit that Aristotle wasn't an Aristotelian, Kant wasn't a Kantian, Mill wasn't a Millian, and Rawls wasn't a Rawlsian. (Well, maybe Aristotle *was* an Aristotelian.) A story that takes our moral sentiments seriously is bound to reflect their eclectic nature.

But, of course, our story isn't about morality alone; it's about ethics. It's not just about what we should do for others; it's about making a life for ourselves. That's where it starts. And then, because it recognizes that everybody has a life to make and that we are making our lives together, it's bound to take morality—our obligations to others—seriously, too. Indeed, it's precisely our recognition that each other person is engaged in the ethical project of making a life that reveals to us our obligations to them. Our having a life to make is what our humanity consists in: and in recognizing and valuing our own humanity—this is a Kantian idea, of course, though not only a Kantian idea—we are bound to see it as the same humanity that we find in others. If my humanity matters, so does yours; if yours doesn't, neither does mine. We stand or fall together.

To see each other person not just as someone with preferences, pleasures, and pains, but as a creature engaged in the project of making a life, striving to succeed on the basis of standards that are partly found and partly made, you will see why you should keep promises and respect property, why you should not gratuitously obstruct other people's ambitions or ignore their material, social, or psychological needs. Morality derives from an understanding of what other people are up to; it's not a system of arbitrary demands. And the central thing that people are up to is the central ethical task: each of us is making a life. That is the human *telos:* to make a good life, to achieve *eudaimonia.* We cannot pursue that end without an understanding of our cultivated natures. Precisely because making a life is an activity, though, we should expect to learn more from experiments in living than from experiments in philosophizing.

The end of philosophical ethics is to make sense of the project of *eudaimonia.* It cannot do that on its own: it needs the assistance of all the moral sciences, from psychology and economics to anthropology and sociology; indeed, it cannot proceed without the aid of all the nine Muses. Its worldly role is doubtless marginal compared to that played by prophets, preachers, politicians, and storytellers of every kind. But to the extent that philosophical ethics can contribute to our own experiments in living, it inches toward one of its long-cherished ambitions: not merely to study the good life, but to sustain what's good in our lives.

NOTES

ACKNOWLEDGMENTS

INDEX

NOTES

1. Introduction

1. "L'oubli, et je dirai même l'erreur historique, sont un facteur essentiel de la création d'une nation, et c'est ainsi que le progrès des études historiques est souvent pour la nationalité un danger." Ernest Renan, "Qu'est-ce qu'une nation?" (1882), ch. 1, para. 7. See www.bmlisieux.com/archives/nation02.htm (accessed March 23, 2007). All translations are my own, unless otherwise noted.

2. René Descartes, "The Passions of the Soul" (1649), in *Selected Philosophical Writings,* trans. J. Cottingham, R. Stoothoff, and D. Murdoch (Cambridge: Cambridge University Press, 1988), 331. The reference to "animal spirits" here suggests to a modern reader something immaterial; so it's as well to remember that Descartes' use of the term, which draws on Galenic medical theory, doesn't imply anything of the sort. See Nicolaus Steno, *Lecture on the Anatomy of the Brain* (1669), introd. Gustav Scherz (Copenhagen: Nyt Nordisk Forlag, Arnold Busck, 1965), 155, note 2.

3. Descartes, "The Passions of the Soul," 352. In 1669, the Danish anatomist and geologist Nicolaus Steno (né Niels Stensen) rebutted Descartes' claims by publishing anatomical research showing that the pineal gland was present in animals as well as in man, was not so richly innervated as Descartes assumed, and, being firmly secured by adjoining tissue, was incapable of the movement Descartes imputed to it. See Steno, *Lecture on the Anatomy of the Brain,* 12ff.

4. Hooke, *Micrographia* (1665), www.roberthooke.org.uk/micro2.htm (accessed March 23, 2007); and see Steven Shapin and Simon Schaffer, *Leviathan and the Air-Pump: Hobbes, Boyle, and the Experimental Life* (Princeton: Princeton University Press, 1985), 38.

5. See Thomas Hobbes, "Physical Dialogue" (1661), trans. Simon Schaffer, in Shapin and Schaffer, *Leviathan and the Air-Pump*, 354–391.

6. But he went on to note, "It is neither from the roots nor from the trunks of trees that we gather the fruit, but only from the extremities of their branches." René Descartes, "Lettre-Préface de l'édition française des *Principes*" (1647), www.ac-nice.fr/philo/textes/Descartes-LettrePreface.htm (accessed March 23, 2007).

"Ainsi toute la philosophie est comme un arbre, dont les racines sont la métaphysique, le tronc est la physique, et les branches qui sortent de ce tronc sont toutes les autres sciences, qui se réduisent à trois principales, à savoir la médecine, la mécanique et la morale. . . .

"Or, comme ce n'est pas des racines ni du tronc des arbres qu'on cueille les fruits, mais seulement des extrémités de leurs branches . . ."

7. Margaret Cavendish, *Observations upon Experimental Philosophy* (1668), ed. Eileen O'Neil (Cambridge: Cambridge University Press, 2001), 44, 49.

8. The fifth edition of the *Dictionnaire de l'Académie Française* (1798) defines *âme* ("soul" or "spirit") as "Ce qui est le principe de la vie dans tous les êtres vivans" ("That which is the principle of life in all living beings"). *Physique* ("physics" or, in the eighteenth-century sense, "science") is defined as "Science qui a pour objet les choses naturelles" ("Science that takes natural things as its object"). This dictionary is one of many older French dictionaries available online from the Project for American and French Research on the Treasury of the French Language (ARTFL) *Dictionnaires d'autrefois* site: portail.atilf.fr/dictionnaires/onelook.htm (accessed March 23, 2007).

9. David Hume, *An Enquiry concerning Human Understanding*, ed. L. A. Selby-Bigge, 2nd ed. (Oxford: Clarendon, 1902), 43–44. This edition, still the standard one, wrongly has "useful" for "usual" in the first quoted line; compare *The Philosophical Works of David Hume: Including All the Essays, and Exhibiting the More Important Alterations and Corrections in the Successive Editions by the Author* (Edinburgh: Adam Black and William

Tait, 1826), vol. 4, 53–54. Hume was not an unalloyed enthusiast of the mechanical turn. In his *History of England,* he writes, about the founding of the Royal Society, "There flourished during this period a Boyle and a Newton; men who trod with cautious, and therefore the more secure steps, the only road, which leads to true philosophy." But he goes on almost immediately to caution, "Boyle was a great partisan of the mechanical philosophy; a theory which, by discovering some of the secrets of nature, and allowing us to imagine the rest, is so agreeable to the natural vanity and curiosity of men." David Hume, *The History of England, from the Invasion of Julius Caesar to the Revolution in 1688,* Foreword by William B. Todd, 6 vols. (Indianapolis: Liberty Fund, 1983), vol. 6, ch. 71, oll.libertyfund.org/ToC/0011-05.php, accessed March 23, 2007. (The final section of this final chapter is, by the way, a wonderful discussion of "manners, arts and sciences" in the period of the Stuarts, from the Restoration of 1660 to the Glorious Revolution of 1688, which brought William of Orange to the throne. Hume's comments on the Royal Society are followed by a complaint against the general tenor of the literature of the period: "Most of the celebrated writers of this age remain monuments of genius, perverted by indecency and bad taste." Hume's history always involves moral analysis.) See also Michael Barfoot, "Hume and the Culture of Science in the Early Eighteenth Century," in M. A. Stewart, ed., *Studies in the Philosophy of the Scottish Enlightenment* (Oxford: Oxford University Press, 1990), 151–190.

10.   The case has been made, notably, by the eminent intellectual historian Knud Haakonssen, who sees Reid and Kant as having "shaped the epistemological paradigm for the history of early modern philosophy that has dominated the subject ever since they wrote. Our notion of the history of post-Renaissance philosophy is, in other words, itself the outcome of a particular episode in that history." Knud Haakonssen, "The Idea of Early Modern Philosophy," in Jerry Schneewind, ed., *Teaching New Histories of Philosophy* (Princeton: University Center for Human Values, 2004), 108. Haakonssen, having recently edited a history of eighteenth-century philosophy, is charmingly skeptical about whether eighteenth-century philosophy exists as such: once you put aside the project of rational reconstruction, "it is not clear in what sense a philosophical canon can be identified," he writes mildly. "The issues that are considered 'philosophical' in our histories of philosophy, such as the epistemic adequacy of ideas or the normative war-

rant of obligation, have been picked out of these contexts"—contexts of taxonomy and explanation that moral philosophy shared with natural philosophy. "It is not at all clear in what sense we can be said to understand such pickings divorced from their explanatory framework, but it is clear that we have excluded a major part of what our forebears thought of as philosophy. It is equally clear that they did not have room for the subdisciplines of either epistemology or of metaethics. . . . Much of moral philosophy was as descriptive and explanatory in intent as natural philosophy, and the basic justificatory mode of argument was often the same in both branches—namely, teleological and, generally, providential" (ibid., 99, 110–111).

11. Thomas Reid, *Essays on the Intellectual Powers of Man*, I.iii, "Of Hypothesis," in *The Works of Thomas Reid* (New York: N. Bangs and T. Mason for the Methodist Episcopal Church, J. and J. Harper, Printers, 1822), vol. 1, 367–368. And the texture of Reid's own style of argument brings together commonsense intuition (hunger includes both "an uneasy sensation and a desire to eat"; *The Works of Thomas Reid*, vol. 3, 82) and experimental results. "Our seeing an object in that particular direction in which we do see it," he writes in his *Inquiry into the Human Mind*, is owing "to a law of our nature, by which we see the object in the direction of the right line that passeth from the picture of the object upon the *retina* to the center of the eye." But he wouldn't have us take his word for it. "The facts upon which I ground this induction, are taken from some curious experiments of Scheiner, in his *Fundament. Optic.* quoted by Dr. Porterfield, and confirmed by his experience," he continues. "I have also repeated these experiments, and found them to answer." Here, he makes a point that the supporting evidence has been triply validated. Thomas Reid, *Inquiry into the Human Mind*, in *The Works of Thomas Reid*, vol. 1, 243. The latter passage moves on to a detailed accounting of four experiments involving vision through a pinhole.

12. *Kant on Education*, trans. Annette Churton (Ann Arbor: University of Michigan Press, 1960), 61. "Über die Vulkane im Monde" (Concerning the Volcanoes on the Moon) is in vol. 8 of the *Akademieausgabe von Kants Gesammelten Werken*, www.ikp.uni-bonn.de/kant/aa08/067.htmL, 67–76 (accessed March 23, 2007).

To historians of psychology, Hume and Kant both figure large; and some hold that contrasting Humean and Kantian traditions in scientific psychology continue to this day—as a measurement-driven experimental psychology, on the one hand, and as the schemas of cognitive science, on the other. See Daniel N. Robinson, *An Intellectual History of Psychology*, 3rd ed. (Madison: University of Wisconsin Press, 1995), 225–226.

13. G. W. F. Hegel, *Lectures on the History of Philosophy*, vol. 3: *Medieval and Modern Philosophy*, trans. E. S. Haldane and Frances H. Simpson (Lincoln: University of Nebraska Press, 1995), 323–324. (According to Hans Aarsleff, Locke wasn't securely classified as an empiricist until after the publication of David Masson's *Recent British Philosophy* in 1865.)

Perhaps the most influential nineteenth-century history of philosophy, and certainly the most widely read, was George Henry Lewes's *Biographical History of Philosophy*, first published in the mid-1840s and revised in 1857. Lewes complained that "the word Philosophy has come to be used with large latitude, designating indeed any and every kind of speculative inquiry"; in contrast to other historians of philosophy, he intended to limit use of the term "exclusively to Metaphysics, in direct antithesis to Science." But the comparison is to philosophy's disadvantage: "Its inferences start from no well-grounded basis; the arches they throw are not from known fact to unknown fact, but from some unknown to some other unknown. . . . Rising from such mists, the arch so brilliant to look upon is after all a rainbow, not a bridge." George Henry Lewes, *The Biographical History of Philosophy: From Its Origins in Greece Down to the Present Day* (London: John W. Parker and Son, 1857), xxvi. But even Lewes's history contained chapters on physiological researches by the physiologist (and phrenologist) Francis Joseph Gall. Besides, Lewes's own history had an arc of its own: philosophy was finally to relinquish its place to "positive science," and, in particular, scientific psychology.

14. Charles Dickens, *Martin Chuzzlewit* (New York: Oxford University Press, 1991), 293.

15. John Stuart Mill, "Examination of the Philosophy of William Hamilton," in *The Collected Works of John Stuart Mill*, 33 vols., ed. John M. Robson (Toronto: University of Toronto Press, 1963–1991), vol. 9, 359.

16. Theodor Lipps, "Die Aufgabe der Erkenntnistheorie und die Wundt'sche Logik, I" (The Task of Epistemology and Wundtian Logic, I), *Philosophische Monatshefte* 16 (1880), 529–539; cited in Edward S. Reed,

From Soul to Mind: The Emergence of Psychology from Erasmus Darwin to William James (New Haven: Yale University Press, 1997). For a historical-sociological account, see Martin Kusch, *Psychologism* (London: Routledge, 1995), which argues that the ascent of both Frege and Husserl was the result of contingent historical factors. It is often said that Husserl was converted to anti-psychologism by Frege's 1894 review of his *Philosophie der Arithmetik.* Husserl's *Logische Untersuchungen* appeared six years later, but there is dispute about whether, in this instance, post hoc meant propter hoc. And Frege's influence on Anglophone philosophy was, of course, largely mediated by Bertrand Russell.

17. Hume, *An Enquiry concerning Human Understanding,* 83.

18. W. H. Auden, *Academic Graffiti* (New York: Random House, 1972), 25.

19. Published as J. L. Austin, *How To Do Things with Words* (Oxford: Clarendon, 1962), 50.

20. W. V. O. Quine, "Epistemology Naturalized," in Quine, *Ontological Relativity and Other Essays* (New York: Columbia University Press, 1969), 82–83.

21. Michael Dummett, *Frege and Other Philosophers* (Oxford: Oxford University Press, 1991), 287.

22. David Hume, *A Treatise of Human Nature,* ed. L. A. Selby-Bigge (Oxford: Clarendon Press, 1896), Book 3, 469. Whether Hume has been correctly read in this respect—whether he anticipated the cognate distinction between facts and values—has long been disputed. Morality, Hume writes, "consists not in any *matter of fact,* which can be discover'd by the understanding"; "can there be any difficulty in proving, that vice and virtue are not matters of fact, whose existence we can infer by reason?" Some modern philosophers have interpreted such passages as meaning that, for Hume, there are no moral facts; others have concluded that, for Hume, there are moral facts, but not the kind that are discovered by reason, as opposed, say, to direct perception. ("Vice and virtue," Hume also writes, "may be compar'd to sounds, colours, heat and cold, which according to modern philosophy, are not qualities in objects, but perceptions in the mind.") See, for instance, A. C. MacIntyre, "Hume on 'Is' and 'Ought,'" *Philosophical Review* 68, no. 4 (1959), 451–468; Nicholas Capaldi, "Hume's Rejection of 'Ought' as a Moral Category," *Journal of Philosophy* 63, no. 5 (March 2, 1966), 126–137; J. L. Mackie, *Hume's Moral Theory* (London: Routledge,

1980), 51–63; Mark Platt, "Hume and Morality as a Matter of Fact," *Mind* 97 (April 1988), 189–204.

23. Hume, *A Treatise of Human Nature*, xvi, xvii.

24. Hume, *An Enquiry concerning Human Understanding*, 6.

25. Cited in John B. Stewart, *The Moral and Political Philosophy of David Hume* (New York: Columbia University Press, 1963), 343, note 16.

26. MacIntyre, "Hume on 'Is' and 'Ought,'" 457–458.

27. Philippa Foot, "Moral Arguments," *Mind* 67, no. 268 (October 1958), 507–508, 510.

28. John R. Searle, "How to Derive 'Ought' from 'Is,'" *Philosophical Review*, 73, no. 1 (January 1964), 43–58. A certain amount of normative work is done by the "ceteris paribus," of course: the fact that Smith, a loan shark, says, "I promise I'll break your legs if you don't pay up," doesn't entail that he ought to do so. But Searle's real argument was that the distinction between "descriptive" and "evaluative" language was a muddle.

29. Richard Wollheim, "Introduction," in F. H. Bradley, *Ethical Studies* (Oxford: Oxford University Press, 1962), xvi.

30. G. E. M. Anscombe, "Modern Moral Philosophy," *Philosophy* 33 (1958), 1–19; reprinted in G. E. M. Anscombe, *Ethics, Religion and Politics* (Minneapolis: University of Minnesota Press, 1981), 26–42, quotations from 27, 33, 32–33.

31. Ibid., 38.

32. Ibid., 27. Hume was not, for Anscombe, a virtue ethicist, and most virtue ethicists today are neo-Aristotelian by self-description; but Hume, too, provided a roster of vices and virtues; and some proponents of virtue theory—most notably Michael Slote—identify themselves as Humean, although the distinction is hardly sharp.

33. W. V. O. Quine, "Two Dogmas of Empiricism," *Philosophical Review* 60 (1951), 20; and idem, "Epistemology Naturalized," 83.

34. Recent and representative work at the intersection of psychology and moral philosophy includes Allan Gibbard, *Wise Choices, Apt Feelings: A Theory of Normative Judgment* (Cambridge, Mass.: Harvard University Press, 1990); Owen Flanagan, *Varieties of Moral Personality* (Cambridge, Mass.: Harvard University Press, 1991); Peter Railton, "Made in the Shade: Moral Compatibilism and the Aims of Moral Theory," in J. Couture and K. Nielsen, eds., *On the Relevance of Metaethics: New Essays in Metaethics*

suppl. vol., *Canadian Journal of Philosophy* 21 (1995), 79–106; Gilbert Harman, "Moral Philosophy Meets Social Psychology: Virtue Ethics and the Fundamental Attribution Error," *Proceedings of the Aristotelian Society* 99 (1998–1999), 315–331; Jonathan Haidt, "The Emotional Dog and Its Rational Tail: A Social Intuitionist Approach to Moral Judgment," *Psychological Review* 108 (2001), 814–834; John Doris, *Lack of Character* (Cambridge: Cambridge University Press, 2002); Joshua D. Greene, "From Neural 'Is' to Moral 'Ought': What Are the Moral Implications of Neuroscientific Moral Psychology?" *Nature Reviews Neuroscience* 4 (October 1, 2003), 847–850; Mark L. Johnson, "How Moral Psychology Changes Moral Philosophy," in *Mind and Morals*, ed. Larry May, Marilyn Friedman, and Andy Clark (Cambridge, Mass.: MIT Press, 1996), 45–68; William Casebeer, *Natural Ethical Facts* (Cambridge, Mass.: MIT Press, 2003); Daniel C. Dennett, *Freedom Evolves* (New York: Viking, 2003); Shaun Nichols, *Sentimental Rules: On the Natural Foundations of Moral Judgment* (New York: Oxford University Press, 2004); Joshua Knobe, "Intention, Intentional Action and Moral Considerations," *Analysis* 64 (2004), 181–187; Richard Joyce, *The Evolution of Morality* (Cambridge, Mass.: MIT Press, 2006); Chandra Sripada and Stephen Stich, "A Framework for the Psychology of Norms," in *The Innate Mind*, vol. 2: *Culture and Cognition*, ed. Peter Carruthers, Stephen Laurence, and Stephen Stich (New York: Oxford University Press, 2006); Marc D. Hauser, *Moral Minds* (New York: Ecco, 2006); Walter Sinnott-Armstrong, "Moral Intuitionism Meets Empirical Psychology," in Terry Horgan and Mark Timmons, eds., *Metaethics after Moore* (New York: Oxford University Press, 2006), 339–365.

2. THE CASE AGAINST CHARACTER

1. Lydia Davis, "Trying to Learn," in Davis, *Almost No Memory: Stories* (New York: Farrar, Straus and Giroux, 1997; rpt. Picador, 2001).

2. Rosalind Hursthouse, *On Virtue Ethics* (Oxford: Oxford University Press, 1999); the précis of "honest" is from Hursthouse, "Virtue Ethics," in Edward N. Zalta, ed., *The Stanford Encyclopedia of Philosophy* (Fall 2003 edition), plato.stanford.edu/archives/fall2003/entries/ethics-virtue/ (accessed March 26, 2007). Other influential expositions of virtue ethics include Julia Annas, *The Morality of Happiness* (New York: Oxford University Press,

1993); Roger Crisp, "Modern Moral Philosophy and the Virtues," in Crisp, ed., *How Should One Live? Essays on the Virtues* (Oxford: Oxford University Press, 1996), 1–18; Philippa Foot, *Natural Goodness* (Oxford: Clarendon Press, 2001); Peter Geach, *The Virtues* (Cambridge: Cambridge University Press, 1977); John McDowell, "Virtue and Reason," *Monist* 62 (1979), 331–350; Michael Slote, *Morals from Motives* (Oxford: Oxford University Press, 2001); Jay Wallace, *Virtues and Vices* (Ithaca: Cornell University Press, 1978).

3. Hursthouse, "Virtue Ethics."

4. Ibid. There is something to be learned from the fact that our vocabulary of vice seems so much richer than our vocabulary of virtue.

5. Aristotle, *Nicomachean Ethics*, trans. H. Rackham, Loeb Classical Library (Cambridge, Mass.: Harvard University Press, 1934), 11. Though Aristotle's focus on the virtues was standard fare among ancient Greeks, his is the version most frequently adapted. In ways I'll return to, "happiness" is famously misleading as a translation of *eudaimonia*, or "flourishing," the activity of the soul in accordance with the greatest virtue, or *arête*. Of course, "virtue" is also a problematic rendering of *arête*, which is alternately rendered as "excellence."

6. John M. Doris, *Lack of Character: Personality and Moral Behavior* (Cambridge: Cambridge University Press, 2002), 61, 62.

7. See Lee Ross and Richard E. Nisbett, *The Person and the Situation* (Philadelphia: Temple University Press, 1991). Situationism of this kind, which holds that, in explaining other people's behavior, we routinely underestimate the role of situation and overestimate the role of dispositions, is not to be confused with the "situation ethics" promulgated by the theologian Joseph Fletcher, according to which "all laws and rules and principles and ideals and norms, are only contingent, only valid if they happen to serve love in any situation." Fletcher, *Situation Ethics: The New Morality* (Philadelphia: Westminster Press, 1966), 30.

8. Doris, *Lack of Character*, 16–19.

9. Hugh Hartshorne and Mark A. May, *Studies in Deceit* (New York: Macmillan, 1928). And see Donelson R. Forsyth, "Overview of Studies of Moral Thought, Behavior, and Action," www.richmond.edu/dforsyth/ethics/ethics.htm#over (accessed March 26, 2007).

10. A. M. Isen and P. F. Levin, "The Effect of Feeling Good on Help-

ing: Cookies and Kindness," *Journal of Personality and Social Psychology* 21 (1972), 384–388; J. M. Darley and C. D. Batson, "'From Jerusalem to Jericho': A Study of Situational and Dispositional Variables in Helping Behavior," *Journal of Personality and Social Psychology* 27 (1973), 100–108; K. E. Matthews and L. K. Cannon, "Environmental Noise Level as a Determinant of Helping Behavior," *Journal of Personality and Social Psychology* 32 (1975), 571–577; R. A. Baron and J. Thomley, "A Whiff of Reality: Positive Affect as a Potential Mediator of the Effects of Pleasant Fragrances on Task Performance and Helping," *Environment and Behavior* 26 (1994), 766–784. All are cited in Doris, *Lack of Character*, 30–34, 181.

11. And people are about one-tenth as likely to help someone behind a curtain who has had what sounds like an accident, if there's someone else standing by who does nothing. B. Latané and J. Rodin, "A Lady in Distress: Inhibiting Effects of Friends and Strangers on Bystander Intervention," *Journal of Experimental Social Psychology* 5 (1969), 189–202. As cited in Doris, *Lack of Character*.

12. Virtue ethicists, Hursthouse says (responding, as you will gather, to those experiments with the Good Samaritans at Princeton Theological Seminary), are "amused to find writers willing to attribute the virtue of charity to inexperienced young men on, apparently, the sole ground that they are at theological college, and then being surprised to discover that their attribution fails" (Hursthouse, "Virtue Ethics," end of section 3). So, in effect, she accuses the situationists of making an attribution error of their own. But, as has been observed, the classic experiments in psychology are usually conceived in theatrical terms as well as empirical ones: the choice of seminarians as subjects heightens the rhetorical force of a finding that has significance whether or not you think the subject population is likely to be especially charitable.

13. E. E. Jones and V. A. Harris, "The Attribution of Attitudes," *Journal of Experimental Social Psychology* 3 (1967), 1–24. The "Fundamental Attribution Error" is introduced in Lee Ross, "The Intuitive Psychologist and His Shortcomings: Distortions in the Attribution Process," in Leonard Berkowitz, ed., *Advances in Experimental Social Psychology*, vol. 10 (New York: Academic Press, 1977). Daniel T. Gilbert and Patrick S. Malone give an elegant summary of much work in "The Correspondence Bias," *Psycho-*

logical Bulletin 117, no. 1 (January 1995), 21–38, and offer explanations of why this disposition might be adaptive.

14. An influential 1977 paper by Richard Nisbett and Timothy D. Wilson suggests that—with respect to processes, not content—our access to what's going on in our heads may be no more privileged than our access to what's going on in our livers. In one experiment, Nisbett and Wilson arrayed four pairs of pantyhose on a table in a bargain store, and, in a "Customer Evaluation Survey," asked customers to say which pair they preferred, and why. People made their choice, typically plumping for the one on the right, and had no problem explaining their choice with reference to its particular features: the knit, the elasticity, the sheerness, and so on. Which is all very well—except that the researchers had previously discovered that people tended to favor items on the right side of the display, and all the pairs of pantyhose were, in fact, identical. Although the preference for the rightmost pair was a pure position effect, the subjects had no trouble coming up with spurious yet sincere explanations for their choices. Indeed, when they were asked whether position might have affected their choices, they loftily denied it. As Nisbett and Wilson conclude: "When people attempt to report on their cognitive processes, that is, on the processes mediating the effects of a stimulus on a response, they do not do so on the basis of any true introspection. Instead, their reports are based on a priori, implicit causal theories, or judgments about the extent to which a particular stimulus is a plausible cause of a given response." Richard Nisbett and Timothy D. Wilson, "Telling More Than We Can Know: Verbal Reports on Mental Processes," *Psychological Review* 84 (1977), 231–259; and see Timothy D. Wilson, *Strangers to Ourselves: Discovering the Adaptive Unconscious* (Cambridge, Mass.: Harvard University Press, 2002), 102–103. In endorsing this picture, Nisbett and Wilson's work echoes a claim made in the 1950s by the philosopher Gilbert Ryle in his book *The Concept of Mind.* Ryle got there (perhaps paradoxically) by sitting in his study and reflecting; Nisbett and Wilson did it by conducting and reviewing experiments. Ryle didn't offer the claim as a hypothesis for experimental investigation, and many of his philosophical readers argued on conceptual grounds that he simply couldn't be right. So while he might not have expected to gain support from the laboratory, he wouldn't have been sur-

prised by these results. Indeed, insofar as he was a conceptual analyst—the book, remember, was called *The Concept of Mind*—he might have thought it strange to do experiments to confirm a conceptual truth!

15. Actually, asking for change for a parking meter is more likely to get change than asking for change period. People are more likely to be helpful, it turns out, if the person asking for help offers them a reason, *even if the reason isn't a good one.* See E. J. Langer, A. Blank, and B. Chanowit, "The Mindlessness of Ostensibly Thoughtful Action: The Role of 'Placebic' Information in Interpersonal Interaction," *Journal of Personality and Social Psychology* 36 (1978), 635–642. Experimenters asked people if they could go ahead of them in a line for a photocopy machine. When they said, "May I use the Xerox machine?" slightly more than half allowed them to. But if they said, "May I use the Xerox machine because I'm in a hurry?" almost everybody agreed. Reasonable, you might think. But pretty much the same result was achieved by saying, "May I use the Xerox machine because I want to make copies?" It looks as if all that was required was the *form* of a reason, not a substantial reason.

16. Of course, its being good because it helps doesn't mean it isn't bad overall: suppose you're a nasty person who offers change only because you know you're being watched by someone who has promised to give you fifty bucks if you ever do anything generous. That's blameworthy: you're trying to fake generosity.

17. Not all the classical authors, by the way, shared Aristotle's views about the constancy of virtue. Xenophon, in *The Memorabilia*, takes issue with those philosophers who claim that "a just man can never become unjust; a prudent man can never become wanton; in fact no one having learned any kind of knowledge can become ignorant of it." "I do not hold with this view," he asserts, and he endorses the poet who says, "Ah, but a good man is at one time noble, at another base." Xenophon goes on, "For many who are careful with their money no sooner fall in love than they begin to waste it: and when they have spent it all, they no longer shrink from making more by methods which they formerly avoided because they thought them disgraceful. How then can it be impossible for one who was prudent to lose his prudence, for one who was capable of just action to become incapable?" Xenophon, *The Memorabilia*, trans. E. C. Marchant, Loeb Classical Library (Cambridge, Mass.: Harvard University Press,

1979), I.2.19, online at www.perseus.tufts.edu/cgi-bin/ptext?lookup (accessed March 26, 2007).

18. Owen Flanagan, *Varieties of Moral Personality* (Cambridge, Mass.: Harvard University Press, 1991), 32. It may be noted that personality psychology and social psychology have taken quite different turns in the past few decades. Among specialists in the first field, there has been a revival of the so-called Big Five Personality Traits, or the Five-Factor Model of personality (FFM). At least in adults, there's good test-retest reliability for personality inventories meant to measure emotional stability, extroversion, agreeableness, conscientiousness, and openness to experience. But the prospects for regrounding character traits in these personality traits are not encouraging. As to how such paper-and-pencil scores relate to actual behavior, research is sparse and evidence is weak.

19. In a well-known paper on nonmoral explanations, Nicholas Sturgeon dealt with a worry about whether nonmoral explanations were undermining of our moral appraisals—one of his examples was the historian David Herbert Donald's account of the nineteenth-century abolitionists as being motivated, in large part, by a rancorous sense of class displacement. Suppose someone became an abolitionist because he came to believe (rightly, as it happens) that slaves were fully human and that slavery thwarted their capacities while promoting cruelty among the masters. This, too, would be (in some sense) a nonmoral explanation—it's just a fact that the person has come to have these beliefs—but it's hardly an undermining one. Nonmoral explanations, in Sturgeon's view, are as likely to amplify as to undercut moral ones. And, he says, it's difficult to come up with "*completely* undermining explanations" of obviously correct moral judgments; even if someone's argument about the evils of slavery was a pretext for another agenda, we'd have to account for the fact that this was taken to be a plausible pretext (which, for Sturgeon, is surely connected to the moral facts of the matter). Nicholas Sturgeon, "Nonmoral Explanations," in James Tomberlin, ed., *Philosophical Perspectives*, vol. 6: *Ethics* (Atascadero, Calif.: Ridgeview, 1992), 99–117.

20. See, e.g., Julia Annas, "Virtue Ethics and Social Psychology," *A Priori* 2 (January 2003), 20–59; and Rachana Kamtekar, "Situationism and Virtue Ethics on the Content of Our Character," *Ethics* 114 (April 2004), 458–491, which, however, acknowledges that "virtue ethics can benefit from

considering the particular situational factors that social psychology suggests have a profound influence on behavior" (461).

21. Theodor Lipps, "Die Aufgabe der Erkenntnistheorie und die Wundt'sche Logik, I" (The Task of Epistemology and Wundtian Logic, I), *Philosophische Monatshefte* 16 (1880), 529–539; and Edward S. Reed, *From Soul to Mind: The Emergence of Psychology from Erasmus Darwin to William James* (New Haven: Yale University Press, 1997), 188.

22. See Frank P. Ramsey, "Truth and Probability" (1926), in *The Foundations of Mathematics: Collected Papers of Frank P. Ramsey* (London: Routledge and Kegan Paul, 1931), 156–198.

23. Sometimes, of course, the best course of action may be to try to get more information. I shall be insisting later that this is not all there is to rationality, so I part company with those in the social sciences today who think means-end rationality just *is* rationality. As we shall see, when I say that this is wrong I mean more than that this is not the right way to use the word "rational."

24. See Gerd Gigerenzer, Peter M. Todd, and the ABC Research Group, *Simple Heuristics That Make Us Smart* (New York: Oxford University Press, 1999). Much previous work on cognitive heuristics—notably the pioneering research of Daniel Kahneman and Amos Tversky, which we'll discuss in the next chapter—has stressed the fallibility of heuristics, the way they generate defections from rationality. For students of naturalistic decision making, though, what's striking is how often they guide us well.

25. The term "moral heuristic" was given currency, I believe, by Ferdinand Schoeman, "Statistical Norms and Moral Attributions," in *Responsibility, Character, and the Emotions: New Essays in Moral Psychology,* ed. Ferdinand Schoeman (New York: Cambridge University Press, 1987), 314; Allan Gibbard, "Why Theorize How To Live with Each Other?" *Philosophy and Phenomenological Research* 55, no. 2 (June 1995), 328–329; and Cass R. Sunstein, "Moral Heuristics and Moral Framing," *Minnesota Law Review* 88 (2004), 1556.

26. "An action is right if and only if it is what an agent with a virtuous character would do in the circumstances," Justin Oakley writes in "Varieties of Virtue Ethics," *Ratio* 9 (1996), 129; "An action is right iff it is what a virtuous agent would do in the circumstances," says Rosalind Hursthouse in "Virtue Theory and Abortion," *Philosophy and Public Affairs* 20 (1990), 225.

27. See W. Kip Viscusi, "Corporate Risk Analysis: A Reckless Act?" *Stanford Law Review* 52, no. 3 (February 2000), 547–597, presenting the results of a study in which five hundred people were asked to consider various car accident scenarios. Higher damages were awarded when the carmaker had performed a cost-benefit analysis that dissuaded it from making a safety improvement. Sunstein, "Moral Heuristics and Moral Framing," goes on to speculate about how a jury would react to a company that markets a product it knows will kill ten people as opposed to a company that sells a product with a one-in-a-million risk of death to ten million customers. To eliminate the risk would cost, in either case, a hundred million dollars. Sunstein predicts that, even though these are, with respect to expected outcome, equivalent cases, the first company would tend to be punished more severely.

28. Of course, there are such proposals. Roger Crisp, in "Utilitarianism and the Life of Virtue," *Philosophical Quarterly* 42, no. 167 (April 1992), 139–160, elaborates a "utilitarianism of the virtues" specifically in response to a problem that has been noticed in utilitarianism: the split between how acts should be motivated and how acts must be justified—between (in Crisp's terms) decision procedures and criteria of rightness. For it might be best (on utilitarian grounds) if we honored promise keeping for its own sake. Yet the virtuous agent, as has been noted, often doesn't do the virtuous thing under that designation. Not only does the courageous person not choose an act *as* courageous, but, if you're really courageous, you may not even recognize your act as being courageous. So in virtue ethics, too, there's a similar split between the perspective of the observer-analyst and the perspective of the agent. See also Julia Driver, *Uneasy Virtue* (Cambridge: Cambridge University Press, 2001), which explores a consequentialist theory of virtues: if they're good, they're good because they reliably have good consequences.

29. The notion that an act is right if and only if it's what a virtuous person would do is open to an immediate objection. Sometimes I shouldn't do an otherwise virtuous act, given that I'm not virtuous and will almost certainly default on a responsibility generated by that act. The virtuous person may volunteer to do a benevolent thing in the future (a thing that is, modulo the promise, supererogatory); but I shouldn't make that sincere promise (act A) to do this fine thing (act B), because I'm likely to fail to keep it,

and my having volunteered to do it will prevent the other party from making alternate arrangements. *Pace* the virtue theorist, my doing A and my failing to do B isn't a conjunction of one right decision and one wrong decision; given what I know of myself, both decisions were wrong.

Other problems have been raised, to do with the match between agent and situation. You might think that, having slept with your best friend's spouse, you should apologize to your friend; but you can't ask what a virtuous person would do in your situation, since a virtuous person would never be in your situation. (An ideally virtuous person, to give another example, would never take the precautions against akrasia—weakness of will—that you might need to.) One could reframe the moral heuristic as, instead, what an ideally virtuous person would do if she were morally limited. But then we would also have to ask: Who would the ideally virtuous person be if she weren't ideally virtuous? Which is about as helpful as asking what a radish would be if it weren't a radish. More promisingly, the question could be recast as one of advice, in a manner analogous to "ideal advisor" theories (wherein what's good for you to do is what an idealized version of yourself—fully informed, perfectly rational—would have you do): but perhaps, like Glinda, the good witch in *The Wizard of Oz,* the ideally virtuous person would refrain from giving you advice, on the grounds that you'll be better off working things out on your own. See Gilbert Harman, "Virtue Ethics without Character Traits," in Alex Byrne, Robert Stalnaker, and Ralph Wedgwood, eds., *Fact and Value* (Cambridge, Mass.: MIT Press, 2001), 117–127; and cf. Connie S. Rosati, "Persons, Perspectives, and Full Information Accounts of the Good," *Ethics* 105 (January 1995), 296–325.

30. Similarly, for Michael Slote, whose account of virtues is meant to be an alternative to the Aristotelian tradition, and rooted, instead, in David Hume and Francis Hutcheson's theories of sentiments, "an act is morally acceptable if and only if it comes from good or virtuous motivation involving benevolence or caring (about the well-being of others) or at least doesn't come from bad or inferior motivation involving malice or indifference to humanity." Slote, *Morals from Motives* (Oxford: Oxford University Press, 2001), 38.

31. Hursthouse, *On Virtue Ethics,* 17.

32. Hurka espouses what he calls an "occurrent-state" account of virtue, which he takes to be commonsense morality, and therefore denies that the

findings of the situationists really threaten our moral common sense. He decries the fallacy of supposing that "if common sense takes dispositions to be central to the psychological explanation of particular acts, it must also take them to be central to their evaluation." Situationist facts are merely of practical concern: "If most people will help another from concern for her happiness in situation A but not in trivially different situation B, situation A causally encourages their acting generously while situation B does not. . . . If we want to promote generous action, we should place people in situations of type A rather than of type B. But the situationist fact will have no effect on the concept of virtuous action, which is just that of action from an occurrent virtuous desire no matter what that desire's causes are." Thomas Hurka, "Virtuous Act, Virtuous Disposition," *Analysis* 66, no. 1 (January 2006), 75.

33. For Thomson, "an act's being just is metaphysically prior, and a person's being just is metaphysically secondary." Virtue properties rest on first-order ways of being good, she argues, and come in clusters: there are reliance virtues (e.g., honesty, justness) and virtues of concern (e.g., generosity, kindness, considerateness). Without a substantial number of just people, for example, we wouldn't be able to form a community, she observes. "Whatever else may be true of the people among whom we live, it is better for us that they be just than that they not be just. . . . We should take this to be, not merely a fact about justice, but what marks it as a virtue." From this account of the virtues, a program of obligation issues: we are required to avoid their contraries (and in this sense, the right rests on the good). Judith Jarvis Thomson, "The Right and the Good," *Journal of Philosophy* 94, no. 6 (June 1997), 280, 282–283. See also Harman, "Virtue Ethics without Character Traits."

34. "And it gives no distinctive guidance about how to analyze a dispute so as to find the common ground from which agreement can be peacefully reached," he further observes. "Natural law theory tries to do precisely that." Jerome B. Schneewind, "Misfortunes of Virtue," *Ethics* 101 (October 1990), 62.

35. John Stuart Mill, *On Liberty,* in *The Collected Works of John Stuart Mill,* 33 vols., ed. John M. Robson (Toronto: University of Toronto Press, 1963–1991), vol. 18, 265–266. He goes on to declare, "Having said that Individuality is the same thing with development, and that it is only the culti-

vation of individuality which produces, or can produce, well-developed human beings, I might here close the argument: for what more or better can be said of any condition of human affairs, than that it brings human beings themselves nearer to the best thing they can be? or what worse can be said of any obstruction to good, than that it prevents this?" This is a manifesto for virtue ethics more sonorous than it has received from any of its current adepts. Elsewhere, in *Utilitarianism,* Mill specifically links the love of virtue for its own sake with man's social nature.

36. Philippa Foot, "Virtues and Vices," in Roger Crisp and Michael Slote, eds., *Virtue Ethics* (Oxford: Oxford University Press, 1997), 163; Mill, *On Liberty,* 263. Again, it clashes with a sedimented disciplinary story that the author of *Utilitarianism* should have captured what we might take to be the core insight of virtue ethics.

37. Charles Dickens, *Martin Chuzzlewit* (New York: Oxford University Press, 1991), 116.

38. Thomson, "The Right and the Good," 276, 287, drawing, she says, on Peter Geach, G. H. Wright, and Philippa Foot. Elizabeth Anscombe was taking a leaf from Aristotle when, in "Modern Moral Philosophy," she proposed, "It would be a great improvement if, instead of 'morally wrong,' one always named a genus such as 'untruthful,' 'unchaste,' 'unjust.' We should no longer ask whether doing something was 'wrong,' passing directly from some description of an action to this notion; we should ask whether, e.g., it was unjust; and the answer would sometimes be clear at once." Given her other beliefs about the connection between the right and the good, it would seem to follow that to be bad (or good) was to be bad (or good) in a particular way.

39. Gilbert Harman, "My Virtue Situation" (December 4, 2005), 14, www.princeton.edu/harman/Papers/Situ.pdf (accessed March 26, 2007).

40. See, for instance, Russell Hardin, *One for All: The Logic of Group Conflict* (Princeton: Princeton University Press, 1997); Donald Horowitz, *Ethnic Groups in Conflict* (Berkeley: University of California Press, 1987); David D. Laitin, "Ethnic Unmixing and Civil War," *Security Studies* 13, no. 4 (Summer 2004), 350–365; James Waller, *Becoming Evil: How Ordinary People Commit Genocide and Mass Killing* (New York: Oxford University Press, 2002).

3. The Case against Intuition

1. Thomas Reid, *Essays on the Intellectual Powers of Man* I.iii, "Of Hypothesis," in *The Works of Thomas Reid*, vol. 1 (New York: N. Bangs and T. Mason for the Methodist Episcopal Church, J. and J. Harper, Printers, 1822), 363, 361.

2. William Whewell, *Lectures on Systematic Morality* (London: J. W. Parker, 1846), 34, 35, 121. (Translating the Latin, we get: "The voice of savage people is not the voice of truth. It would be more suitable to say that the voice of human kind is the voice of truth.")

3. Henry Sidgwick, "My Station and Its Duties," *International Journal of Ethics* 4, no. 1 (October 1893), 9, 10.

4. W. D. Ross, *The Right and the Good* (Oxford: Oxford University Press, 1930), 40.

5. "The procedure is somewhat analogous to evidencing a proposition or theory in the real sciences, except that in oral discussions we try to validate or invalidate decisions and the action consequent thereto, given the circumstances and the interest in conflict (not acts of believing given a proposition or theory and its evidence), and the criteria we use are the principles of justice (and not the rules of inductive logic)." John Rawls, "Outline of a Decision Procedure for Ethics," *Philosophical Review* 60, no. 2 (April 1951), 195–196. Intuitions are the "data," in the consonant words of Nicholas Rescher, that "the theoretician must weave into a smooth fabric" in a process that is "closely analogous with the systematization of the 'data' of various levels in natural science." Rescher, "Reply to Hare," in Ernest Sosa, ed., *The Philosophy of Nicholas Rescher: Discussion and Replies* (Dordrecht: D. Reidel, 1979), 153–155. Nelson Goodman, writing in 1954, advanced the procedure as a general one for theory building. A given deductive argument, he wrote, is justified by being seen to accord with the rules of deductive inference. "Yet, of course, the rules themselves must eventually be justified. . . . Principles of deductive inference are justified by their conformity with accepted deductive practice. Their validity depends upon accordance with the particular deductive inferences we actually make and sanction. If a rule yields unacceptable inferences, we drop it as invalid. . . . The point is that rules and particular inferences alike are justified by being brought into agreement with each other. A rule is amended if it

yields an inference we are unwilling to accept; an inference is rejected if it violates a rule we are unwilling to amend." Nelson Goodman, *Fact, Fiction, and Forecast*, 4th ed. (Cambridge, Mass.: Harvard University Press, 1983), 63–64.

6. Frank Jackson, *From Metaphysics to Ethics* (Oxford: Clarendon, 1998), 134, 133, 135.

7. W. D. Ross, *The Right and the Good* (Oxford: Oxford University Press, 1930), 40.

8. I've discussed this passage previously myself in *The Ethics of Identity* (Princeton: Princeton University Press, 2005). Ironically, a remark attributed to Fénelon suggests an impartialist perspective that Godwin might have commended. Camille Desmoulins, in a talk to the Club des Jacobins, cites him as saying, "I love my family more than myself, my fatherland more than my family, and the universe more than my fatherland" ("J'aime mieux ma famille que moi, ma patrie que ma famille, et l'univers que ma patrie"). Quoted in Desmoulins, "Sur la situation politique de la nation à l'ouverture de la seconde session de l'Assemblée Nationale," Club des Jacobins, October 21, 1791; cited at www.royet.org/nea1789-1794/archives/discours/desmoulins_situation_politique_nation_21_10_91.htm (accessed March 27, 2007).

9. At the same time, these moral radicals enlist intuition, too. If one of two people must die, and one is an insignificant wretch and the other a great humanitarian, wouldn't most people feel relieved to learn the great humanitarian survived? Or consider a revisionist line of argument that was first advanced by Bentham and has reached its greatest force and influence in the works of Peter Singer. If you agree that it's wrong to mistreat an infant, whose sentience surely compares unfavorably to that of a mature horse or dog, doesn't it stand to reason that the capacity to suffer, not the capacity to think, is what entitles a creature to considerate treatment? Such arguments seek to overturn one element of common sense by appealing to another.

10. It won't help, of course, to say that we should aim at truth here, because, in each case, it looks like we have access to the truth only by way of the phenomena. This is the thought that leads to anti-realism. See my book *For Truth in Semantics* (Oxford: Blackwell, 1986).

11. Here's one counterproposal that has been bruited: give up the de-

mand that our intuitions and our theory never clash. On this view—engagingly advanced by the philosopher Ben Eggleston—what matters is not that the theory always gives us the outcome that accords with our intuition; what matters is whether the theory can endorse our having the intuition in question. Act utilitarianism may recommend telishment while also endorsing our intuitive revulsion at it, since such an intuition might conduce to acts that maximize utility. See Ben Eggleston, "Practical Equilibrium: A New Approach to Moral Theory Selection" (January 12, 2002), www.ku.edu/utile/unpub/pe.pdf (accessed March 27, 2007). The fact that this approach is more conserving of our actual intuitions is put forward as a recommendation. Whether you take it as one will depend, of course, on your intuitions about the reliability of people's intuitions. I'll return to the point that one might distinguish—as not all the literature does—between intuitions about cases and intuitions about principles. We have intuitions when confronted with general propositions—cruelty is bad, punishing the innocent is wrong—but further inquiry would be necessary to determine whether our intuitions in response to stated principles conform with our intuitions in response to the actual phenomena. Yet there's another ambiguity that bedevils the subject. We sometimes conflate "intuitions" (as specific responses to specific cases) with "intuition" (as a general disposition to respond to certain generalizable features across a range of cases). The first looks like the sort of raw data we can collect; the second—in which we distill a pattern from these specific responses—necessarily requires various background assumptions, inferences, and theories. In the account of "practical equilibrium" that Eggleston advocates, the intuitions to be endorsed cannot be the particular judgment in a particular case, but some larger disposition that's taken to issue in that judgment; and identifying that larger disposition is a far from trivial task, as we'll see. This problem should, of course, remind us of the discussion of what it is to identify the maxim of an action in Kant.

12. See, for example, Richard Brandt, *A Theory of the Good and the Right* (Oxford: Clarendon, 1979), 21–22; or, more recently, David Papineau, "The Tyranny of Common Sense," *Philosophers' Magazine* 34 (April–June 2006), 19–25, available at www.philosophersnet.com/magazine/article.php ?id=1005 (accessed March 27, 2007). "In ethics, as in mathematics, the appeal to intuition is an epistemology of desperation," Philip Kitcher writes

in "Biology and Ethics," in David Copp, ed., *The Oxford Handbook of Ethical Theory* (New York: Oxford University Press, 2005), 176. R. M. Hare, in "Rawls' Theory of Justice, I," *Philosophical Quarterly* 23, no. 91 (April 1973), 146, started a list of Rawls's appeals to common sense and accused Rawls of "monistic intuitionism." Because these arguments, in various ways, reprise John Stuart Mill's critique of Whewell's moral theory—and because Mill's critique is better known than its object—it should be noted that Whewell's rationalist intuitionism is closer to the constructivism that Rawls espoused than to the moral-sense varieties of intuitionism in which moral truths are directly apprehended; for Whewell, elevated intuition was a starting point—it did not define the right answer (our conscience was as fallible as our reason); and he believed that progress was possible in the moral realm as much as in the scientific realm. "Conscience," he readily acknowledged, is "a subordinate and fallible Rule," for man's "moral and intellectual progress is still incomplete; and this incompleteness is no justification for what is done under its influence." William Whewell, *The Elements of Morality* (New York: Harper and Brothers, 1845), 246. And cf. J. S. Mill, "Whewell on Moral Philosophy" (1852), in *The Collected Works of John Stuart Mill*, ed. J. M. Robson, vol. 10 (Toronto: University of Toronto Press, 1969), 167–201. It will be clear, I hope, that the intuition problem is hardly confined to those approaches to morality that are labeled "intuitionist."

13. This story, which I learned in college, is presumably about G. H. Hardy, who, in his book *A Course of Pure Mathematics,* said of a certain proposition, "This is almost obvious" . . . but then added in a footnote: "There is a certain ambiguity in this phrase which the reader will do well to notice. When one says 'such and such a theorem is almost obvious' one may mean one or other of two things. One may mean 'it is difficult to doubt the truth of the theorem,' 'the theorem is such as common sense intuitively accepts,' as it accepts, for example, the truth of the propositions '2 = 4' or 'the base angles of isosceles triangles are equal.' That a theorem is 'obvious' in this sense does not prove that it is true, since the most confident of the intuitive judgments of common sense are often found to be mistaken; and even if the theorem is true, the fact that it is also 'obvious' is no reason for not proving it, if a proof can be found. The object of mathematics is to prove that certain premises imply certain conclusions; and the

fact that the conclusions may be as 'obvious' as the premises never detracts from the necessity, and often not even from the interest of the proof.

"But sometimes (as for the example here) we mean by 'this is almost obvious' something quite different from this. We mean 'a moment's reflection should not only convince the reader of the truth of what is stated, but should also suggest to him the general lines of a rigorous proof.' And often, when a statement is 'obvious' in this sense, one may well omit the proof, not because the proof is unnecessary, but because it is a waste of time to state in detail what the reader can easily supply for himself."

Cited in Andrew Lenard, "What Can Be Learned from n<n!?" *Mathematics Magazine* 71 (February 1998), 58.

14. Brandt, *A Theory of the Good and the Right.* Some philosophers have argued that it is *impossible* to distance oneself from one's own moral perspective. I should be clear that this is a claim (putting aside the sense in which it is trivially true, taking whatever perspective one adopts to be one's perspective) that I do not endorse. See Kwame Anthony Appiah, "Metaphys Ed.," *Village Voice* (September 19, 1989), 55, a discussion of irony in Richard Rorty's *Contingency, Irony, and Solidarity.*

15. Amos Tversky and Daniel Kahneman, "The Framing of Decisions and the Psychology of Choice," *Science* 221 (1981), 453–458. In the original experiment 72 percent preferred A to B and 78 percent preferred D to C (453).

16. Of course, even economists and philosophers know that some irrational people will be lucky and some rational people will be unlucky. Lotteries are designed to make money for the people that run them. As a result, usually when someone wins the lottery, they've made out on an investment that had a negative financial expected value; and, conversely, the person who takes a drug with a small risk of negative side effects and a large prospect of medical benefits, and then becomes one of the rare people who suffer the side-effects, was nevertheless doing the rational thing. Given this fact, people sometimes respond to the maximizing argument by saying, "How can it be the best policy if rational people can suffer so badly and irrational people can profit so much?" The question presupposes that the best policy ought to guarantee rewards for those who adhere to it. As I've said, I'll generally be sticking to intuitions about cases; but you could call that presupposition an intuition, too, if you like. And it's a mistaken in-

tuition, because it ignores the reality that we live in a world of chance, where the best you can do is try to maximize the probability of getting what you want. There are, generally speaking, no guarantees. But this mistaken thought is not the sort of intuition I have in mind, because it's a thought, as I say, about a principle. And the intuitions I have in mind are intuitions about cases, scenarios like the Asian Flu scenario: they are what happens when we read or hear a scenario described and just find we have a view about what is the right thing to do.

17. Of course, a judgment in a social-policy scenario like this one is, in an important sense, normative; and you can imagine a morally fraught argument between those who favor different choices. Imagine an Option D partisan arguing with an Option C partisan: "What kind of monster are you that you would countenance the certain death of 400 people!" Imagine an Option A partisan arguing with an Option B partisan: "What kind of monster are you that you could risk the deaths of all 600?" In fact, there might be relevant differences between the probabilistic outcomes and the determinate ones, such that I should prefer one to the other, depending on other background assumptions—especially those relating to further consequences that have been cropped out by the scenario. Perhaps my community of 600 would be so devastated by grief and despondency were 400 to die that it would be utility-maximizing to pursue the one-third chance of no deaths. Perhaps the survival of the germline is what's most important, so that people would prefer the guaranteed survival of a few to the possible extinction of all. And of course the actual policies that would achieve these results would have to be different, even if the outcomes were not. The Kahneman and Tversky scenario brackets a question that preoccupies deontologists—namely, how these results are arrived at. Suppose the choice were between (a) murdering 400 people in order to extract enough gamma globulin from their serum to save 200; and (b) injecting the 600 with a vaccine that would save only a third of them. (In each case, let the alternative be that all 600 people die.)

18. Thomas C. Schelling, "Economic Reasoning and the Ethics of Policy," *Public Interest* 63 (Spring 1981), 37–61.

19. Thalia Wheatley and Jonathan Haidt, "Hypnotic Disgust Makes Moral Judgments More Severe," *Psychological Science* 16, no. 10 (October 2005), 780–784.

20. Philippa Foot, "The Problem of Abortion and the Doctrine of the

Double Effect," *Oxford Review* 5, nos. 8–9 (1967), reprinted in Foot, *Virtues and Vices and Other Essays in Moral Philosophy* (Berkeley: University of California Press, 1978), 19, 23. Judith Jarvis Thomson, "Killing, Letting Die, and the Trolley Problem," *Monist* 59 (1976), 204–217, reprinted in Thomson, *Rights, Restitution, and Risk,* ed. William Parent (Cambridge, Mass.: Harvard University Press, 1986); Judith Jarvis Thomson, "The Trolley Problem," *Yale Law Journal* 94 (1985), 1395–1415, reprinted in Thomson, *Rights, Restitution, and Risk,* 94. Thomson's earlier arguments concerning the trolley-car cases centered on claims to rights and "origin of harm"; in *The Realm of Rights* (Cambridge, Mass.: Harvard University Press, 1990), she has turned to the notion of "hypothetical consent." In the bystander-at-the-switch case, a person, even if he knew that he would later be one of the people on the tracks, would rationally consent (here, the notion of "rationally" is normatively fraught). Cf. William Godwin: "It would have been just in the chambermaid to have preferred the archbishop to herself. To have done otherwise would have been a breach of justice." Godwin, *An Enquiry concerning Political Justice, and Its Influence on General Virtue and Happiness* (London: G. G. J. and J. Robinson, 1793), book 2, 83.

21. Researchers have collected data from around the world, and the results are quite robust. Some deeply held convictions, though, turn out to be surprisingly culturally variable, including our repugnance toward telishment. One study asked students to respond to a "magistrate and the mob" scenario: if authorities don't falsely convict and punish an innocent man, murderous ethnic rioting will break out, resulting in many deaths and injuries. Chinese students were much more likely to consider telishment in this scenario to be justified than were American students. The work, by Kaiping Peng, John Doris, Shaun Nichols, and Stephen Stich, is described in John M. Doris and Alexandra Plakias, "How To Argue about Disagreement: Evaluative Diversity and Moral Realism," in Walter Sinnott-Armstrong, ed., *Moral Psychology,* vol. 2: *The Cognitive Science of Morality: Intuition and Diversity* (Cambridge, Mass.: MIT Press, 2008).

22. Discussion of this question usually assumes that we can decide what someone intended, independently of a moral evaluation of their action. Not so, according to experiments I'll discuss later in this chapter. See Joshua Knobe, "The Concept of Intentional Action: A Case Study in the Uses of Folk Psychology," *Philosophical Studies* 130, no. 2 (August

2006), 203–231, available at www.unc.edu/knobe/PhilStudies.pdf (accessed March 27, 2007).

23. These scenarios are, of course, extraordinarily artificial; but there are real situations where we have to contemplate killing the innocent in order to save lives. When the attacks on the World Trade Center and the Pentagon occurred on September 11, 2001, the U.S. military sent up fighter jets whose job, if they had been successful, would have been to kill the many innocent passengers on such planes, in order to save other people's lives. Now, of course, the people on the planes were going to be dead in either case. But suppose the president had been asked for permission to use fighter jets, or some sort of avionic intervention, to get the plane to crash not in Manhattan but in White Plains, where the death toll on the ground would be a good deal lower. This choice is structurally identical to the choice in the trolley problem. There are people you can save by stopping a dangerous vehicle in one place, thus killing fewer people than if you had let the vehicle travel on. The deaths in White Plains are foreseen but unintended side effects of saving Manhattan. Here most people would respond (and expect the president to respond) as in the trolley problem: authorizing someone to cause the death of some people in order to save the lives of many more.

24. Nor do trolley ethicists restrict themselves to the rails. To exemplify a situation that produces a response similar to that of the footbridge scenario, philosophers often mention the fact that every transplant surgeon knows he could extend the lives of at least five people by killing a random healthy adult, who is the potential source, after all, of two kidneys, a liver, a heart, and a pair of lungs. There are people waiting for just such organs right now in many hospitals in the world. Without them, they'll soon die. Yet not only do most people think it's completely obvious that it would be wrong to take the life of a healthy person for this purpose; we don't even allow people to take these organs from *dead* people without their consent or that of their relatives. So all the time, faced with the option of killing someone to save the lives of several others, doctors abstain . . . exactly as most people say they would do in the footbridge scenario. We can call it the organ-harvesting problem. This generalizes a scenario—the "Transplant Case"—that was introduced by Philippa Foot in "The Problem of Abortion and the Doctrine of Double Effect," *Oxford Review* 5 (1967),

28–41, and elaborated in Judith Jarvis Thomson, "Killing, Letting Die, and the Trolley Problem," *Monist* 59 (1976), 204–217, and that stipulated a choice between killing one particular healthy person and letting five patients die. Though the scenarios differ in important ways, it's plausible to suppose that our response to the Transplant Case is influenced by our response to the organ-harvesting nightmare, which is a low-level generalization of it. That's why it's perfectly reasonable to forbid the surgeon from killing his healthy visitor even if you favor toppling large men on footbridges to stop runaway trolleys. Who would want to live in that fear-stricken society, where any board-certified surgeon had a license to kill? Indeed, a policy of allowing any surgeon who needs two kidneys, a heart, and a liver to grab and kill the first healthy person who comes along would mean that a lot of other people would be sick and dying because they had decided that it was risky to be around doctors.

25. Robert Nozick, *The Nature of Rationality* (Princeton: Princeton University Press, 1993), 60. And cf. Tamara Horowitz, "Philosophical Intuitions and Psychological Theory," in M. DePaul and W. Ramsey, ed., *Rethinking Intuition: The Psychology of Intuition and Its Role in Philosophical Inquiry* (Lanham, Md.: Rowman and Littlefield, 1998), 153. Nozick's suspicion isn't accepted by everyone, and Frances Kamm, in a lucid discussion of the general issues of method raised here, has marshaled the pertinent objections to conflating the loss-versus-no-gain distinction with the aiding-versus-harming distinction; see Kamm, "Moral Intuitions, Cognitive Psychology, and the Harming-versus-Not-Aiding Distinction," *Ethics* 108 (April 1998), 463–488. If our baseline is what would happen without our intervention—a thesis she ascribes to the psychologist Jonathan Baron—then, as she notes (skeptically), we would always worry less about not preventing deaths than about causing them.

26. Joshua D. Greene, R. Brian Sommerville, Leigh E. Nystrom, John M. Darley, and Jonathan D. Cohen, "An f MRI Investigation of Emotional Engagement in Moral Judgment," *Science* 293, no. 5537 (September 14, 2001), 2105–2108.

27. Ibid. In a more recent experiment, two researchers at Northwestern University, Piercarlo Valdesolo and David DeSteno, found a link between mood and moral judgment. Before presenting their subjects with the two trolley-car scenarios, they had half of their subjects watch five minutes of

Saturday Night Live, and the other half watch an unengaging documentary about a Spanish village. Those buoyed by the comedy show were more likely to say they would topple the large man. The researchers concluded that the negative emotions inspired by contemplating the up-close-and-personal homicide were offset by the cheerful spirits inspired by the TV show. See Piercarlo Valdesolo and David DeSteno, "Manipulations of Emotional Context Shape Moral Judgment," *Psychological Science* 17, no. 6 (June 2006), 476. (So there are times when cheerful people may be less pleasant to be around!)

28. There are plenty of skeptics who have proposed other explanations for these data (or who don't believe they're reliably reproducible). As I say, my interest here isn't so much in whether these claims are true as in what would follow if they were. After all, we need to know *that* in order to decide what to think if they *are* true.

29. See Frances Kamm, "Toward the Essence of Nonconsequentialism," in Alex Byrne, Robert Stalnaker, and Ralph Wedgwood, eds., *Fact and Value: Essays on Ethics and Metaphysics for Judith Jarvis Thomson* (Cambridge, Mass.: MIT Press, 2001), 155–182.

30. Joshua Greene, "From Neural 'Is' to Moral 'Ought': What Are the Moral Implications of Neuroscientific Moral Psychology?" *Nature Reviews Neuroscience* 4 (October 1, 2003), 846–850. It isn't irrelevant, perhaps, that Greene's own inclinations are utilitarian. Suppose you were persuaded by the neural scans that we were indeed reluctant to push the big man from the footbridge because, crudely, emotion overrode reason in this case—but you also believed that pushing that man was wrong. Then you could enlist Greene's research to support the thesis that, in confusing circumstances, emotion can provide deeper moral insight than a calculation of consequences.

31. The survey was conducted by the BBC. See news.bbc.co.uk/2/hi/uk_news/magazine/4954856.stm (accessed April 17, 2007). By April 17, 2007, at 4:00 P.M., the website had collected votes from 18,739 people, 74.13 percent of whom had voted yes and 25.87 percent no, to the question, "Should you blast Big Jack out?" The stakes for the actor count. We can use a trolley case (as always) to make the point. Imagine a conductor of an out-of-control trolley who, approaching a fork, must choose one of two tracks, one with five pedestrians who will die if he hits them, the other with just

one. Suppose, perversely, he chose the track with the five pedestrians. We'd condemn his decision. Yet even if the solitary pedestrian had the ability (via some remote-control device) to switch the train back to his own track, and save their lives at the cost of his own, almost nobody would consider that sacrifice to be obligatory. That sacrifice, if he made it, would be viewed as one of heroic supererogation, and venerated as such.

32. Indeed, experimental research into "affective forecasting" raises some skepticism about our ability to predict how we will feel in some future situation, although (so far as I know) none of this research—pioneered by Jonathan Schooler, Timothy Wilson, and Daniel T. Gilbert—involves moral appraisal in any obvious way.

33. Shaun Nichols and Joshua Knobe, "Moral Responsibility and Determinism: The Cognitive Science of Folk Intuitions," *Nous,* forthcoming. (Available at www.unc.edu/knobe/Nichols-Knobe.pdf, accessed March 27, 2007; quotation from page 12, figure of 86 percent from page 13.) Their study draws on and expands research published in Eddy A. Nahmias, Stephen Morris, Thomas Nadelhoffer, and Jason Turner, "Surveying Freedom: Folk Intuitions about Free Will and Moral Responsibility," *Philosophical Psychology* 18, no. 5 (October 2005), 561–584. These researchers tend to describe the deterministic universe in scientific terms to their subjects (there may be talk of the laws of physics, or of a supercomputer able to predict events with complete accuracy); but the basic concept has been familiar to people from other times and cultures under other terms: curses, oracles, predestination, and so on. A Greek from the fifth century B.C. could ponder whether Oedipus was fully morally responsible for his actions. See A. W. H. Adkins, *Merit and Responsibility* (Oxford: Clarendon, 1960).

34. P. F. Strawson, "Freedom and Resentment," *Proceedings of the British Academy* (1962), 187–211. Reprinted in Strawson, *Freedom and Resentment, and Other Essays* (London: Methuen, 1974).

35. Gilbert Ryle, *The Concept of Mind* (Chicago: University of Chicago Press, 1949; rpt. 2002), 71. Ryle is probably right about "most ordinary employments" of the terms "voluntary" and "involuntary," but it's easy to come up with not-very-exotic counterexamples—as, for instance, if you find out that someone has been kind to you because he's been coerced; or when we commend a soldier's brave act as especially heroic because he volunteered for a risky mission, rather than having been ordered to do it.

36. At the same time, media scholars have shown that the way people apprehend narratives will be shaped by what they take to be common sense. For instance, researchers found that a group of Israeli Arabs watching the TV show *Dallas* wrongly assumed that the character Sue Ellen, having left her husband, had sought refuge with her father, because returning to your family in those circumstances is what made sense to them. Their effort to make the show culturally intelligible overrode the information that she'd actually taken refuge at the family home of her previous lover. See Tamar Liebes and Elihu Katz, *The Export of Meaning: Cross-Cultural Readings of "Dallas"* (London: Polity, 1994).

37. Knobe, "The Concept of Intentional Action." "The existence of the general framework of attitudes itself is something we are given with the fact of human society," Strawson argues. "As a whole, it neither calls for, nor permits, an external 'rational' justification." The optimist is prone to an "incomplete empiricism, a one-eyed utilitarianism. He seeks to find an adequate basis for certain social practices in calculated consequences, and loses sight (perhaps wishes to lose sight) of the human attitudes of which these practices are in part the expression. . . . It is a pity that talk of the moral sentiments has fallen out of favor. The phrase would be quite a good name for that network of human attitudes in acknowledging the character and place of which we find, I suggest, the only possibility of reconciling these disputants to each other and the facts" (Strawson, "Freedom and Resentment," 210).

38. Joshua Knobe, "Folk Psychology and Folk Morality: Response to Critics," *Journal of Theoretical and Philosophical Psychology*. Available at www.unc.edu/knobe/ResponseCritics.pdf (accessed March 27, 2007). "People do not normally praise or blame agents for reluctant side-effects, and the process is therefore constructed in such a way that it classifies all reluctant side-effects as unintentional," he elaborates. "In certain cases, however, reluctant side-effects may still elicit feelings of blame. In those cases, people's feelings of blame end up diverging in tell-tale ways from their intentional action intuitions." When a drunk driver runs over a child, the fact of intoxication has two faces: it tends to exempt him from direct responsibility in the act while inculpating him in (let's say) an act of criminal negligence.

39. Knobe, "The Concept of Intentional Action."

40. Josh Knobe and John Doris, "Strawsonian Variations: Folk Morality and the Search for a Unified Theory," forthcoming in John Doris et al., *The Handbook of Moral Psychology* (Oxford: Oxford University Press). Available at www.unc.edu/knobe/Knobe-Doris.pdf (accessed March 27, 2007). Notice that all these patterns have criminal-justice correlatives. Accidentally causing a death in the course of committing a felony, for instance, is usually an offense in itself, punished more severely than the accidental death would be otherwise. A driver who runs over a child who has suddenly darted into the road may be held blameless—but not if he was also drunk, or had run a light, or was racing from a bank he'd robbed, even when there's no specific causal link between the two circumstances. As Bernard Williams has famously observed, in our intuitions about responsibility, we have more in common with the authors of the Greek tragedies than we often suppose.

41. Paul Churchland, "The Neural Representations of the Social World," in Larry May, Marilyn Friedman, and Andy Clark, eds., *Mind and Morals* (Cambridge: MIT Press, 1996), 103. "People with unusually penetrating moral insight will be those who can see a problematic moral situation in more than one way, and who can evaluate the relative accuracy and relevance of those competing interpretations," Churchland argues. "Such people will be those with unusual moral *imagination,* and a critical capacity to match." In his view, "The morally successful person has acquired a complex set of subtle and enviable skills: perceptual, cognitive, and behavioral," and he draws a connection to Aristotle's insistence that virtue involved skills accumulated over a lifetime of experience, and consisted in "largely inarticulable skills, a matter of practical wisdom. Aristotle's perspective and the neutral network perspective here converge" (105, 106). What this (otherwise rather plausible) account of moral expertise leaves out is the task of providing explicit moral justification, which can also be a practical affair.

42. Bernard Williams, *Moral Luck* (Cambridge: Cambridge University Press, 1981), 52.

43. There are many disanalogies, to be sure. Usually, for example, reasons for action are generated by way of our imagining a situation, not by our observing one.

44. Ross made a similar move when he suggested that we cast duties in

terms of "tendencies"—for example, it tends to be our duty to pay our debts or to relieve others' distress—and thus resolves the "theoretical problem of conflict of duties," by allowing that the two may conflict (even if we decide that, on the whole, it's our duty to do one rather than another). "The absoluteness of the law of justice and of the law of benevolence is preserved if they are stated as laws of tendency," he concluded. W. D. Ross, "The Basis of Objective Judgments in Ethics," *International Journal of Ethics* 37, no. 2 (January 1927), 127. Though he became identified with the less felicitous term "prima facie duties" (which gives the impression they may vanish upon inspection, rather than being trumped), Ross intended the tendency interpretation; these duties (including duties of fidelity, reparation, gratitude, justice, beneficence, self-improvement, and nonmaleficence) were, as he also put it, "conditional duties," and one became actual when an agent decided that it was "more incumbent than any other." Obviously, some ostensible duties may be prima facie in the sense that they aren't really duties at all.

45. I should make a technical aside here: the state of affairs which warrants not pushing the heavy stranger off the bridge is not its being wrong (which is a state of affairs that some people don't believe in) but your having the intuition that it's wrong (which is a state of affairs whose existence is sometimes quite uncontroversial). But sometimes you ought to believe something not because you are aware of a state of yours but because you are aware of the world. So something's being blue is also a (boring) pro tanto reason to believe that it's blue. If you're aware that it's blue you have a reason to believe that it is. So, too, an act's being wrong is a pro tanto reason not to do it; awareness of this fact gives you reason not to do it.

46. Perhaps we ought to modify our attitudes in the light of such studies, Strawson allowed; but we should not expect our moral sentiments—our reactive attitudes—to disappear. "What *is* wrong is to forget that these practices, and their reception, the reactions to them, really *are* expressions of our moral attitudes and not merely devices we calculatingly employ for regulative purposes. Our practices do not merely exploit our natures, they express them." Strawson, "Freedom and Resentment," 210.

47. David Hume, *An Enquiry into the Principles of Morals* (1777), section 9, "Conclusion," part I. Available at etext.library.adelaide.edu.au/h/hume/david/h92pm/chapter9.html (accessed March 27, 2007).

48. Ross, "The Basis of Objective Judgments in Ethics," 113.

4. The Varieties of Moral Experience

1. Immanuel Kant, *The Moral Law: Kant's Groundwork of the Metaphysic of Morals,* trans. H. J. Paton (New York: Harper and Row, 1964), 118.

2. For example: There's often a man other than the husband who might be persuaded to help a woman with her children, namely her brother. And he doesn't have to worry about whether he's biologically related to her children, so long as he's biologically related to her. In a society where maternal uncles play a big role in childrearing, people need to worry less about marital fidelity. And, in fact, so far as I can tell—having grown up in such a place—they do indeed worry less about this. If that's the case, then whatever the innate mechanisms are that shape jealousy, they must have a component that is sensitive to issues of family structure.

3. I am relying here on Anscombe's account of the way in which acts come "under a description." See section 23 of G. E. M. Anscombe, *Intention* (Oxford: Basil Blackwell, 1972), 37–41; and idem, "Under a Description," *Nous* 13 (1979), 219–233, where she rightly points out that the different descriptions of a given action don't, of course, designate different actions. Some people—Jerry Fodor springs to mind—have argued that there's a sense in which all concepts are innate; it's just that they're triggered by culture. Even on this view, though, which ones you'll be able to act on will depend on what your culture triggers. A final caveat: when I said that when we act intentionally, there is something we think we are doing, I'm not claiming that we constantly bear these intentions and descriptions in our consciousness; for one thing, we often go through our routines quite inattentively, on autopilot. See the fascinating research done by John Bargh and others on the automaticity of cognition, motivation, and conduct—for example: John A. Bargh, M. Chen, and L. Burrows, "Automaticity of Social Behavior: Direct Effects of Trait Construct and Stereotype Priming on Action," *Journal of Personality and Social Psychology* 71 (1996), 230–244; John A. Bargh and T. L. Chartrand, "The Unbearable Automaticity of Being," *American Psychologist* 54 (1999), 462–479; and John A. Bargh and M. L. Ferguson, "Beyond Behaviorism: On the Automaticity of Higher Mental Processes," *Psychological Bulletin* 126 (2000), 925–945; Daniel Kahneman and Anne Treisman, "Changing Views of Attention and Automaticity," in R. Parasuraman and R. Davies, eds., *Varieties of Attention*

(New York: Academic Press, 1984), 29–61. Cf. Gilbert Ryle's critique of the "intellectualist legend," in Ryle, *The Concept of Mind* (Chicago: University of Chicago Press, 1949), 25–60; and his critique of the myth of "Privileged Access," the supposed transparency of self-knowledge, ibid., 154–198. More confirmation of Ryle's skepticism can be found in Timothy D. Wilson, *Strangers to Ourselves* (Cambridge, Mass.: Harvard University Press, 2004). It would be an error, to whose significance I'll return, to think that these findings reveal conscious deliberation on moral judgment to be little more than a charade. Let me adumbrate my position with two quick observations. You may brush your teeth on "autopilot," but if stopped and required to say why you are scrubbing your teeth, you could readily do so, and it matters that you could. Conversely, the fact that a chess master (and her coach) may be unable to articulate persuasive reasons for some move she plans to make—she speaks vaguely and intuitively of "taking control of the center"—doesn't mean that there isn't a best move, or set of equi-optimal moves, available to be made; and it doesn't mean that there's no connection between the optimality of the move and her decision to make it.

4. Somewhat different versions of the classification have been advanced, inter alia, in Jonathan Haidt and Craig Joseph, "Intuitive Ethics: How Innately Prepared Intuitions Generate Culturally Variable Virtues," *Daedalus* (Fall 2004), 55–66; and Jonathan Haidt and Fredrik Björklund, "Social Intuitionists Answer Six Questions about Moral Psychology," in Walter Sinnott-Armstrong, ed., *Moral Psychology*, vol. 3: *The Neuroscience of Morality: Emotion, Brain Disorders, and Development* (Cambridge, Mass.: MIT Press, 2008), available at faculty.virginia.edu/haidtlab/articles/haidt .bjorklund.social-intuitionists-answer-6-questions.doc (accessed March 28, 2007). Among the works Haidt and Björklund survey, in identifying normative clusters, are Donald Brown, *Human Universals* (Philadelphia: Temple University Press, 1991); Franz de Waal, *Good Natured: The Origins of Right and Wrong in Humans and Other Animals* (Cambridge, Mass.: Harvard University Press, 1996); S. H. Schwartz and W. Bilsky, "Toward a Theory of the Universal Content and Structure of Values: Extensions and Cross-Cultural Replications," *Journal of Personality and Social Psychology* 58 (1990), 878–891; and the influential "three ethics" proposal elaborated in Richard Shweder et al., "The 'Big Three' of Morality (Autonomy, Community, and Divinity), and the 'Big Three' Explanations of Suffering," in

A. Brandt and Paul Rozin, eds., *Morality and Health* (New York: Routledge, 1997), 119–169.

5. See Jerry Fodor, "The Modularity of Mind," *Behavioral and Brain Sciences* 8 (1985), 1–42; and Dan Sperber, *Explaining Culture: A Naturalistic Approach* (Oxford: Blackwell, 1996). For an overview of recent controversies about the notion, see H. Clark Barrett and Robert Kurzban, "Modularity in Cognition: Framing the Debate," *Psychological Review* 13, no. 3 (2006): 628–647.

6. Less compactly, Fiske's categories are: communal sharing (an ethic of "share and share alike" within a group of people who regard themselves as equivalent, but who may take aggressive action against an outside group); authority ranking (whereby subordinates obey their superiors, who are, in turn, bound by custodial duties to their wards); equality matching (marked by fairness norms like turn-taking and reciprocity); and market pricing (the ethic of the marketplace, the realm of wages, taxes, rents, and cost/benefit calculation, with value reduced to a unitary metric). See Alan P. Fiske, *Structures of Social Life: The Four Elementary Forms of Social Relationships* (New York: Free Press, 1991). For a fairly Fiskean account of moral modularity, see John Bolender, "The Genealogy of the Moral Modules," *Minds and Machines* (2003) 13, 233–255; see www.sscnet.ucla.edu/anthro/faculty/fiske/RM_PDFs/Bolender_Moral_Modules_2003.pdf (accessed March 27, 2007).

7. Shaun Nichols, *Sentimental Rules: On the Natural Foundations of Moral Judgment* (New York: Oxford University Press, 2004), reporting Zahn-Waxler and Eadke-Yarrow, "The Development of Altruism: Alternative Research Strategies," in N. Eisenberg-Berg, ed., *The Development of Prosocial Behavior* (New York: Academic Press, 1982), 124; Nichols, *Sentimental Rules*, 58 (on autism), 59 (on psychopathy). A distinction is sometimes made between sympathy proper and distress-at-another's-distress, which may precede it developmentally.

8. Interestingly, studies involving psychopaths show that they tend to appeal to social convention in explaining why, for instance, it might be wrong to hit another child, whereas the control groups of criminals—the nonpsychopaths—speak in terms of the victim's distress. Nichols observes, "This does not mean that the psychopaths are unaware of the fact that the general category that is discouraged is the category of harming others.

However, lacking an intact Concern Mechanism for processing distress attributions, they presumably regard the social-convention explanation as more informative than the fact that the transgression involves harming." See Shaun Nichols, "Mindreading and the Core Architecture of Moral Psychology," at snipurl.com/v6b8 (accessed March 28, 2007).

9. Arthur Schopenhauer, *On the Basis of Morality,* trans. A. F. J. Payne (Indianapolis: Bobbs-Merrill, 1965), 172; and cf. Alvin Goldman, "Ethics and Cognitive Science," *Ethics* 103 (1993), 355.

10. John Stuart Mill, *Utilitarianism,* in *The Collected Works of John Stuart Mill,* 33 vols., ed. John M. Robson (Toronto: University of Toronto Press, 1963–1991), vol. 10, 245ff.

11. Here is a representative experiment, described in Ernst Fehr and Simon Gächter, "Altruistic Punishment in Humans," *Nature* 415 (January 10, 2002), 137–140. I've changed their monetary units ("MU's," they call them) to dollars.

First you give four people each $20. You tell them they can "invest" as little or as much of it as they like in a group project with three anonymous strangers. Any money they don't contribute, they can keep for themselves. If a person invests in the group project, you say, then for each dollar they put in, every member of the group gets another 40 cents. (As a result, every time someone puts a dollar into the pool, $1.60 gets paid out; but the person who put the money in sustains a net loss of 60 cents.) So, as the authors of the paper say, "it was always in the material self-interest of any subject to keep all" the money, "irrespective of how much the other three subjects contributed." But (as a quick calculation will show you) whereas if everyone did this, each would take away just $20, if they all invested all their money, they'd walk away with $32 apiece.

As in the ultimatum game—and remember the players never get to meet each other—people don't behave like collections of rational profit maximizers. (If they did, they'd always end up with $20 here, because, if everyone assumes the other three players are just pursuing their own interests, they have no incentive to invest at all.) And indeed in a typical such game, most people do, in fact, end up with more than $20, presumably because most people are willing to bet that strangers will see the virtues of cooperation. Notice that if the world contains many situations like these, where cooperation is to the adaptive advantage of all if everyone plays their part, there'd be some selection pressure for (genes that make likely) behavior that secures these advantages. Our disposition to punish those who deviate from norms of cooperation—combined with the fact that we know this about one another—thus looks like it can be given an evolutionary explanation.

12. Fehr and Gächter, "Altruistic Punishment in Humans," 137. Let me underline the fact that, as Fehr and Gächter indicate, a large number of evolutionary models now exist that show how genetically fixed tendencies to biological altruism—costly behavior that confers benefits on other people—could come to be adaptive provided there was also an inherited tendency to punish those who fail to conform to social norms. (This is "biological altruism," by the way, because it's what evolutionary biologists mean by "altruism." Moral altruism, of course, involves the intent to benefit others, and that's not evident in these cases.)

If that willingness to punish is extended to those who themselves fail to punish offenders, such prosocial behavior is even easier to establish evolutionarily. Indeed, Robert Boyd and Peter Richerson, who have constructed many computer models of the evolution of norms, once published a paper on this topic in a sociobiology journal: "Punishment Allows the Evolution of Co-operation (or Anything Else) in Sizable Groups," *Ethology and Sociobiology* 13 (1992), 171–195, reprinted as ch. 9 of Boyd and Richerson, *The Origin and Evolution of Cultures* (New York: Oxford University Press, 2005).

These effects go beyond kin selection—the stabilization of traits that are selected for because the survival of close kin entails the likely survival of an individual's own genes; and they work in models that assume that human beings evolved in competing social groups on the order of 100 people in size, with relatively little migration across groups, conditions that we have reason to think may indeed have obtained before the development of settled agriculture in the past ten thousand or so years. We can also show that many of the advantages of collaboration with strangers beyond a basic human band will be available only to creatures that are disposed to enjoy cooperation independently of its current benefits. Brain studies have confirmed that the reward centers of the brain light up when people detect cooperation.

Another mechanism for securing cooperation is identified in recent studies with oxytocin (a hormone present in men but best known for its role in inducing labor in pregnant women), which show that people are more likely to be trusting after inhaling this compound. See Ernst Fehr and Urs Fischbacher, "The Nature of Human Altruism," *Nature* 425 (October 23, 2003), 785–791.

There can also be genetically based abilities to detect whether people have the psychological traits that make them worth cooperating with. And the better individuals get at detecting noncooperators and denying them the advantages of sociability, the more likely it is that the easiest way to gain those advantages will be to *be* reliable rather than merely feigning to be so. An evolutionary "arms race" might ensue here, with growing skill in deception making its detection more adaptive; and increasing skill in deception-detection raising the pressure to develop new forms of deception.

13. Gretchen Vogel, "The Evolution of the Golden Rule," *Science* 303, no. 5661 (February 20, 2004), 1128–1131.

14. Reflections on justice may invite the thought that the notion of fairness and reciprocity is too accommodating. It's only fair to give people what they deserve; it's only fair to treat people equally; it's only fair to remember and return a favor: Aren't these three distinct kinds of obligation? The political philosopher David Schmidtz has suggested that justice is plural in exactly this way. There are principles of equality, desert, reciprocity, and need; in different contexts, he argues, different principles will come to the fore, and sometimes they'll overlap, even clash. Talk of *need* evokes the Concern Mechanism, compassion, the ideal of harm avoidance; but the other principles suggest that the proposed "fairness and reciprocity" module might harbor some discordant values. Very roughly, he suggests, children are due what they need; citizens are due equal treatment; partners are due reciprocity; contestants are due "fair acknowledgement of demonstrated merit"; employees are due what they've earned; the poor are due a chance. David Schmidtz, *Elements of Justice* (Cambridge: Cambridge University Press, 2006), 18.

15. John Seldon, *The Duello, or Single Combat* (1610), as quoted in Robert Baldick, *The Duel* (London: Chapman and Hall, 1965), 32; Francis Bacon, "The Charge of Sir Francis Bacon, Knight, His Majesty's Attorney Generall, Touching Duels," in Francis Bacon, *The Major Works,* ed. Brian Vickers (Oxford: Oxford University Press, 2002), 304. Bacon's observation may recall one of Oscar Wilde's: "As long as war is regarded as wicked, it

will always have its fascination. When it is looked upon as vulgar, it will cease to be popular." Wilde, "The Critic as Artist," in *The Artist as Critic: Critical Writings of Oscar Wilde,* ed. Richard Ellmann (Chicago: University of Chicago Press, 1969; rpt. 1982), 405.

16. "Tiele est la dueté des Roys, / Amer et servir dieu aincois, / Et sainte eglise maintenir, / Et garder salvement les loys." These lines are from the *Mirour de l'Omme,* cited in Bernard F. Huppé, "The Authorship of the A and B Texts of Piers Plowman," *Speculum* 22, no. 4 (October 1947), 588, note 17.

17. This is, of course, a somewhat anomalous moment for Cicero, who complained of democracy that it permitted no "degrees of dignitas" (*De Re Publica,* 1.43). But, as I say, the very acknowledgment that dignity comes in degrees opens the door to the thought that some measure of dignity might be the possession of everyone.

18. See Michael Walzer, *The Revolution of the Saints: A Study in the Origins of Radical Politics* (Cambridge, Mass.: Harvard University Press, 1965); and Peter Singer, *The Expanding Circle* (New York: Farrar, Straus and Giroux, 1981). Don Herzog, *Poisoning the Minds of the Lower Orders* (Princeton: Princeton University Press, 2000), has a fine analysis of the recruitment of contempt by conservatives and democrats alike in eighteenth-century England. And see the discussion in Kwame Anthony Appiah, *The Ethics of Identity* (Princeton: Princeton University Press, 2005), ch. 5, section entitled "Globalizing Human Rights."

19. T. M. Scanlon, *What We Owe to Each Other* (Cambridge, Mass.: Harvard University Press, 1998), 197.

20. Jonathan Haidt, Silvia Koller, and Maria G. Dias, "Affect, Culture, and Morality, or Is It Wrong To Eat Your Dog?" *Journal of Personality and Social Psychology* 65 (1993), 613–628. The narrow compass of these conundrums may mislead us: we should not assume, as a sociological matter, that a liberal sophisticate is really free of purity-and-pollution intuitions. His feelings about food—to move within the penumbra of their proper domain—are complicated, but he objects (let's suppose) to the way the factory-farming system doses livestock with drugs and hormones. He prizes organic foods that are uncontaminated by pesticides and additives, and shudders at how agribusiness has despoiled the environment. His commitment to organic, locally produced food is more than a consumer

preference; it's a politics, and an ethics. He deplores, too, what he considers the toxic effluents of mass-media corporations—trash in the service of mindless consumerism, which fouls the minds of the young. He splashes red paint on fur-coat-wearing fashion editors, to make their moral contamination visible to all. I'll grant this is a cartoon, but it should make us think twice about the irrelevance of the purity module to the moral intuitions of progressive souls.

21. Bernard Williams, "Conflicts of Value," in Williams, *Moral Luck* (Cambridge: Cambridge University Press, 1981), 81.

22. As in the title of Sartre's play *Les Mains Sales* (Dirty Hands; 1948), which explores the theme in the realm where it has usually been considered: that of warfare and statecraft. The philosophical literature on the subject is extensive and of long standing. Michael Walzer has cited the advice dispensed by the Bishop of Caesarea in the fourth century A.D.: "Killing in war was differentiated by our fathers from murder. . . . Nevertheless, perhaps it would be well that those whose hands are unclean abstain from communion for three years." Walzer comments, "Here dirty hands are a kind of impurity or unworthiness, which is not the same as guilt, though closely related to it." Michael Walzer, "Political Action: The Problem of Dirty Hands," *Philosophy and Public Affairs* 2, no. 2 (Winter 1973), 167. See also the useful discussion in Michael Stocker, *Plural and Conflicting Values* (Oxford: Clarendon, 1990), 9–37.

Williams introduced Jim and Pedro in his essay "A Critique of Utilitarianism," in J. J. C. Smart and Bernard Williams, *Utilitarianism: For and Against* (Cambridge: Cambridge University Press, 1973), 98ff. The trouble that dirty-hands cases create for utilitarianism, in Williams' view, isn't that utilitarianism gives the wrong answers; it is that "if the situations are essentially as described and there are no further special features, it regards them, it seems to me, as *obviously* right answers." The reference to what is "obvious" suggests that the account is to be faulted, at least in part, for its failure to accord with our (presumably conflicting) moral sentiments. Elsewhere, Williams argues that the pro tanto reason not to do something doesn't disappear, even when trumped by another reason; not all moral conflict is "soluble without remainder." Bernard Williams, "Ethical Consistency," in Williams, *Problems of the Self* (Cambridge: Cambridge University Press, 1973), 179. Yet all sorts of *faute de mieux* acts might seem to have such "remainders," and only a special subset of them (those involving what could be called abominations) pose the problem of dirty hands.

23. Josiah Royce, *The Philosophy of Loyalty* (Nashville: Vanderbilt University Press, 1995; orig. pub. 1908), 48, 56, 74.

24. Martin Hoffman, "The Contribution of Empathy to Justice and Moral Judgment," in Nancy Eisenberg and Janet Strayer, eds., *Empathy and Its Development* (Cambridge: Cambridge University Press, 1987), 47–90; David Hume, *A Treatise of Human Nature*, ed. L. A. Selby-Bigge (Oxford: Clarendon, 1988), 581; and cf. Alvin Goldman, "Ethics and Cognitive Science," *Ethics* 103 (1993), 359. The research on "kind-mindedness" is engagingly explored in David Berreby, *Us and Them: Understanding Your Tribal Mind* (New York: Little, Brown, 2005).

25. As I pointed out in *Cosmopolitanism* (New York: Norton, 2006), we may suppose that racists or chauvinists of one kind or another think that other classes of people simply don't matter. But these victimizers never stop with that claim; they tell you why their victims—Jews or Aztecs or Tutsi—*deserve* what's being done to them.

26. Jonathan Haidt, "Elevation and the Positive Psychology of Morality," in C. L. M. Keyes and Jonathan Haidt, eds., *Flourishing: Positive Psychology and the Life Well-Lived* (Washington, D.C.: American Psychological Association, 2003), 275–289.

27. See, for instance, John Mikhail, Cristina M. Sorrentino, and Elizabeth Spelke, "Toward a Universal Moral Grammar," in Morton A. Gernsbacher and Sharon A. Derry, eds., *Proceedings of the Twentieth Annual Conference of the Cognitive Science Society* (Mahwah, N.J.: Erlbaum, 1998); John Mikhail, "Aspects of the Theory of Moral Cognition: Investigating Intuitive Knowledge of the Prohibition of Intentional Battery and the Principle of Double Effect" (May 2002). Georgetown Public Law Research Paper no. 762385, available at ssrn.com/abstract762385 (accessed March 28, 2007); and Marc Hauser, Liane Young, and Fiery Cushman, "Reviving Rawls' Linguistic Analogy: Operative Principles and the Causal Structure of Moral Actions," in Walter Sinnott-Armstrong, ed., *Moral Psychology and Biology* (New York: Oxford University Press, forthcoming), available at www.wjh.harvard.edu/mnkylab/publications/recent/ReviveRawslChpt.pdf. And see John Rawls, *A Theory of Justice* (Cambridge, Mass.: Harvard University Press, 1971), 46–47.

28. In Kazuo Ishiguro's novel *Never Let Me Go* (in which clones are

raised without knowing that they will be slaughtered for their organs) or the movie *Logan's Run* (where people approaching their thirtieth birthday are promised the chance of "renewal," but are actually to be killed), consent is predicated upon prevarication. Suppose we throw our eldest sons into a volcano to appease the sun god, and they are happy to accede because they think paradise awaits them. Ask a member of these societies why their moral system is just, and you may hear about what's owed to the sun god; you won't hear that the mere fact of acceptance constitutes justice. Facts about the sun god and the nature of the hereafter are relevant to their evaluations. (The contractualists who talk about "reasonable acceptance" pack an enormous bale of normative constraints into the slim valise of the word "reasonable.")

29. Aldous Huxley, *Ends and Means: An Inquiry into the Nature of Ideals and into the Methods Employed for Their Realization* (London: Chatto and Windus, 1938), 13.

30. Harry Harrison, "I Always Do What Teddy Says," in Harrison, *50 in 50* (New York: Tor, 2001), 228–235, originally published in *Ellery Queen's Mystery Magazine* 258 (June 1965).

31. Moral justifications, as I've said, always have a universal aspect in this way. Earlier, I mentioned Williams' remark (à propos of abortion) that "You can't kill that, it's a child" is a stronger reason than any reason we could come up with for why it's a reason. That's so: but it's important to recognize that it *is* a reason. (That reason, more wordily, is: you can't kill that, because it is a child and killing children is, self-evidently, impermissible. As G. E. Moore noted, even casuistry wasn't just about particular cases; its judgments were less general than were appropriate to ethics, he thought, but they were still general.) By contrast, "You can't kill that child," though perhaps a self-validating truth, isn't a reason.

32. Mark Johnston, "The Authority of Affect," *Philosophy and Phenomenological Research* 63, no. 1 (July 2001), 189.

33. There are two problems about evaluations. One is whether we should give what I call a "subjective evaluation" any weight at all. Should I count the fact that I feel disgust as a pro tanto reason? This is the question I am raising here. A second question is: What further considerations ought to override a pro tanto reason? When should I override my revulsion against killing the innocent (as in the scenario I discussed in note 23 of Chapter 3, where we expect the fighter pilot to overcome his revulsion)?

The first question strikes me as the deeper one. But the second raises complex issues about the proper weighing of considerations, which is part of what Aristotle meant by *phronesis*.

34. Years ago, the philosopher Frank Jackson came up with a scenario about Mary the Color Scientist, who, by hypothesis, knows everything there is to know about color—all the physical facts, anyway, including neurophysiology—but, confined to a black-and-white habitat, has never seen color. One day she ventures out into the world and sees, say, yellow for the first time, and the question arises: Has she learned anything about color?

Now imagine a psychopath who knows all the social facts about morality, appears to be a competent user of moral terms, but has never experienced a moral sentiment. Shaun Nichols actually put something like this scenario to people: John the psychopath says he knows that hurting others is wrong but he hurts people anyway because he doesn't care. Nichols asked whether the psychopath understood that hurting others is morally wrong. People mostly said yes. What can you conclude from this? Not, as Nichols suggests, that people are "externalists" about morality and motivation: you can't infer that from a single yes-or-no question about a freak of nature.

Suppose, further, that John the psychopath turns out to have had a tumor pressing against his prefrontal cortex, and after undergoing an operation, he has normal moral sentiments and regards his past misdeeds with horror and regret. "Now I truly know how wrong my actions were," he says. Is he right? Has John learned anything? Does he know or perceive anything he didn't before?

Here we might think that the psychopath is in the situation of the blind color scientist who, having the right frequency-detection equipment always available in his pocket, has been able to use the word "yellow" correctly. Does he know what "yellow" means? Well, he knows a good deal about yellow, but you might say he doesn't know *everything* there is to know about yellow. Similarly, post-operative John has reason to doubt he knew everything about cruelty. But I don't expect people to have tight intuitions about the use of the word "know" in this strange case. I'm inclined to say that John has gained a *capacity:* he may have no more propositional knowledge about the nature of cruelty in itself, but he has now come to respond to it in a new (and proper) way.

35. Martin Gilbert, *The Righteous* (London: Black Swan, 2003), 11.

36. Marissa L. Greif, Deborah G. Kemler Nelson, Frank C. Keil, and Franky Gutierrez, "What Do Children Want to Know about Animals and Artifacts? Domain-Specific Requests for Information," *Psychological Science* 17, no. 6 (June 2006), 455–556.

5. THE ENDS OF ETHICS

1. I am not going to challenge here the coherence of this notion of happiness; though I do, as it happens, think that there is something incoherent in the general idea (which goes back at least to Descartes) of a mental state infallibly known to the person who has it. I'm also bracketing accounts of well-being in terms of counterfactually "rational" or "fully informed" desires or preferences.

2. Robert Nozick, *Anarchy, State, and Utopia* (New York: Basic Books, 1974), 43.

3. G. E. M. Anscombe, in *Intention,* observed: "It is a familiar doctrine that people can want anything." But, she went on to suggest, this apparent truism, like many such familiar doctrines, is mistaken:

"It will be instructive to anyone who thinks this to approach someone and say: 'I want a saucer of mud' or 'I want a twig of mountain ash.' He is likely to be asked what for; to which let him reply that he does not want it *for* anything, he just wants it. It is likely that the other will then perceive that a philosophical example is all that is in question, and will pursue the matter no further; but supposing that he did not realize this, and yet did not dismiss our man as a dull babbling loon, would he not try to find out in what aspect the object desired is desirable? Does it serve as a symbol? Is there something delightful about it? Does the man want to have something to call his own, and no more? Now if the reply is: 'Philosophers have taught that anything can be an object of desire; so there can be no need for me to characterize these objects as somehow desirable; it merely so happens that I want them,' then this is fair nonsense. . . . To say, 'I merely want this' without any characterization is to deprive the word of sense." G. E. M. Anscombe, *Intention* (Oxford: Basil Blackwell, 1972), 70–71 (I have silently Americanized punctuation and spelling).

Anscombe's view here can be put in terms she herself would not have favored: roughly speaking, wants make sense only if they connect with intelligible human purposes.

4. Philip Larkin, "Annus Mirabilis," in Larkin, *High Windows* (London: Faber and Faber, 1974).

5. Derek Parfit, "What Makes a Life Go Best," in Parfit, *Reasons and Persons* (New York: Oxford University Press, 1986), 499. Other variants of this approach include T. M. Scanlon's "substantive goods" account and James Griffin's catalogue of the "ends of life." See also the discussion of various such theories of well-being in Kwame Anthony Appiah, *The Ethics of Identity* (Princeton: Princeton University Press, 2005), ch. 4.

6. John Stuart Mill, *On Liberty*, in *The Collected Works of John Stuart Mill*, 33 vols., ed. John M. Robson (Toronto: University of Toronto Press, 1963–1991), vol. 18, 270.

7. From the perspective of the *Verstandeswelt*, we are responding to values, not inventing them. So this view differs crucially from the last element of the subjective conception of happiness that I sketched above: the view that we simply make up for ourselves the standards by which our life will be evaluated as more or less successful. Once again, Mill has a wonderful passage to this point:

"He who lets the world, or his own portion of it, choose his plan of life for him, has no need of any other faculty than the ape-like one of imitation. He who chooses his plan for himself, employs all his faculties. He must use observation to see, reasoning and judgment to foresee, activity to gather materials for decision, discrimination to decide, and when he has decided, firmness and self-control to hold to his deliberate decision. And these qualities he requires and exercises exactly in proportion as the part of his conduct which he determines according to his own judgment and feelings is a large one. . . . Among the works of man, which human life is rightly employed in perfecting and beautifying, the first in importance surely is man himself" (Mill, *On Liberty*, 262–263).

The forms of "observation" that matter include an attention to our own capacities and our own social and historical situation; the "discrimination" we must exercise requires us to distinguish what is valuable from what is not; and we need judgment to match our own talents and our situation to values that we can live by.

8. Aristotle, *Nicomachean Ethics*, trans. H. Rackham, Loeb Classical Library (Cambridge, Mass.: Harvard University Press, 1934), 44–45.

9. If, like most of us, you are not beautiful, you can, at least, despite what Aristotle said, make your looks matter less to the evaluation of your life by avoiding professions—like modeling, say—in which beauty is of central instrumental importance. But you cannot, even by an act of will, make it true that your life wouldn't have been intrinsically better if you had been more beautiful. For beauty is a good thing, is it not? It is of value. (Not obviously of moral value; but not all values are moral. That something is beautiful is a pro tanto reason to respond to it in a certain way. *Which* way depends, in part, on what kind of thing it is.)

Of course, most of us, being, by definition, ordinary looking, may think that not being beautiful is not a very substantial reduction in the value of our lives; that it would be shallow to care about it too much; and that, therefore, though the film actor Brad Pitt and the fashion model Iman have lives made better by their looks, we shouldn't worry too much about the absence of this element in our own *eudaimonia*. But if, for some reason, you did come to care about your looks, there are ways even for the unbeautiful to compensate for that loss by picking a life in which looking as they do is central in a positive way: as you might, for example, think it is to some acting careers. Think of Peter Lorre or Willem Dafoe, or Rossy de Palma in the films of Pedro Almodóvar. All three of them would have to have had different careers if they'd been conventionally attractive. They've made, as we say, the best of a bad situation, with respect to their looks, at least.

10. Think how the *eudaimonia* of German patriots was affected by the Nazi regime and the shame of the Holocaust; or how that of British patriots was affected by the triumph over fascism. It wasn't just that many lives were made instrumentally better by that military triumph. Their lives were improved intrinsically by it. As Ronald Dworkin puts it, nationality can be one of the *parameters* of your life. Some of our circumstances (including our own physical, mental, and social attributes) act as *parameters*, in his terms, when they help define what it is for us to have lived a successful life. They are, so to speak, part of the challenge that we must meet. Others are *limits*—obstacles that get in the way of our making the ideal life that the parameters help define.

Each person, in thinking about her own life, must decide how to allocate her circumstances between these categories, just as an artist must decide which aspects of the tradition she inherits define what her art is and which are barriers to or instruments for her creativity. Dworkin writes: "We have no settled template for that decision, in art or in ethics, and no philosophical model can provide one, for the circumstances in which each of us lives are enormously complex. . . . Anyone who reflects seriously on the question which of the various lives he might lead is right for him will consciously or unconsciously discriminate among these, treating some as limits and others as parameters." Dworkin, *Sovereign Virtue: The Theory and Practice of Equality* (Cambridge, Mass.: Harvard University Press, 2000), 260.

11. "In short, man is a social being; he is real only because he is social, and can realize himself only because it is as social that he realizes himself. The mere individual is a delusion of theory." F. H. Bradley, *Ethical Studies*, ed. Richard Wollheim (Oxford: Oxford University Press, 1962), 174 and 160–206. Compare, say, Charles Taylor's critique of the "punctual self," which he associates with John Locke and his intellectual heirs, and Michael Sandel's critique of what he regards as the "unencumbered self" central to much liberal theory. (Bradley held that we also had duties to ourselves and still other duties that went beyond our station, which could involve "what might be called cosmopolitan morality" [*Ethical Studies*, 204]. He was not so much assigning primacy to station-related obligations as compensating for what he saw as an omission in the theories favored by his contemporaries.)

12. Mab Segrest, *Memoir of a Race Traitor* (Boston: South End Press, 1994). There's a long tradition here: the role of white abolitionists in the eighteenth and nineteenth centuries was, inevitably, distinct from the role of their black counterparts. Segrest's book also belongs to the morally powerful genre of the "conversion narrative."

13. Lydia Davis, "Happiest Moment," in Davis, *Samuel Johnson Is Indignant* (New York: McSweeney's Books, 2001).

14. As Michael Krausz wrote to me after the third of my Flexner Lectures: "Inevitably one of the considerations that enter into 'what one should do' involves a judgment of its accord with what sort of person one takes oneself to be, and whether doing or not doing something violates (or

is expected to violate) one's capacity to recognize one's self or who one wishes to be." My talk of "balancing" here (and of "trade-offs" later) should be taken loosely: there is a sense of who one wishes to be; there is not an ethical scale with two pans. If I stand you up at a restaurant, we would agree, I would only compound the injury occasioned by the broken promise if I offered you a hundred dollars in compensation. Few would balk at the seeming pluralism here. But, as I'll be pointing out, such pluralism extends to the zone between project-dependent and moral values.

15. William Godwin, *Thoughts Occasioned by the Perusal of Dr. Parr's Spital Sermon, Preached at Christ Church, April 15, 1800: Being a Reply to the Attacks of Dr. Parr, Mr. Mackintosh, the Author of an Essay on Population, and Others* (London: Printed by Taylor and Wilks, Chancery-Lane; and sold by G. G. and J. Robinson, Paternoster-Row, 1801). At snipurl.com/v8fu (accessed March 28, 2007).

16. Mill, *On Liberty*, 281, 261.

17. Here's how the discussion goes: "Das ist es aber gerade. Die gibt es doch gar nicht. Jede Zahl, ob sie nun positiv ist oder negativ, gibt zum Quadrat erhoben etwas Positives. Es kann daher gar keine wirkliche Zahl geben, welche die Quadratwurzel von etwas Negativem war." "Ich glaube, wenn man allzu gewissenhaft wäre, so gäbe es keine Mathematik." "Darin hast du recht. Wenn man es sich so vorstellt, ist es eigenartig genug. Aber das Merkwürdige ist ja gerade, dass man trotzdem mit solchen imaginären oder sonstwie unmöglichen Werten ganz wirklich rechnen kann und zum Schluss ein greifbares Resultat vorhanden ist." Robert Musil, *Die Verwirrungen des Zöglings Törless* (Reinbek bei Hamburg: Rowohlt, 1978), 103.

18. I will not attempt to do justice to the disputes over the "fact-stating" claims of moral sentences, but will content myself with an observation about the diversity of ways in which facts can be factual. No, moral facts are not just like physical facts; but neither is one physical fact just like every other. The fact that cobras are dangerous is not like the fact that two plus two equals four, which is not like the fact that a cup of Coca-Cola contains a hundred calories—or the fact that Carl Czerny's musical talent was dwarfed by Haydn's; that one second is defined as the time it takes an atom of cesium-133 to emit or absorb 9,192,631,770 cycles of microwave light; that, at a pressure of one atmosphere, water freezes at zero degrees Celsius; that Pluto is not a planet; that Hesperus is Phosphorus; that the

city of Catal Hoyuk was established on the Anatolian plain almost ten thousand years ago; that the sky is blue; or that a bachelor is an unmarried man. Some of these facts (if they are facts) are a priori and true in all possible worlds; some are a posteriori necessary truths; some are anthropocentric; some embody institutionally ratified, and perhaps reversible, definitions; some are known through complex chains of inferences; some are self-evident; and on and on. Mill, though he sometimes wrote about well-being as if it were a purely nonnormative phenomenon—it would be question-begging to say "natural"—is best read as holding a complex, fact-and-value-laden view of the subject. So he was not the "naturalist" that Moore took him for. The naturalistic fallacy is to define (indefinable) goodness in terms of natural properties; the naturalistic-fallacy fallacy is to assume that such putative "definitions," when fully spelled out, wouldn't contain other appeals to value, or that the natural property in question is really, in Moorean terms, natural.

19. Stephen Jay Gould, "Nonoverlapping Magisteria," *Natural History* 106 (March 1997), 16–22.

20. As Ryle wrote, "The fear that theoretically-minded persons have felt lest everything should turn out to be explicable by mechanical laws is a baseless fear. And it is baseless not because the contingency which they dread happens not to be impending, but because it makes no sense to speak of such a contingency." Gilbert Ryle, *The Concept of Mind* (Chicago: University of Chicago Press, 1949), 76.

21. Richard Joyce, *The Evolution of Morality* (Cambridge, Mass.: MIT Press, 2006), 219, 229–230.

22. *The Complete Essays of Montaigne*, trans. Donald M. Frame (Stanford: Stanford University Press, 1958), 83, 85, 88, 85.

23. Isaiah Berlin, "The First and the Last," *New York Review of Books*, 45, no. 8 (May 14, 1998), 53–60.

24. Saul Kripke, *Naming and Necessity* (Cambridge, Mass.: Harvard University Press, 1972), 83–84. Incidentally, the Gödel scenario is anything but far-fetched. The statistician Stephen M. Stigler maintains that most named theorems in math and statistics are misattributed; see his delightful essay "Stigler's Law of Eponymy," in Stigler, *Statistics on the Table* (Cambridge, Mass.: Harvard University Press, 1999); Stigler's law, he insists, is self-instantiating, having really been devised by Robert K. Merton.

25. Edouard Machery, Ron Mallon, Shaun Nichols, and Stephen P. Stich, "Semantics, Cross-Cultural Style," *Cognition* 92 (2004), B1–B12. "We find it wildly implausible that the semantic intuitions of the narrow cross-section of humanity who are Western academic philosophers are a more reliable indicator of the correct theory of reference"—if one exists—"than the differing semantic intuitions of other cultural or linguistic groups," the authors conclude. The basic complaint here echoes one made by Ernest Gellner in *Words and Things*, his notorious attack on "ordinary language" philosophy. Gellner thought it rich that linguistic philosophy was hostile to sociology: "It is ironical that this should be so, for a number of reasons. Linguistic Philosophy is itself a pseudosociology, just as it is a pseudo-metaphysics. Secondly, some of its insights logically call for sociological enquiry, if indeed they do not imply that sociology should replace philosophy. Thirdly, social factors which affected the nature of Linguistic Philosophy are themselves rather conspicuous." Ernest Gellner, *Words and Things* (London: Gollancz, 1959), 230. (The last remark hints at an analysis similar to Auden's.)

26. Montaigne quotes the relevant passage in his *Complete Essays*, 79. "Non pudet igitur physicum, id est speculatorem venatoremque naturae, ab animis consuetudine inbutis petere testimonium veritatis?" (Isn't it therefore shameful for a natural scientist—that is, an investigator and hunter of nature—to seek testimony as to the truth from minds imbued with custom?") Cicero, *De Natura Deorum*, I.83.

27. In Aristotle's famous observation, "Our treatment of this science will be adequate, if it achieves the amount of precision which belongs to its subject matter. The same exactness must not be expected in all departments of philosophy alike, any more than in all the products of the arts and crafts." Aristotle, *Nicomachean Ethics*, 7. There have been some engaging and intelligent efforts to sketch decision procedures that acknowledge pluralism. Peter Railton, for example, once proposed that an enlightened consequentialist should seek to develop "rules of thumb" that lead to the best action within "a pluralistic approach in which several goods are viewed as intrinsically, non-morally valuable—such as happiness, knowledge, purposeful activity, autonomy, solidarity, respect, and beauty. These goods need not be ranked lexically, but may be attributed weights, and the criterion of rightness for an act would be that it most contributes to the

weighted sum of these values in the long run." Railton, "Alienation, Consequentialism, and the Demands of Morality," in Samuel Scheffler, ed., *Consequentialism and Its Critics* (New York: Oxford University Press, 1988), 109–110. But, of course, this is a theory of practice, not a practical theory (moral physics, then, not moral engineering).

28. Edmund Pincoffs, "Quandary Ethics," *Mind* 80 (1971), 552–571; see also idem, *Quandaries and Virtues: Against Reductivism in Ethics* (Lawrence: University of Kansas Press, 1986).

29. "The Death of Ivan Ilyich," in Leo Tolstoy, *The Death of Ivan Ilyich; The Cossacks; Happy Ever After,* trans. Rosemary Edmonds (New York: Penguin, 1960), 137.

30. G. E. M. Anscombe, "Modern Moral Philosophy," *Philosophy* 33 (1958), 34, reprinted in Anscombe, *Ethics, Religion, and Politics* (Minneapolis: University of Minnesota Press, 1981). Elizabeth Anscombe had a normative objection to scenarios like the footbridge dilemma: "The point," she said, "of considering hypothetical situations, perhaps very improbable ones, *seems* to be to elicit from yourself or someone else a hypothetical decision to do something of a bad kind. I don't doubt that this has the effect of predisposing people—who will never get into the situations for which they have made the hypothetical choices—to consent to similar bad actions, or to praise or flatter those who do them, so long as their crowd does so too, when the desperate circumstances imagined don't hold at all" (ibid., 37). This is, of course (despite Anscombe's breezy "I don't doubt"), an empirical hypothesis. But if it were right, then just inviting people to think about all those trolleys could do harm. Actually, however, the demoralizing effect of these stories is not likely to be all that substantial. Because of the very extensive capacities for rationalization uncovered by the moral psychologists—our powers of confabulation, as they might say—you don't need much help to come up with reasons for doing what you are going to do anyway.

31. Thomas Hobbes, *The Elements of Philosophy: Concerning Body,* ch. 2, sect. 3, reprinted in *Hobbes: Selections,* ed. F. J. E. Woodbridge (New York: Scribner's, 1958), 15. There are very different routes that lead to adjoining errors. A point of agreement among some Wittgensteinians and some cognitive and experimental psychologists is that moral evaluation is primarily a matter of tacit skills, or ways of going on, as with the capacities that let us count or walk. Expertise of this sort is part of the story; but if we think the

nontacit stuff is somehow epiphenomenal, we'll have a hard time explaining why we spend so much time *talking* about, and through, such judgments, as we do not when it comes to walking or counting. Allan Gibbard—in a series of wise and apt discussions in *Wise Choices, Apt Feelings: A Theory of Normative Judgment* (Cambridge, Mass.: Harvard University Press, 1990)—gets at something critical, as I say, when he emphasizes the "norm expressive" dimension of moral discourse, the more-than-instrumental importance of normative conversations.

32. Actually, this question conflates two of Mill's thoughts, but it makes the point. What Mill said, of course, is "It is better to be a human being dissatisfied than a pig satisfied; better to be Socrates dissatisfied than a fool satisfied." John Stuart Mill, *Utilitarianism,* in *The Collected Works of John Stuart Mill,* vol. 10, 212. Mill's formulation of lower and higher pleasures may have been a response to a line of criticism from William Whewell, who argued that animals could be an object of moral concern—it was wrong to treat them cruelly—but could not be the subject of morality, inasmuch as they were not moral actors, capable of responding to moral reasons. Mill, he thought, gave us no reason to prefer the well-being of a human to the pleasures of pigs or geese. See William Whewell, *Lectures on the History of Moral Philosophy in England* (London: John W. Parker and Son, 1852), 223ff. Whewell was in favor of laws against cruelty to animals, but in his view "the word *Rights* has no meaning as applied to animals, which cannot understand the word." To have rights, he thought, you must be capable of acting morally. "Animals offer to us images of some of the lower parts of our nature; but except so far as these elements are directed and governed by the higher elements, they are not subjects of moral consideration." William Whewell, *Elements of Morality, Including Polity* (New York: Harper and Brothers, 1856), 365, 366; his discussion of laws against cruelty is on pages 310–311. See also Laura J. Snyder, *Reforming Philosophy: A Victorian Debate on Science and Society* (Chicago: University of Chicago Press, 2006), 248–249.

ACKNOWLEDGMENTS

This book began as the 2005 Mary Flexner Lectures at Bryn Mawr College (which were entitled, a little too provocatively I now think, "The End of Ethics?"). So I want, first, to thank the Flexner committee and President Nancy Vickers for inviting me to talk at Bryn Mawr. I was deeply honored to be asked, not least because I was conscious of the eminence of my predecessors; and, mindful of their distinction, I was also daunted by the standards they had set.

In revising these lectures (indeed, in preparing the later ones) I was stimulated and challenged by many of those I met at Bryn Mawr. I am particularly conscious that the final chapters were shaped by my discussions with faculty and students at the college, and especially by a discussion with Haverford and Bryn Mawr philosophy and politics professors on Friday, November 4, 2005, attended by Cheryl Chen, Robert Dostal, Jeremy Elkins, Jeremy Fantl, Aryeh Kosman, Christine Koggel, Danielle Macbeth, Jerry Miller, Stephen Salkever, Jill Stauffer, and Kathleen Wright. Danielle Macbeth was particularly responsible for getting me to say more about the ways in which human nature is cultural; Christine Koggel and Aryeh Kosman for getting me to focus on the problems of quandary ethics. Kathleen Wright seeded the talk of the "cultivation" of our natures.

I have made some further specific acknowledgments in the notes, along with the standard references to works I have quoted or found useful; but, no doubt, as usual, I have missed some of those I should have acknowledged by name. And so, if you do not find your name where you think it should be, please accept my thanks (and my apologies) here.

I am especially grateful to Lydia Davis for generously agreeing to my incorporating two of her short stories, "Trying to Learn" and "Happiest Moment," in this book. Sharing them with the audience at Bryn Mawr was one of the great pleasures of my lectures for me; and, as I learned, for many who heard them there.

I would like also to express my gratitude both to the referees whose reports allowed me to improve upon the version I initially submitted and to those who shepherded my manuscript through the process of publication. Referees are offered anonymity; I am glad that Walter Sinnott-Armstrong emerged from behind the veil, so that I can thank him by name. Lindsay Waters, my editor, orchestrated the process; Maria Ascher copyedited gracefully; and Lisa Clark designed the inventive and arresting cover. Thanks, too, to Alexander O. Trotter for the index.

Finally, I owe a great debt to Henry Finder, who has read the manuscript of this book with his usual loving, careful intelligence and given me many helpful suggestions for improving it.

At the turn of the 1930s, the philosopher Alfred North Whitehead delivered Flexner Lectures that became part of his *Adventures in Ideas;* in that same decade, a classic of literary criticism, I. A. Richards' *The Philosophy of Rhetoric* (1936), and a classic of art historical scholarship and theory, Erwin Panofsky's *Studies in Iconology* (1937), began as Flexner Lectures, too. Isaiah Berlin's *Political Ideas in the Romantic Age* (published posthumously in 2006) is based on his notes for the 1952 Flexner Lectures; and Frank Kermode's *The Sense of an Ending*, another monument in literary studies, grew out of his 1965 lectures entitled "The Long Perspective." Bernard Flexner surely cannot have anticipated—but must, I am sure, have hoped—that in honoring his sister Mary by endowing this series he would be responsible for connecting his family's name with some of the most distinguished figures in twentieth-century humanistic scholarship.

Faced with these antecedents, a sensible person would not expect himself to live up to them. In the humanities we really do have classics and, as I have indicated, many previous Flexner Lectures are among them; but I do not have the hubris to aim to add to them. My form of homage to these great predecessors has not been to try to join their company but rather to take inspiration from their achievements.

INDEX

261

PSALM 91
God's Umbrella
Of Protection

Peggy Joyce Ruth

Psalm 91 God's Umbrella of Protection

Peggy Joyce Ruth

Printed in the United States of America by Kairos Printing and Production

ISBN 978-1-942757-04-7
Library of Congress Control Number: 2002110752

Eleventh Printing, 2020

Cover by Marcus Stallworth
Edit by Roberta Wescott

Contents

4

Psalm 91 Testimonies

Foreword

In the midst of these turbulent times, God has anointed Peggy Joyce to write this wonderful book, *Psalm 91 God's Umbrella of Protection*.

When someone has walked in a Truth of God for over 40 years, there is a depth of insight incomparable to anything else. Such is the case of Peggy Ruth, our dear friend and partner in the ministry. What a gift she is to the Body of Christ! She is a pastor's wife, Bible teacher, radio host and author. And there is no fluff to Peggy! She is Rock solid and has earned the right to be listened to. From her personal furnace of affliction, she has effectively explained this famous psalm and challenged us to new levels of faith and trust in God.

This is more than an inspiring book. It is a parent's manual, a leader's handbook, a pastor's promise and a Christian's covenant. I wholeheartedly recommend this book. It contains both inspiration and information which remains Biblically sound.

Along with this much-needed book, Tommy and I applaud both Jack and Peggy Joyce for their unwavering faithfulness to their many assignments from the Lord. Their lives are a book!

Rachel Burchfield
President of Texas Bible Institute

Foreword

I have always loved the 91st Psalm, and I've known it to be the chapter of God's promises of protection for believers. It has been very helpful to read the books that Peggy Joyce Ruth has written on Psalm 91, because Holy Spirit has helped her dissect it and get the meat out to feed those of us who are hungry to know everything that will nourish us, give us strength, and allow us to grow and mature into the sons and daughters of The Most High God.

I have hidden the Word in my heart and found that in my times of need, Holy Spirit brings it to my remembrance. When I receive it, and speak it, it brings results. In the beginning was the Word, and the Word was with God, and the Word was God! That settles it! We need to know the Promises of God in His Word to apply to our lives until our faith grows to the stature and measure of Jesus Christ.

THANK YOU Peggy Joyce Ruth for digging into the Word of Psalm 91 to help us digest the strength made available to those who have ears to hear. God bless you, and all who hunger and thirst for TRUTH! It will set you FREE!

Love in Him who Loved us first...

Mama Shirley Boone
WE WIN MINISTRIES
RyansReach.com
The Boone Center for the Family at Pepperdine University
Mercy Corps International Humanitarian Organization

Introduction

Are you tired of tormenting fear thoughts that seem to always be lurking just below the surface, ready to control your life and steal your peace and well-being? If so, I think you will find the message in this book is the answer you've been searching for.

Maybe you fear the dangers that face your children every day—peer pressure, drugs or alcohol. I, too, faced those fears. I battled the nagging anxiety over what I would do if my husband, Jack, was in a car wreck, had a sudden heart attack or was involved in some other tragedy.

Those fears that tormented my imagination used to be my constant companions. Yet, it was easy to justify them with all that was going on in the world!

Back in the 1950s things were fairly predictable, but the word *predictable* was becoming more obsolete with each passing decade. Fear was running rampant because of the uncertainty of the times—cancer, natural disasters, financial difficulties and terrorism were everywhere I turned. But after all, didn't the Bible tell us in Matthew 24, *"In the last days men's hearts will fail because of fear?"* Somehow it consoled me to know I was not alone in my dilemma.

But one Sunday changed everything. That's the day the Lord miraculously, through a dream, spoke to me from a psalm I had never heard of before and answered my question— "*Is there any way to be protected from all the things that are coming on the earth?*" When I awoke, peace—like warm oil—flowed over me.

From that supernatural Word from God and the months of research that followed, I came to realize Psalm 91 was not merely something to bring comfort to me during times of sorrow. I saw it was there to take me *victoriously* though *any* crisis I might encounter.

This book is the result of the longing in my heart to help people who are struggling with the same fears I agonized over for so long. If this is something you already know, then God wants to remind you of this truth.

I encourage you to mark these scriptures in your own Bible as we go straight through this psalm. This is God's *covenant of protection* for you personally.

My prayer is that Psalm 91 will give you the **courage to trust!**

Setting the Scene

Sundays were usually a comfort. For some reason being inside the church building made the fears temporarily disappear—but not on this particular Sunday!

Our pastor looked unusually serious that day as he made the announcement that one of our most beloved and faithful deacons had been diagnosed with leukemia and had only a few weeks to live. Only the Sunday before this robust-looking deacon in his mid-forties had been in his regular place in the choir—looking as healthy and happy as ever. Now, one Sunday later, the entire congregation was in a state of shock after hearing such an unexpected announcement.

Several of the members got upset with the pastor when he said, "*Get out all of your silly little get-well cards and start sending them.*" But I completely understood the frustration that had initiated the remark. However, little did I know this incident would pave the way to a message that was *GOING TO FOREVER BURN IN MY HEART.*

Surprisingly, I had gone home from church that day feeling very little fear, perhaps because I was numb from the shock of what I had heard. I vividly remember sitting down on the edge of the bed that afternoon and saying out loud, "*Lord, is there any way to be protected from all the evils that are coming on the earth?*"

I was not expecting an answer. I was merely voicing the thought that kept going over and over in my mind. I remember lying across the bed and falling immediately to sleep, only to wake up a short five minutes later. However, in those five minutes I had a very unusual dream.

In the dream I was in an open field, asking the same question I had prayed earlier—"*Is there any way to be protected from all the things that are coming on the earth?*" And in my dream I heard these words:

"*In your day of trouble call upon*
**Me, and I will answer you!*"

Suddenly, I knew I had the answer I had so long been searching for. The ecstatic joy I felt was beyond anything I could ever describe. And instantly, to my surprise, there were hundreds of Christians with me in the dream out in that open field, praising and thanking God for the answer. But it wasn't until the next day when I heard the 91st Psalm referred to on a tape by Shirley Boone that suddenly—I *knew in my heart* that **whatever** was in that psalm was God's answer to my question. I nearly tore up my Bible in my haste to see what it said. And there it was in verse 15—the *exact statement* God had spoken to me in my dream. I could hardly believe my eyes!

I believe that you who are reading this book are among the many Christians who were pictured with me in that open field, who will, through the Message in this book, get your answer to the question, "Can a Christian be protected through these turbulent times?"

Since the early 1970s, I have had many opportunities to share this message. I believe God has commissioned me to write this book to proclaim God's *Covenant of Protection*. May you be sincerely blessed by it.

Peggy Joyce Ruth

Psalm 91

He who dwells in the shelter of the Most High
Will abide in the shadow of the Almighty.
I will say to the Lord, "My refuge and my fortress,
My God, in whom I trust!"
For it is He who delivers you from the snare of the trapper
And from the deadly pestilence.
He will cover you with His pinions,
And under His wings you may seek refuge;
His faithfulness is a shield and bulwark.

You will not be afraid of the terror by night,
Or of the arrow that flies by day;
Of the pestilence that stalks in darkness,
Or of the destruction that lays waste at noon.
A thousand may fall at your side,
And ten thousand at your right hand;
But it shall not approach you.
You will only look on with your eyes,
And see the recompense of the wicked.
For you have made the Lord, my refuge,
Even the Most High, your dwelling place.

No evil will befall you,
Nor will any plague come near your tent.
For He will give His angels charge concerning you,
To guard you in all your ways.
They will bear you up in their hands,
Lest you strike your foot against a stone.
You will tread upon the lion and cobra,
The young lion and the serpent you will trample down.

Because he has loved Me, therefore I will deliver him;
I will set him securely on high,
Because he has known My name.
He will call upon Me, and I will answer him;
I will be with him in trouble;
I will rescue him, and honor him.
With a long life I will satisfy him,
And let him behold My salvation.

Chapter 1

Where Is My Dwelling Place?

He who dwells in the shelter of the Most High will abide in the shadow of the Almighty. —Psalm 91:1

HAVE YOU EVER BEEN inside a cabin with a big roaring fire in the fireplace, enjoying this wonderful feeling of safety and security as you watched an enormous electrical storm going on outside? It was a warm, wonderful sensation, knowing you were being sheltered and protected from the storm. **That is what Psalm 91 is all about—shelter!**

Did you know there is a place in God—a secret place—for those who want to seek refuge? It is a *literal* place of physical safety and security that God is referring to.

Dwelling in the shelter of the Most High is the Old Testament's way of teaching faith. This gives us the most intense illustration of the very essence of personal relationship. Man has no innate built-in shelter. Alone, he stands shelterless against the elements and must run to the shelter, which is God Himself. In verse one, God is offering us more than protection; it is as if He rolls out the hospitality mat and personally invites us in.

I am sure every one of you can think of something that represents *security* to you. When I think of security, shelter and protection, I have a childhood memory that automatically comes to mind. My parents would take me and my younger brother and sister out to a lake to fish for an afternoon of fun.

Dad had a secluded place on this lake near Brownwood where he would take us to fish for perch. That was the second greatest highlight of the outing. I loved seeing the cork begin to bobble, and then, suddenly, it would go completely out of sight. There were only a few things that could thrill me more than jerking back on that old cane pole and landing a huge perch right in the boat. I think I was grown before I realized Dad had an ulterior motive in taking us for an afternoon of perch fishing. Those perch were his bait for the trotline he had stretched out across one of the secret coves at the lake.

Dad would drive the boat over to the place where his trotline was located, then he would cut off the boat motor and inch the boat across the cove as he *"ran the trot line."* That's what he called it when he would hold onto the trotline with his hands and pull the boat alongside all the strategically placed, baited hooks to see if any of them had caught a large catfish.

I said that catching the perch was the *second* greatest highlight of the outing. By far, the greatest thrill was the times when Dad would get to a place where the trotline rope would begin to jerk almost out of his hand. It was then that we three siblings would watch wide-eyed as Dad would wrestle with the line until finally, in victory, he would flip that huge catfish over the side of the boat, right on the floor board at our feet. Money couldn't buy that kind of excitement! The circus and carnival, all rolled up into one, couldn't compete with that kind of a thrill.

One of these outings proved more eventful than most—turning out to be an experience I will never forget. It had been a beautiful day when we started out, but by the time we had finished our perch fishing and were headed toward the cove, everything changed. A storm came up on the lake so suddenly that there was no time to get back to the boat dock. The sky turned black, lightning flashed, and drops of rain fell with such force they actually stung when they hit. Then, moments later we began to be pelted by large, marble-sized hailstones.

I saw the fear in my mother's eyes, and I knew we were in danger. But, before I had time to wonder what we were going to do, Dad had driven the boat to the rugged shoreline of the only island on the lake. Boat docks surround that island now, but back then it just looked like an abandoned island with absolutely no place to take cover.

Within moments Dad had us all out of the boat and ordered the three of us to lie down beside our mother on the ground. He quickly pulled a canvas tarp out of the bottom of the boat, knelt down on the ground beside us and thrust the tarp up over all five of us. That storm raged outside the makeshift tent he had fashioned over us; the rain beat down, the lightning flashed and the thunder rolled, yet I could think of nothing else but how it felt to have my dad's arms around us. There was a certain calm under the protection of the shield my father provided that is hard to explain now.

In fact, I had never felt as safe and secure in my entire life. I can remember thinking I wished the storm would last forever. I didn't want anything to spoil the wonderful security I felt that day *in our secret hiding place*. Feeling my father's protective arms around me, I never wanted the moment to end.

Although, I have never forgotten that experience, today it has taken on new meaning. Just as Dad had put a tarp over us that day to shield us from the storm, our Heavenly Father has a *Secret Place* in His arms that protects us from the storms raging in the world around us.

That *Secret Place* is literal, but it is also conditional! In verse one of Psalm 91, God lists our part of the condition before He even mentions the promises included in His part. That's because *our part* has to come first. In order to abide in the *shadow* of the Almighty, we must *choose to dwell* in the shelter of the Most High.

The question is—"*How do we dwell in the security and shelter of the Most High?*" It is more than an intellectual experience. It is a dwelling place where we can be physically protected if we run to Him. You may utterly believe that God is your refuge, you may give mental assent to it in your prayer time, you may teach Sunday school lessons on this concept of refuge, and you may even get a warm feeling every time you think of it, but unless you do something about it—*unless you actually get up and run to the shelter*—you will never experience it.

You also might call that place of refuge—a *Love Walk!* In fact, the secret place is, in reality, the intimacy and familiarity of the presence of God Himself. When our grandchildren, Cullen and Meritt, were young they would often stay overnight with us. The moment they would finish breakfast they would each run to his own secret place to spend some time talking with God. Cullen found a place behind the couch in the family room, and Meritt would go behind the lamp table in the corner of our bedroom. Those places became very special to them.

Where is your secret place? You, too, need the security and shelter of a secret place with the Most High. This place of refuge is actually a relationship with the Father you have cultivated and developed by investing enough time into it to make it very personal and intimate.

Chapter 2

What Is Coming Out Of My Mouth?

I will say to the Lord, "My Refuge and my Fortress, my God, in whom I trust!" —Psalm 91:2

NOTICE VERSE TWO SAYS, "*I will say...*" Circle the word "*say*" in your Bible because we must learn to verbalize our trust. We answer back to God what He said to us in the first verse. There is power in saying His Word back to Him!

We are not told to just *think* the Word. We are told to *say* the Word. For example, Joel 3:10 tells the weak to say, "*I am a mighty man.*" Over and over we find great men of God such as David, Joshua, Shadrach, Meshach and Abednego declaring their confessions of faith out loud in dangerous situations. Notice what begins to happen on the inside when you say, "*Lord, You are my Refuge—You are my Fortress—You are my Lord and my God! It is in You that I put my total trust!*" The more we say it out loud, the more confident we become in His protection.

So many times, as Christians, we mentally agree that the Lord is our Refuge—but that is not good enough. *Power is released* in saying it out loud. When we say it, and mean it, we are placing ourselves in His shelter. By *voicing* His Lordship and His Protection we *walk in the door* to the secret place.

One cannot miss the fact that this verse uses the word *my* three times: "my refuge...my fortress...my God!" The psalmist makes a personal claim to God. The reason we can trust is that we know who God is to us. This verse makes the analogy of who God is; He is a refuge and a fortress. God Himself becomes the defensive site for us against all invading enemies. He is personally our protection.

Some quote Psalm 91 as though it were some *magical wand*, but there is nothing magical about this psalm. It is powerful and it works simply because it is the Word of God—alive and active. And, we confess it out loud, simply because the Bible tells us to.

There is, however, a uniqueness about this psalm. Promises of protection can be found throughout the Bible; but Psalm 91 is the only place in the Word where all of the protection promises are brought together in one collection —forming a covenant written through the Holy Spirit. How powerful that is!

Have you ever tried to protect yourself from all the bad things that can happen? It's like trying to keep the whole law. God knows we can't do it. Psalms 60:11b tells us *"...deliverance by man is in vain."* God has to be our source before the promises in Psalm 91 will ever work.

We could go to the doctor once a month for a checkup. We could double check our cars every day to see that the motor, the tires and the brakes were all in good running order. We could fireproof our houses and store up food for a time of need. Yet, we still couldn't do enough to protect ourselves from every potential danger. It's impossible!

It isn't that any one of these precautions is wrong. It is that not one of these things, in and of itself, has the power to protect. God has to be the One to whom we run first. **He is the only One who has an answer for *whatever* might come.**

> *"For I know the plans that I have for you," declares the Lord, "plans for welfare and not for calamity to give you a future and a hope."* –Jeremiah 29:11

When I think of how utterly impossible it is to protect ourselves from all the evils that are in the world, I always think of a sheep. A sheep has no real protection other than its shepherd. In fact, it is the only animal I can think of that has *no* built-in protection. It has no sharp teeth, no offensive odor to spray to drive off its enemies, no loud bark, and it certainly can't run fast enough to escape danger. That's why the Bible calls us God's sheep! God is saying, *"I want you to see Me as your Source of protection. I am your Shepherd."* Now, He may use doctors, storm cellars or bank accounts to meet our specific needs, but our hearts have to run to Him first as our Shepherd and our Protector. Then, *He* will choose the method He desires to bring about the protection.

When I'm facing a challenge I have learned to say out loud, *"In this particular situation* _____ (name the situation out loud) *I choose to trust you, Lord."* The difference it makes when I proclaim my trust out loud is amazing.

Take notice of what flies out of your mouth in times of trouble. The worst thing that can happen is for something to come out that brings death. Cursing gives God nothing to work with. This psalm tells us to do just the opposite—speak life! One of those times that brought life to a death situation really stands out in my mind: The whole family was rejoicing when our daughter-in-law, Sloan, received a positive pregnancy test report and found that she was going to have the first grandchild on either side of the family. Since she'd had a tubal pregnancy once before that resulted in a miscarriage, making her highly susceptible for another, the doctor then ordered a sonogram as a precautionary measure.

The disturbing result of the sonogram was—"*no fetus found, a great deal of water in the uterus and spots of endometriosis.*" With only a two-hour notice, emergency surgery was quickly underway, at which time the doctor performed a laparoscopy, drained the uterus, and scraped away the endometriosis. After the surgery the doctor's words were, "*During the laparoscopy we carefully looked everywhere, and there was no sign of a baby, but I want to see you back in my office in one week to be sure fluid doesn't build back up.*" When Sloan argued that the pregnancy test had been positive, he said there was a 99 percent chance the baby had naturally aborted and had been absorbed back into the uterine lining.

After he left the room Sloan was the only one not fazed by the doctor's report. What she said next surprised everyone. She emphatically stated that even the doctor had left her with a one percent chance, and she was going to take it. From that moment, no amount of discouragement from well-meaning friends who didn't want her to be disappointed had any effect on her. Never once did she veer from confessing out loud Psalm 91 and another Scripture promise that she had found:—*"My child will live, and not die, and declare the wonderful works of God (Psalm 118:17)."* A treasured book that was very important to Sloan during this time was *Supernatural Childbirth* by Jackie Mize.

A strange look came on the technician's face the next week as she administered the ultrasound. She immediately called for the physician. Her reaction was a little disconcerting to Sloan until she heard the words—*"Doctor, I think you need to come here quickly. I've just found a six-week old fetus!"* It was nothing short of a miracle that such severe, invasive procedures had not damaged or destroyed this delicate beginning stage of life. When I look at my grandson, it is hard to imagine life without him. I thank God for a daughter-in-law who believes in her covenant and is not ashamed *to confess it out loud* in the face of every negative report.

Our part of this protection covenant is expressed in verses one and two—"he who *dwells…*" and "he who *says…*" This releases His power to bring about the promises in verses three through sixteen.

Chapter 3

Two-Way Deliverance

For it is He who delivers you from the snare of the trapper and from the deadly pestilence.   –Psalm 91:3

HAVE YOU EVER SEEN a movie where a fur trapper travels deep into the mountains in the cold climate? He baits big, steel traps, covers them over with branches and then waits for some unsuspecting animal to step into the trap. Those traps were not there by chance. The trapper had taken great care in placing them in very strategic locations.

That is a picture of what the enemy does to us. That's why he is called the *trapper!* The traps set for us are not there by accident. It is as if your name is on it. They are custom made, placed and baited specifically for each one of us. But like an animal caught in a trap, it is a slow, painful process. You don't die instantly. You are ensnared until the trapper comes to destroy you.

The enemy knows exactly what will most likely hook us, and he knows exactly which *thought* to put into our minds to lure us into the trap. That is why Paul tells us in 2 Corinthians 2:11 that we are *"...not to be ignorant of the schemes (traps) of the enemy."* Then he says:

> For the weapons of our warfare are not of the flesh but divinely powerful for the destruction of fortresses. We are destroying speculations and every lofty thing raised up against the knowledge of God, and we are taking every thought captive to the obedience of Jesus Christ.
>
> –2 Corinthians 10:4-5

God not only delivers us from the snare laid by the trapper (Satan), but according to the last part of verse three, He also delivers us from the deadly *pestilence.* I always thought a pestilence was something that attacked crops—bugs, locusts, grasshoppers, spider mites, mildew and root rot. After doing a word study on the word *pestilence,* however, I found, to my surprise, that pestilence attacks people—not crops! A pestilence is any lethal disease.

Webster's New World Dictionary says pestilence is *"any virulent or fatal disease; an epidemic that hits the masses of people—any deadly disease that attaches itself to one's body with the intent to destroy."* But, God says, *"I will deliver you from the deadly disease that comes with the intent to destroy."*

There are all kinds of enemies: temptations, spiritual enemies, and physical enemies. Initially, I was in a quandary wondering if God really meant *literal* pestilence. It took me awhile to see the internal workings of warfare in the body as a parallel concept with disease. Only man tries to choose between physical and spiritual deliverance; the Scripture encases both. (Notice how Jesus demonstrates that His power operates at all levels with a very literal, physical fulfillment in Matthew 8:16-17). When evil is served it looks the same on the platter. Scripture deals with both through clear verses that promise physical healing and literal deliverance.

God is so good to confirm His Word when one seeks Him with an open heart. Right after I had received the dream about Psalm 91 and was trying to digest all of these protection promises and comprehend the fact that God is the One who always sends good and not evil, Satan was on the other end trying to discourage my faith at every turn. Because I was very young in my conviction and struggling hard to maintain it in the midst of a world that does not believe in the supernatural *goodness* of God, I was devastated when a thought came into my mind one morning as I was getting ready to go to church. *"If God wants us to walk in health, why did He create germs?"* That one thought was attempting to completely dismantle my faith in this *new-found truth* that God had provided healing in the atonement. In fact, I was so distraught that I didn't even think I could motivate myself to go to church that morning. I remember I went into my bedroom and literally fell on my face before God, asking Him how those two facts could possibly be reconciled. As clear as a bell, God spoke in my spirit, "*Trust Me, get up and go, and I will give you an answer.*" I got up with mixed emotions. I had unmistakably heard God speak to my spirit, but I could see no way in which He could satisfactorily resolve the question that had struck in my head. *Why would God create a germ to make us sick, if He did, in fact, want us to walk in divine health?*

I went to church that morning under a cloud of heaviness, and I couldn't tell you what subject the pastor preached on. But, somewhere in the middle of his sermon he made a random statement, "God made everything good. Take germs, for instance—germs are nothing more than microscopic plants and animals that *the enemy* perverted and uses to spread disease." Then, he just stopped and with a very strange look on his face said, "I have no idea where that thought came from. It was not in my notes," and went right on with his sermon. I must admit I almost disturbed the entire service because I couldn't keep from bouncing up and down on the pew. The awesomeness of God was more than I could take in without it erupting out of me. God could not have done anything that would have strengthened my faith for healing more than that incident did that morning.

Do you sometimes feel you have opposition facing you from every side? This verse is addressing the enemy's assignments from both the physical, as well as the spiritual. One of our family members went to a certain country as a missionary and made the comment, "This is a country where there are numerous ways to die." Both the poor health conditions and the hostility in the country provided many dangers. There are enemies that attack your mind (thoughts), some that attack your body (germs) and some who attack you physically (people). This is your verse that ensures your deliverance from all the varieties of harm.

Consider with me one more area of physical protection from harm. When Jesus sent the disciples out, He gave these instructions, *"I send you out as sheep among wolves. Be as wise as serpents, but be harmless as doves (Matthew 10:16)."* It is an interesting piece of information to be told to have the cleverness of a snake (in order not to be harmed), but also the innocence of a dove (in order not to cause harm).

Each year at the Texas Rattlesnake Show, snakes are skillfully handled to educate and entertain the audience. Often the pit is several feet deep in snakes. Before milking the snake of its poison, the rattlesnake handlers slice open the thick, scaly skin covering with its agile muscular structure and pry open the snake's mouth to reveal the fangs. After seeing the internal workings, it becomes obvious that the snake is geared for causing harm. Not so with the dove. When a hunter cleans a dove, first he pulls off the feathers. There are no thick scales, no dangerous claws, no poisonous venom… The dove has nothing in him that causes harm. In this analogy we are advised as sheep among wolves to be as clever as the snake, but as innocent as the dove. This takes care of harm in two directions. I believe you can claim the promise of this verse—for God to protect you from being harmed and from your harming innocent people. Defensively pray, for example, that God protects you from ever hitting a child on a bicycle, being involved in a wreck that kills another person, causing someone to walk away from the faith... Many a person has been traumatized from inadvertently hurting someone he never intended to hurt. God has this preventative promise in verse three for us to stand on for protection from both ways in which harm can destroy a life.

In the same way, notice the two-fold aspect to this deliverance in verse three: from the **snare of the trapper** and from the **deadly pestilence**. This covers being delivered from *temptation* and being delivered from *harm*. It *is similar to the request in the Lord's Prayer. "Lead us away from temptation and deliver us from evil."* What good would it do to be delivered from harm—only to be caught in a sin that destroys us? On the other hand, what good would it do to be delivered from a sin—only to be destroyed by a deadly pestilence? This verse covers both. Thank God for His deliverance from both *traps* and *pestilence*.

Chapter 4

Under His Wings

He will cover you with His pinions, and under His wings, you may seek refuge. —Psalm 91:4a

WHEN YOU PICTURE a magnificent flying bird, it is usually not a chicken that comes to mind. I've never seen a chicken pictured in flight—many eagles, but no chickens. We quote the Scripture from Isaiah 40:31 that talks about being borne up on the wings of eagles or with wings like eagles. There is a difference, however, between being "on" His wings and being "under" His wings. This promise in Psalm 91 is not elaborating on the *flying* wing—but on the *sheltering* wing. One indicates strength and accomplishment, while the other denotes protection and familiarity. When you picture the warmth of a nest and the security of being under the wings of the nurturing love of a mother hen with chicks, it paints a vivid picture of the sheltering wing of God's protection that the psalmist refers to in this passage.

Is everyone protected under the wings? Did you notice it says He will cover you with His pinions (feathers), and under His wings, you *may* seek refuge? Again, it's up to us to make that decision! We can seek refuge under His wings, if we *choose* to.

The Lord gave me a vivid picture of what it means to seek refuge under His wings. My husband, Jack, and I live out in the country, and one spring our old mother hen hatched a brood of baby chickens. One afternoon when they were scattered all over the yard, I suddenly saw the shadow of a hawk overhead. I then noticed something very unique that taught me a lesson I will never forget. That mother hen did not run to those little chicks and jump on top of them to try to cover them with her wings. No!

Instead, she squatted down, spread out her wings and began to cluck. And those little chickens, from every direction, came running *to her* to get under those outstretched wings. Then, she pulled her wings down tight, tucking every little chick safely under her. To get to those babies, the hawk would have to have gone through the mother.

When I think of those baby chicks running to their mother, I realize it is under His (God's) wings where we *may* seek refuge—but we have to run to Him. *"He will cover you with His pinions, and under His wings, you may seek refuge."* That one little word **may** is a strong word! It is up to us! All that mother hen did was cluck and expand her wings to tell them where to come.

> *Oh, Jerusalem, Jerusalem... How often I wanted to gather your children together, the way a hen gathers her chicks under her wings, and you were unwilling.*
> –Matthew 23:37

Notice the contrast between His willingness and our unwillingness—His *wanting to* against our *not willing to*—His *would* against our *would not*. What an amazing analogy to show us theologically that there is protection offered that we don't accept!

It is interesting that Jesus uses the correlation of maternal love to demonstrate His attachment to us. There is a certain fierceness to motherly-love we cannot overlook. God is deeply committed to us—yet, at the same time, we can reject His outstretched arms if we so choose. It is available, but not automatic. God does not run here and there, trying to cover us. He said, *"I have made protection possible. You run to Me!"* And, when we do run to Him in faith, **the enemy will have to go through God to get to us!** What a comforting thought!

Chapter 5

A Mighty Fortress Is My God

His faithfulness is a shield and bulwark.   –Psalm 91:4b

I T IS *GOD'S FAITHFULNESS* to His promises that is our shield. It is not just *our* faithfulness! God will be faithful to the promises He has made. When the enemy comes to whisper fearful or condemning thoughts in our mind, we can ward off his attack by saying, *"My faith is strong because I know My God is faithful, and His faithfulness is my shield!"*

How often I've heard people say, *"I can't dwell in the shelter of God. I mess up and fall short too many times. I feel guilty and unworthy."* God knows all about our weaknesses. That's why He gave His Son. We can no more earn this protection, or deserve it, than we can earn or deserve our salvation. The main thing is—if we slip and fall, we must not stay down. Get up, repent and get back under that shield of protection. Thankfully this verse says it is His faithfulness, not ours, that is our shield.

If we are faithless, He remains faithful; for He cannot deny Himself. —2 Timothy 2:13

We must not point to what we've done, or haven't done. We must point to what Jesus has done for us. We dwell in His shelter by faith in God's grace (Ephesians 2:8-9). And faith is not hard. It is simply our response to what Jesus has already provided through His Blood. We cannot perform enough good deeds to keep ourselves in His shelter anymore than we can do enough to keep ourselves saved. We have to realize we dwell in His shelter, not in our own righteousness, but in the righteousness of Jesus Christ.

*For by His doing, you are **in Christ Jesus who became to us** wisdom from God, and **righteousness**...* —1 Corinthians 1:30

There is a difference, however, between making an occasional mistake and staying in willful sin. Self-will and rebellion will keep us out of the secret place of protection because self-will is a wall we build between God and us.

Our daughter slipped and fell face down in the busiest 4-way intersection in our city. Embarrassment made her want to keep lying there so she didn't have to look up and show her face to so many people who would know her in a small town. Yet, the worst thing she could have done was to lie there in that heavy traffic area. This is a humorous illustration of what it looks like when we fall spiritually. When you think of my daughter lying face down in the middle of the street, don't ever forget that the worst thing you can do after you fall spiritually is **fail to get up!**

Psalm 91:4b expresses again God's commitment and faithfulness to being our shield of protection. It is His faithfulness that gets us back on our feet and moving again. His unshakable faithfulness is a literal shield. I have this awesome mental picture of a huge shield in front of me, completely hiding me from the enemy. And, the shield is God Himself. His faithfulness to His promises guarantees us that His shield will remain forever steadfast and available, but whether or not we stay behind the protection of that shield is our choice.

Dunkirk, in World War II, is another example. During the dreadful, yet heroic week in May of 1940, when the British army had been forced into total retreat and lay exposed on the sandy shores of Dunkirk, many miracles occurred. Lying hopelessly exposed, pinned down by Nazi planes and heavy artillery, and armed only with their rifles, the brave troops were seemingly trapped by the channel with no place to turn for protection. A British chaplain told of lying face down in the sand for what seemed an eternity on the shell-torn beach at Dunkirk. Nazi bombers dropped their lethal charges causing shrapnel to kick up sand all around him while other planes repeatedly strafed his position with their machine guns blazing.

Although dazed by the concussions around him, the British chaplain suddenly became aware that, in spite of the deafening roar of the shells and bombs falling all around him, he had not been hit. With bullets still raining down about him, he stood and stared with amazement at the outline of his own shape in the sand. It was the only smooth and undisturbed spot on the entire bullet-riddled beach. His heavenly shield must have fit the exact shape of his body.

Psalm 91:4b also tells us that God's faithfulness is our *bulwark*. According to *Nelson's Bible Dictionary*, "*a bulwark is a tower built along a city wall from which defenders shoot arrows and hurl large stones at the enemy.*" Think about that! From that tower, God is faithful to point out the enemy so he can't sneak up on our blind side. Note that this verse declares God's faithfulness to us as both a shield and a bulwark in a two-layered analogy. The passage is using two images of fortification and protection. God is our tower—our wall of protection in a collective sense; and He is our shield—a very personal and individualized defense. This verse indicates *double* protection.

Chapter 6

I Will Not Fear The Terror

You will not be afraid of *the terror by night*...–Psalm 91:5a

I T IS INTERESTING to note that verses five and six of Psalm 91 cover an entire 24 hour period emphasizing *day and night* protection. But, what is more important is that these two verses encompass **every evil known to man**.

The psalmist divides the list into four categories. We will look at those categories one at a time, chapter by chapter. The first—*terror by night*—includes all the evils that come through man: kidnapping, robbery, rape, murder, terrorism, wars…! It is the dread—or horror—or alarm that comes from what man can do to you. God is saying, *"You will not be afraid of any of those things…because they will not approach you" (Psalm 91:5-7).* The first thing verse five deals with is *fear.*

Never before in our history has there been so much talk of *terrorism* and *violence,* but to the surprise of so many people, God is not shocked or caught off guard by these things. Do we think *chemical warfare* is bigger than God?

Long before man ever discovered biological weapons, God had made provision for the protection of His people—if they would believe His Word.

These signs will accompany those who have believed…
if they drink any deadly poison, it will not hurt them.
                                                                    –Mark 16:17-18

According to the Strong's Concordance, the word *drink* in this Scripture comes from the Greek word *imbibe* which means "to drink, to absorb, to inhale or to take into the mind." No evil has been conceived by man against which God has not provided a promise of protection for any of his children who will choose to believe and act on it.

What about the fear that has come on mankind regarding our polluted water supplies, foods contaminated by pesticides…? I believe the Word of God advocates using wisdom, but all the precautions in the world cannot protect us from every harmful thing that could be in our food and water. Therefore, God's instruction to bless our food and water before eating is not merely some ritual to make us look more spiritual. Rather, it is another provision for our safety, playing an important role in God's protective plan.

But the Spirit explicitly says that in later times...men will advocate abstaining from food, which God has created to be gratefully shared in by those who believe and know the truth. For everything created by God is good, and nothing is to be rejected, if it is received with gratitude; for it is sanctified by means of the Word of God and prayer.   –I Timothy 4:1-5

But you shall serve the Lord your God, and He will bless your bread and your water; and He will remove sickness from your midst.   –Exodus 23:25

It is the goodness of God that He made provision before we ever asked! This is not for everyone; it is for those who *know and believe the truth.* Blessing the food with gratitude literally brings about sanctification—a cleansing of our food and water.

Over and over Jesus told us, "Do not fear!" Why do you think He continually reminds us not to be afraid? Because it is through faith in His Word that we are protected—and since fear is the opposite of faith, the Lord knows fear will keep us from operating in the faith that is necessary to receive. It is no wonder God addresses *the fear of terror* first.

So, how do we keep from being afraid? Very simply! Fear comes when we think we are responsible for bringing about this protection ourselves. Too often, we think—"*Oh, if I can just believe hard enough, maybe I'll be protected!*" That's wrong thinking! The protection is already there. It has already been provided, whether we receive it or not. Faith is simply the **choice to receive** what Jesus has *already* done. The Bible has classic examples of how to deal with fear.

The answer is in the *Blood of Jesus.* Exodus 12:23 tells us when Israel put blood on the door facings, the Destroyer could not come in. The animal blood they used then serves as a *type and shadow,* or a picture, of the Blood of Jesus which ratifies our *better* protection—under our *better* Covenant.

When we confess out loud, *"I am protected by the Blood of Jesus"*—and believe it, the devil literally cannot come in! Remember verse two tells us, *"I will say…the Lord is my refuge and my fortress."* It is *heart and mouth*—believing with our heart and confessing with our mouth.

Our physical weapons are operated with our hands, but we operate our *spiritual* weapons with our mouths. The Blood is applied by *saying it* in faith. Confessing with our mouth and believing with our heart starts with the new birth experience and sets precedence for receiving all of God's good gifts (Romans 10:9-10).

If we find ourselves being afraid of the *terror by night* that is our barometer to let us know we are not dwelling and abiding up close to the Lord in the shelter of the Most

High and believing His promises. Fear comes in when we are confessing things other than what God has said. When our eyes are not on God, fear will come. But let that fear be a reminder to repent.

We walk by faith, not by sight.   −2 Corinthians 5:7

We have to choose to believe His Word more than we believe what we see—more than we believe the terror attack. Not that we deny the existence of the attack. The attack may be very real, but God wants our faith in His Word to become more of a reality to us than what we see in the natural.

For example, gravity is a fact! No one denies the existence of gravity, but just as the law of aerodynamics can supersede the law of gravity, Satan's attacks can also be superseded by a higher law—the law of faith and obedience to God's Word. Faith does not deny the existence of *terror*. There are simply higher laws in the Bible for overcoming it.

David did not deny the existence of the giant. Fear has us compare the size of the giant to ourselves. Faith, on the other hand, had David compare the size of the giant to the size of his God. David's eyes saw *the giant*, but his faith saw *the promises* (I Samuel 17).

Our daughter had a friend, Julee, living in an apartment in Fort Worth, Texas. She was getting ready for church one Sunday morning when someone knocked on her door. Never dreaming it wasn't someone she knew, she opened the door, only to be almost knocked over by a strange man who shoved his way in and attacked her.

Julee started using the Word of God as her defense. In the natural, there was no way for a young girl to escape from a strong man, but confidence in her God allowed her not to give up!

It took forty-five minutes of spiritual battle as he came at her time after time. But, her persistence in quoting these words out of Psalm 91 brought confusion and immobility on him, thwarting every attempted attack. And, during one of those times when he was at a standstill, she was able to get out the door and escape unharmed.

Later, after he was apprehended and held in custody, she found out he had sexually assaulted numerous young women, and she was the only one of his victims who had been able to escape without harm. We do not have to be afraid of the terror *of what man can do to harm us.* Praise God for our higher law! God's laws triumph over man's laws.

Chapter 7

I Will Not Fear The Arrow

You will not be afraid of... *the arrow* that flies by day.
—Psalm 91:5b

THE SECOND CATEGORY of evil is the *arrow that flies by day*. An arrow is something that pierces or wounds spiritually, physically, mentally or emotionally. This category indicates that you are in a spiritual battle zone—specific enemy assignments that are directed toward your life to defeat you.

Arrows are deliberately sent by the enemy and meticulously aimed at the spot that will cause the most damage. They are targeted toward the area where our mind is not renewed by the Word of God—perhaps an area where we are still losing our temper, or an area where we are still easily offended, or perhaps, an area of rebellion or fear.

Seldom does the enemy attack us in an area where we are built up and strong. He attacks us where we're still struggling. That's why we have to run to God! And when we do battle using our spiritual weapons, his arrows will not approach us.

God tells us in Ephesians 6:12 that we have a *"shield of faith to extinguish all the **flaming** darts of the enemy."* These are not just plain arrows, they are "on fire". And, God doesn't say we can miss most of them. He says that we can extinguish *"all"* of them. When arrows are sent to wound us spiritually, physically, emotionally or financially, God wants us to ask and believe by faith that He *will pick us up out of harm's way* and deliver us from calamity.

Long before my husband and I moved into full-time ministry, we owned and operated a soft drink bottling plant that his dad had started the year before Jack was born. Several years before we sold the business, one of the other bottling plants in our area changed management, and the new manager told us he was going to spare no expense in putting us out of business.

He told the truth! We could never have anticipated how much money he was going to spend trying to fulfill his promise. He literally went all over town, placing free vending machines wherever our venders were located, and store owners were continually calling us to come and pick up our equipment. Financially, there was no way to compete, especially when the manager also started product price-cutting and flooding the market with advertising. The outlook in the natural was pretty dismal, but, we had something he didn't have. We had a *covenant* with God, telling us *not to be afraid of the arrow that flies by day.*

And, God is faithful. Those arrows—or circumstances—that had looked impossible for us to overcome, finally passed, and our business was left standing long after the competition was gone. The competitor had obviously expected our business to fold quickly under the intense financial pressure, but, when we were able to survive longer than he anticipated, it was *he* who went under financially.

We have a covenant with God telling us not to be afraid of the arrow that flies by day. Assignments will rise up, but don't be afraid. He has promised to protect us and He has promised the arrows will not hit their target.

Chapter 8

I Will Not Fear The Pestilence

You will not be afraid of the *pestilence* that stalks in darkness. 　　　　　　　　　　　　 -Psalm 91:6a

FEAR GRIPPED MY heart and beads of perspiration popped out on my forehead as I feverishly ran my fingers over what felt like a lump in my body. How I dreaded that monthly self-examination the doctor had suggested. My fingertips were as cold as ice from the panic I had worked up just thinking about what I might find, and the turn my life would take from there.

On that particular day it turned out to be a false alarm, but the dread of what I might find in the coming months was constantly in the back of my mind until this promise came alive in my heart. If you fight fears of fatal diseases, then this is the Scripture for you to take hold of.

The third category of evil that God names is **pestilence**. This is the only evil He names twice! Since God doesn't waste words, He must have a specific reason for repeating this promise.

Have you noticed when a person says something more than once, it is usually because he wants to emphasize a point? God knew the pestilence and the fear that would be running rampant in these end days. The world is teeming with fatal epidemics that are hitting people by the thousands, so God catches our attention by repeating this promise.

It's as though God is saying, *"I said it in verse three, but did you really hear Me? Just to be sure, I am saying it again in verse six—you do not have to be afraid of the deadly pestilence!"* This is so contrary to the world in which we live that we have to renew our thinking before we can comprehend the fact we do not have to be afraid of the sicknesses and diseases that are epidemic in the world today.

When I first started studying this psalm, I remember thinking, *"I don't know whether I have the faith to believe these promises!"* This thought stretched my faith and my mind until I thought it would snap like a rubber band that was being pulled too tightly.

God, however, reminded me that faith is not a feeling. Faith is simply *choosing* to believe what He says in His Word.

The more I chose to believe God's Word, the more I had a *knowing* I could trust and rely on it completely.

> *Heaven and earth will pass away, but My Words will not pass away.* —Mark 13:31

Our inheritance is not limited to what is handed down to us genetically from our ancestors. Our inheritance can be what Jesus provided for us if we believe the Word and put it to work.

> *Christ redeemed us from the curse of the law having become a curse for us...* —Galatians 3:13

The pestilence mentioned here in Psalm 91 is spelled out in detail in Deuteronomy 28. This scripture in Galatians tells us we are *redeemed* from every curse (including pestilence), if we will simply believe and appropriate the promise.

In Bible days when they mentioned pestilence, they were thinking of diseases like leprosy. Luke 21:11 states that part of the signs of the end times is an outbreak of pestilence. And, today we have many widespread diseases such as Alzheimer's, cancer, heart disease... But, no matter what pestilence we might be facing, His promise never ceases to be true. The enemy may try to cause sudden surprises to catch us unaware and knock us down, but God is faithful. His Word is true no matter what the circumstances look like. I shudder to think what we might open ourselves up to without the promise of Psalm 91 and without the determination to stand firm and refuse to entertain fearful thoughts.

I wish I had kept a diary through the years of the healing miracles that I have seen personally. I remember the night our son was born and we were told he had a lung disease and could not be taken out of the incubator, even to be fed. After we got over the initial shock, God seemed to just drop faith in our hearts and there was never another question in our minds whether or not he would be normal. Two perfectly healthy lungs demonstrated God's healing power.

I remember when Mary Ann, a friend of mine with three incurable diseases, was practically carried into one of my Bible study meetings and laid on the couch. Her little eighty-seven-pound body looked beyond hope, but the group prayers that morning incited a miracle and thirty years later she was still alive. She often showed the picture on her old driver's license to illustrate the shocking difference in her appearance.

I remember the night that a member of the staff at the Texas Youth Commission approached my husband and daughter. He had been listening to their Bible studies each Monday night and wanted prayer. Two tests showed his unborn child to have Down's Syndrome, but he and his wife had chosen against the recommendation to have the baby aborted and just wanted Jack and Angie to pray for them as parents. Instead, they asked if they could pray that God would bring forth a miracle. Several months later his wife gave birth to a completely whole and healthy baby. Time and space prevent my sharing all the wonderful miracles I have witnessed through the years—some instantaneous, some through a miracle process, but all brought about by the hand of God.

What we allow our mind to dwell on is *our* choice. Therefore, if we desire to operate in this protection covenant, taking authority over negative thoughts and emotions is imperative. It is amazing how the simple phrase, *"I am just not going there,"* will dispel those fears immediately.

I'm sure this promise of protection from plagues and pestilence reminds you of Israel's complete immunity from the Egyptian plagues in the land of Goshen. The destroyer could not come in where the blood was applied. The Bible claims that over one million people in the wilderness did not get sick. Even before the completed work on the cross, the Old Testament covenant declared, *"You will not be afraid of the pestilence that stalks in darkness—it will not approach you."*

Chapter 9

I Will Not Fear The Destruction

You will not be afraid of the *destruction* that lays waste at noon.
                                                    –Psalm 91:6b

THIS FOURTH CATEGORY of evil is **destruction**. Destruction takes in the *evils over which mankind has no control*—those things that the world ignorantly calls *acts of God:* tornadoes, floods, hurricanes, fire…! God very plainly tells us that we are not to fear destruction. These natural disasters are not coming from God.

In Mark 4:39, Jesus rebuked the storm and it became perfectly calm, demonstrating that God is not the author of such things—otherwise, Jesus would never have contradicted His Father by rebuking something sent by Him.

There is no place in the physical world where you can go and be safe from every *destruction*—every natural disaster. We can never anticipate what might come when we least expect it. But, no matter where you are in the world, God says to run to His shelter where *you will not be afraid of the destruction...it will not approach you!*

Late one night, soon after building our new home in the country, we were faced with a severe weather alert. The local radio station was warning that a tornado had been sited just south of the country club—the exact location of our property. We could see several of the React Club vehicles parked on the road below our hill as the members watched the funnel cloud that seemed to be headed straight for our house.

I had never seen such a strange, eerie color in the night sky or experienced such a deafening silence in the atmosphere. You could literally feel the hair on your body standing on end. Some of our son's friends were visiting, and, to their surprise, Jack quickly ordered our family to get outside with our Bibles and start circling the house—reading Psalm 91 and taking authority. Jack had the children out speaking directly to the storm, just like Jesus did.

The weird silence suddenly turned into a roar, with torrents of rain coming down in what seemed like bucketfuls, rather than drops. Finally, Jack got a peace that the danger had passed, even though by sight nothing had changed.

We walked back into the house just in time to hear the on-location radio announcer exclaim with so much excitement that he was almost shouting, *"This is nothing short of a miracle—the funnel cloud south of the Brownwood Country Club has suddenly lifted back in the sky and vanished before our very eyes."*

You should have seen those kids jumping and hollering. It was the friends' first time to observe the supernatural at work. Their surprise, however, was no greater than that of the professor the next day when he asked the students what they were doing during the storm. Several said that they were in the bathtub under a mattress—some were in closets and one was in a storm cellar!

You can imagine the astonishment when he got around to our daughter, Angie, who said, "With the tornado headed our direction, my family was circling the house, quoting from Psalm 91—we *will not be afraid of the destruction that lays waste...it will not approach us."*

***

Did you know that every extreme evil known to man will fall into one of these four categories that we have named in chapters six through nine (verses 5-6): terror, arrows, pestilence, or destruction? And the amazing thing is that God has offered us deliverance from them all!

God lets us know in Psalm 91, *"You will not be afraid of* **terror**, **arrows**, **pestilence** *or* **destruction** *because I have said in My Word that* **it will not approach you**—*if you are obedient to* *verses one and two to dwell in My shelter and abide in My shadow."* And, of course, we cannot dwell and abide in Him apart from Jesus. But, praise God!—because of the shed Blood of the Cross, it has now been made possible.

We can receive anything that God has already provided. The secret is knowing that *everything for which God has made provision* is clearly spelled out and defined in the Word of God. If you can find where God has offered it— you can have it! It is never God holding it back. His provision is already there—waiting to be received.

Faith is not a tool to manipulate God into giving you something *you* want. Faith is simply the means by which we accept what God has already made available.

Our goal needs to be the *renewal* of our minds, to such an extent that we have more faith in God's Word than in what we see. God does not make promises that are out of our reach.

When the Lord first began showing me these promises and my mind was struggling with doubt, He took me to a portion of His Word that helped to set me free.

> *What then? If some did not believe, their unbelief will not nullify the faithfulness of God, will it? May it never be! Rather, let God be found true, though every man be found a liar, as it is written: that thou mightest prevail when thou art judged.* —Romans 3:3-4

God is telling us that, even though there may be some who don't believe, their unbelief will never nullify His promises to the ones who do believe. A very important part of that verse in Romans 3 is the reminder, in a quote from the Old Testament, that what we as individuals choose to believe and confess will determine our own individual judgment.

Without the promises of protection throughout the Word of God, and especially, without our Psalm 91 covenant—listing all of the protection promises in one chapter—we might feel rather presumptuous, if, on our own, we prayed *asking* God to protect us from all the things covered in these four categories. In fact, we probably would not have the nerve to ask for all of that, but God is so good. **He offered this protection to us before we even had a chance to ask!** It was God's plan to provide protection for His children, even before the foundation of the world.

Chapter 10

Though A Thousand Fall

A thousand may fall at your side and ten thousand at your right hand; but it shall not approach you.   –Psalm 91:7

DO WE EVER STOP to consider what this is saying to us? Do we have the courage to trust God's Word enough to believe **that He means this literally?** And, is it possible for it to be true, and yet still miss out on these promises? Jesus answers the last question in Luke 4:27, *"There were many lepers in Israel in the time of Elijah, but none of them was cleansed."* Only Naaman, the Syrian, was healed when he obeyed in faith. **Not everyone will receive the benefits of this promise in Psalm 91.** Only those who believe God and hold fast to His promises will profit; none-the-less, it *is* available. And to the measure we trust Him, we will in the same measure reap the benefits of that trust.

What an awesome statement! God wants us to know that even though there will be a thousand falling by our side and ten thousand at our right hand, it does not negate the promise that destruction will not approach the one who chooses to believe and trust His Word. The *Amplified Bible* says, "...*it shall not approach you for any purpose*" *(emphasis added)*. He means exactly what He says.

It is no accident that this little statement is tucked right here in the middle of the psalm. Have you noticed how easy it is to become fearful when disaster starts striking all around you? We begin to feel like Peter must have felt as he walked on the water to Jesus. It is easy to see how he started sinking with the waves when he saw all the turbulence of the storm going on around him.

God knew there would be times when we would hear so many negative reports, see so many needs and encounter so much danger around us that we would feel overwhelmed. That is why He warned us ahead of time that *thousands would be falling all around us.* He didn't want us to be caught off guard. But, at that point, we have a choice to make. The ball is then in our court! We can either choose to run to His shelter in faith and it will not approach us or we can passively live our lives the way the world does, not realizing there is something we can do about it.

What tremendous insight, after our minds have been renewed by the Word of God, to realize, contrary to the world's thinking, that we do not have to be among *the ten thousand who fall at our right hand.*

Psalm 91 is the *preventive* measure that God has given to His children against every evil known to mankind. No place else in the Word are all of the protection promises (including help from angels, as well as promises ensuring our authority) accumulated in one covenant to offer such a total package for living in this world. It is both an *offensive* and *defensive measure* to ward off every evil before it has had time to strike. This is not only a *cure*, but a plan for *complete prevention!*

A year after Hurricane Ivan hit, Jack and I stayed at the beach home of our friends, John and Virginia Loyd in Orange Beach, Alabama. For one week we just drove through the area, appalled at the devastation we saw—even after that many months of repairs had taken place. A stone's throw from their house all the decking at the public boat docks, the gigantic dry dock building, and the restaurant glass had all been blown away. What was left of the marina building was under three feet of water. On the other side of the house, we saw what once was a shopping center had been reduced to a pile of rubble. Condos and hotels were completely gutted. Even after that length of time, mounds of siding and roofing shingles from the homes next to our friends' beach house still littered the adjacent properties.

Only after seeing the destruction with our own eyes did we realize the supernatural protection the Loyds had received. Prior to and during the hurricane the year before, they had called us declaring their total trust in the Lord's Psalm 91 covenant promise of protection and getting us to join in faith with them. **When they returned to the area there was NO damage to their beach house or property.** When a hurricane passes over, flooding brings much of the destruction because the water goes everywhere. Only God knows how He kept the water out of their beach home! The Word works! And, did I mention that at the time, the Loyds also owned a beachfront condo just three blocks away that was for sale. In spite of the fact that the condo was directly on the ocean, when John opened the door to the condo not even a picture on the wall had been disturbed nor was the (not covered with plywood) patio glass broken. Yet, the eye of Hurricane Ivan had gone directly over the top of their building. Coincidence? If you had driven down Beach Rd (even a year later, when we did) you would know that it was nothing but the power of God's protection that had shielded them. Praise God! Psalm 91 is not limited to areas where hurricanes can't reach. We can even be immune in the midst of mass destruction.

You will only look on with your eyes, and see the recompense of the wicked. —Psalm 91:8

You will see recompense (payment) being doled out at times. There is judgment. There is justice. Every sin will be exposed sooner or later and paid for. An evil dictator falls, an unrighteous aggressor is stopped, a tyrant faces his crimes against humanity, a wrong is rectified—*the recompense of the wicked speaks of justice.* Wars have been fought where one side had a righteous cause, and eventually, good won over evil. The justness of God is that evil will not triumph—that Hitlers do not win—that communistic governments fall—that darkness does not extinguish light.

This verse says that we will "*only look on and see*" it happening. The word "only" denotes a protection of only seeing and not experiencing the evil; and it denotes detachment in that the evil we see does not get inside of us. We are set apart in that we do not allow our enemy's hate to change us.

Let's look for just a moment at this Scripture with our faith in mind. Do we sometimes fall short into unbelief? Faith in God, in His Son Jesus Christ and in His Word is *counted* in God's eyes as righteousness. But, when we are in unbelief, to a degree we are placing ourselves in the category of the *wicked.* Sometimes, even as a Christian, I have been an *unbelieving* believer when it comes to receiving *all* of God's

Word. Jesus says in Matthew 5:18, *"Not the smallest letter or stroke of His Word will pass away until it is all accomplished."* Even if believers have never utilized this psalm in its full potential the truth has never passed away or lost one ounce of its power.

Many people think of the Gospel as an insurance policy, securing only their eternity and their comfort after disaster strikes. They are depriving themselves of so much. Perhaps, we all need to ask ourselves the question, *"What kind of coverage do I have—fire or life?"* God's Word is more than just an escape from Hell; it is a handbook for living a victorious *life* in this world.

There is a difference, however, between the destruction that comes from the enemy and persecution for the Gospel's sake. 2 Timothy 3:12 tells us, *"all who desire to live godly in Christ Jesus will be persecuted."* There are times when we will be mistreated because of our stand for the cause of Christ. But, persecution for living a Godly life is totally different from the evil talked about in Psalm 91. Psalm 91 is not dealing with persecution. Jesus suffered persecution, but He did not have calamity, disaster and mishap. Accidents never even approached Him.

> *A thousand may fall at your side and ten thousand at your right hand, but it shall not approach you...for you have made the Lord, my refuge, even the Most High, your dwelling place.* —Psalm 91:9

Have you ever been in spiritual warfare where it seemed that everyone was falling around you? If this verse isn't a description of actual combat, I don't know what is—yet, tied to it is a promise of protection beyond anything that can be envisioned. There is a place where calamity literally does not even approach us. This concept is hard to imagine in a peaceful season of life—yet, how much more remarkable is this promise when it's given in connection with the spiritual battle described above. The portrayal of people falling is directly connected to the promise that it will *not even come near us.* Two opposite poles joined together! This psalm is making its strongest offer of protection right in the midst of chaos. And, it is a type of protection that stands in a category all its own.

Too many people see Psalm 91 as a beautiful promise that they file right alongside all of their other good quality reading material and it makes them feel comforted every time they read it. But, I do not want anyone to read this book and fail to see the *superior significance* to these promises in this psalm. These are not written for our inspiration, but for our protection. These are not words of comfort *in* affliction, but words of deliverance *from* affliction.

Chapter 11

No Plague Comes Near My Family

No evil will befall you, nor will any plague or calamity come near your dwelling.　　　　　　　−Psalm 91:10

ARE YOU WORRIED ABOUT your family? This part of Psalm 91 addresses that very concern. After God repeats our part of the condition in verse nine, He then re-emphasizes the promise in verse ten: "*...nor will it come near your dwelling place (your household).*" It is at this point in the psalm that the Bible makes this covenant more comprehensive than just being about ourselves!

God has just *added a new dimension* to the promise: the opportunity to exercise faith, not only for ourselves, but also for the protection of our entire household. If these promises were only available to us as individuals, it would not be very comforting. Because God has created within us both an instinct to be protected and a need to protect those who belong to us, He has assured us here that these promises are for you *and your household.*

It appears that the Old Testament leaders had a better understanding of this concept than we who are under the New Covenant. That is why Joshua chose for himself *and for his household.*

*If it is disagreeable in your sight to serve the Lord, then choose for yourselves today whom you will serve; but as for me **and my house**, we will serve the Lord.*
—Joshua 24:15

As Joshua made the decision that his household would serve God with him, he was influencing their destiny and declaring their protection at the same time. In much the same way, Rahab bargained with the Israelite spies for her whole family (Joshua 2:13).

When our hearts are truly steadfast and when we are trusting in His faithfulness to fulfill His promises, we'll not be constantly afraid that something bad is going to happen to one of our family members.

You will not be afraid of evil tidings because your heart is steadfast—trusting in His Word. —Psalm 112:7

Negative expectations will begin to pass away, and we will start expecting good reports. According to this verse, we can grab our ears and proclaim, "These ears were made to hear good tidings." The fear of bad tidings can plague our very existence. That fear of the phone ringing in the night, of that knock on the door, or of the siren of an ambulance...this is the verse that gives the promise that a steadfast heart will not live in constant fear of tragic news. Someone once said, "Fear knocked, faith answered, and no one was there." When fear knocks, let your mouth say this verse out loud, *"I will not fear evil tidings, my heart is steady, trusting in you!"*

Several years ago as I was cooking breakfast, Jack walked into the kitchen with one of the glands under his chin so swollen that it looked as though he had attempted to swallow a large softball that had lodged on one side of his throat. I rushed him to a close physician friend of ours, and I thought I could tell by the expression on the doctor's face that he was concerned. But, when the first words out of his mouth were, *"I am going to call in another doctor to have a look at you,"* my worst fear was confirmed, and, I then knew he was suspecting that there was something seriously wrong.

At that point, the enemy tried to unload a whole carload of fear thoughts and fear pictures in my mind, but when God's Word has been stored in the heart, it has a way of surfacing just when it's needed. This Scripture in *Psalm 91:10* *"No evil will befall you, nor will any plague or calamity come near your dwelling"* was more than just a *comforting* thought. It brought *life* and *hope* to the situation.

I sat there in the waiting room, thanking God for this promise and rejoicing over the outcome long before the doctor ever poked his smiling face around the corner to tell me that everything was fine. It turned out to be just a sore throat that had settled in the gland on one side of Jack's throat. Even the swelling had gone down by the next morning. It is so rewarding to have Psalm 91 promises that include more than just our own life. It is a family that is under that umbrella of protection, based on the extension of this promise in verse ten that moves us from just the individual to the household.

In Matthew 13:32, Jesus makes reference to a mustard seed starting as an herb but growing into a tree with birds nesting in the branches. Others can find protection in our faith, as well, when we plant the seed of the Word.

Towns are one big collection of families, and family protection could not have been more clearly demonstrated than by what took place in Seadrift, Texas, during World War II. The town's citizens decided to pray Psalm 91 collectively over every one of their husbands, sons, grandsons, cousins, uncles and friends who were going to war. A bulletin board was made with photos of every serviceman and a commitment made that every single day intercessors would cover them in prayer. Every time they met they would read from Psalm 91.

It seemed that everyone had a family member who had gone to fight. What a testimony to this promise of family protection when every single man returned safely home from war—from all over the world. THIS TOWN DID NOT SUFFER A SINGLE COMBAT CASUALTY while so many other towns and families experienced much grief and heartache, and often, multiple casualties.

The beauty of this psalm is that when someone prays for more than himself, he brings the entire family under a shield of God's Word. It is an added dimension to us as individuals to be able to apply the richness of this covenant to our entire household. What a joy to know you have promises in Psalm 91 that will not only protect you, but also those in your family and *near your dwelling*.

I thank God for this added dimension of being able to apply *His Covenant Umbrella of Protection* for your entire household. What a joy to know that your family is safe.

Chapter 12

Angels Watching Over Me

For He will give His angels charge concerning you, to guard you in all your ways. They will bear you up in their hands, lest you strike your foot against a stone.   –Psalm 91:11-12

IN VERSES ELEVEN and twelve God makes another unique promise concerning an additional dimension of our protection. This is one of the most precious promises of God, and He put it right here in Psalm 91.

Most Christians read past this promise with very little, if any, thought about the magnitude of what is being said. Only after we get to Heaven will we realize all the things from which we were spared because of the intervention of God's angels on our behalf.

I am sure you have read stories about missionaries whose lives were spared because would-be murderers saw large bodyguards protecting them—when, in fact, there was no one there in the natural. And, we can all recall close calls where we escaped a tragedy, and there was no explanation in the natural. It is possible *"to entertain angels without knowing it"* as it says in Hebrews 13:2, but sadly, I believe most Christians have a tendency to disregard the ministry of angels altogether.

Floyd, a friend of ours who was working in the potash mines in Carlsbad, New Mexico, had the responsibility of setting off the explosives. One particular day he was ready to push the switch when someone tapped him on the shoulder. To his surprise, no one was anywhere around. Deciding that it must have been his imagination, he started once again to detonate the explosion when he felt another tap on his shoulder. Again, no one was there, so he decided to move all the ignition equipment several hundred feet back up the tunnel. When he finally plunged the charger, the whole top of the tunnel caved in exactly where he had been standing. A coincidence? You could never make our friend believe that. He knew *someone* had tapped him on the shoulder.

This verse 11 says, *"For He will give His angels charge concerning you!"* What does that mean? Think with me for a moment! Have you ever *taken charge* of a situation? When you take charge of something, you put yourself in a place of leadership. You begin telling everyone what to do and how to do it. If angels are taking charge of the things that concern us, God has given the angels, ***not the circumstances,*** the authority to act on our behalf. That same truth is repeated in Hebrews.

Are they (angels) not all ministering spirits, sent out to render service for the sake of those who will inherit salvation? —Hebrews 1:14

Have you ever been fishing on a lake in the middle of the night? Some people think that is the very best time to catch fish. When my husband was seven years old, all the people who worked for his father took their boats to Lake Brownwood to do some night fishing. Jack was placed in a boat with five adults so he would be well supervised. Since one of the men in the boat was an expert swimmer, his mother and dad thought he would be in especially good hands.

Later that night during one of the times when the boats were going back and forth to shore for bait, Jack had gotten out of his boat and into another one without anyone noticing. Then, off they went—without Jack—back onto the lake in the dark. This was back before there were rules about life jackets and lights on your fishing boats, so no one could see in the dark what actually happened. Perhaps, they hit a stump, but for some reason, the boat Jack had been in sank. All five of the people in it drowned, including the expert swimmer. Was Jack directed to another boat by *angels who serve God and are sent to help those who will receive salvation?* Until we get to heaven, we will not know the full extent of the angelic protection on our lives.

When we look to God as the source of *our* protection and provision, the angels are constantly *rendering us aid* and *taking charge* of our affairs. Psalm 103:20 says, *"His angels mighty in strength…obey the voice of His Word."* As we proclaim God's Word, the angels hasten to carry it out.

Verse eleven also says *"Angels will guard you in all your ways."* Have you ever seen a soldier standing guard, protecting someone? That soldier stands at attention: alert, watchful and ready to protect at the first sign of attack. How much more will God's angels stand *guard* over God's children, alert and ready to protect them at all times? Do we believe that? Have we ever even thought about it? Faith is what releases this promise to work on our behalf. How comforting it is to know that God has placed these heavenly guards to have charge over us.

Psalm 91 names so many different avenues through which God protects us. It is exciting to realize from this Old Testament psalm that protection is not just an idea in God's Mind—He is committed to it. Angelic protection is just another one of the *unique* ways in which God has provided that protection. What an unusual idea to add actual beings designed to protect us. He charged angels *to guard us in all our ways.*

Chapter 13

The Enemy Under My Feet

You will tread upon the lion and cobra, the young lion and the serpent (*dragon* in the KJV) you will trample down. —Psalm 91:13

HERE IN VERSE THIRTEEN God transitions to another topic. He takes us from the subject of our being protected *by Him,* and puts emphasis on *the authority in His Name* that has been given to us as believers. Make a note of the corresponding New Testament Scripture that deals with the authority that has been given to us:

> *Behold, I [Jesus] have given you authority to tread upon serpents and scorpions, and over all the power of the enemy, and nothing shall injure you.* —Luke 10:19

We, as Christians, have been given authority over the enemy. *He does not have authority over us!* We need to take the time to allow that fact to soak in! However, our authority over the enemy is not automatic.

My husband says that too many Christians *take authority* when they should be *praying*, and they *pray* when they should be *taking authority!* For the most part, Jesus prayed at night and took authority all day. When we encounter the enemy—that is not the time to start praying. We need to be already "prayed up". When we encounter the enemy, we need to be speaking forth the authority that we have in the Name of Jesus.

If a gunman suddenly faced you, would you be confident enough in your authority that you could boldly declare, *'I am in covenant with the Living God, and I have a Blood covering that protects me from anything that you might attempt to do. So, in the Name of Jesus, I command you to put down that gun!'*?

If we do not have that kind of courage, then we need to meditate on the authority Scriptures until we become confident in who we are *in Christ*. At new birth, we immediately have enough power placed at our disposal to tread upon the enemy without being harmed. Most Christians, however, either do not know it, or they fail to use it. How often do we believe the Word enough to act on it?

Now, let's look at what this verse is actually saying. What good does it do to have authority over lions and cobras unless we are in Africa or India or some exotic place like that? What does the Word mean when it says, *"We will tread on the lion, the young lion, the cobra, and the dragon?"* This is a graphic illustration of things that are potentially harmful in our daily lives. These terms are just an unforgettable means of describing the different types of satanic oppression that come against us. So, what do these terms mean to us today? Let's break them down...

First of all, there are **"lion problems"**—those problems that are bold, loud and forthright—problems that come out in the open and hit us face on. At one time or another, we have all had something come against us that was blatant and overt. It might have been a car wreck or a boss who chewed us out royally in front of our fellow employees. Or, it might have been an unexpected bill at the end of the month that caused a chain reaction of checks bouncing. Those are *lion* problems—obvious difficulties that often seem insurmountable. Yet, God says that we will tread on them—they will not tread on us.

The **"young lions"** can grow into full-grown problems if we don't handle them. These young lion problems come against us to harass and destroy gradually, like little foxes. Subtle negative thoughts that tell us we will not survive or that our spouse no longer loves us or that we are no longer in love with our mate are good examples of this category. And, those little foxes will grow into big ones if they are not taken captive and destroyed (2 Corinthians 10:4-5). Answer those little foxes with the Word of God. Small harassments, distractions and irritations are young lions.

> *Catch the foxes for us, the little foxes that are ruining the vineyards, while our vineyards are in blossom.*
> –Song of Solomon 2:15

Next, God names **"cobra"** problems. These are the problems that seem to sneak up on us like a *snake in the grass* throughout our day, while minding our own business. They are what we might call an *undercover* attack that brings sudden death—a deceptive scheme that keeps us blinded until it devours us.

How many times have you witnessed an unexpected church split or a marriage that fell apart so suddenly that you couldn't imagine what had happened—only to find out later that there had been offenses, gossip, and undermining of authority going on behind the scenes? By the time the cause was uncovered, the poison has had its effect on its victims. Puncture wounds from fangs are hard to detect, and no one sees the poison as it travels through a body, but the results are always damaging, and, oftentimes, deadly. We definitely need God's protection from *cobra* attacks.

The previous figurative examples we might have guessed, but what are the **"dragon"** problems? I looked up that Hebrew word in the *Strong's Concordance* and it listed "*sea monster.*" Fictitious or extinct—like a dragon—have you ever had a fear that was totally ungrounded? Have you ever experienced fears that were a figment of your imagination? Sure you have! We all have!

Dragon problems represent our unfounded fears— phantom fears or mirage fears. That sounds harmless enough, but are you aware that phantom fears can be as deadly as the reality fears—if we believe them?

Some people's *dragon* fears are as real to them as another person's *lion* problems. That is why it is important to define your fears. So many people spend all of their lives running from something that is not even chasing them.

The wicked flee when no one is pursuing…
–Proverbs 28:1

This verse is a good definition of phantom fears. We have had a great many people share testimonies of God's deliverance from things like fear of the unknown, fear of the dark, fear of clowns, fear of dolls, fear of vampires, fear of facing the future alone, fear of loss, fear of death, tormenting suspicions, claustrophobia, etc.

Television and horror movies have built some very realistic imaginary fears. Fantasy fears can cause us to do a lot of unnecessary running in life, so authority over *dragons* is not a mental game.

But the *Good News* is—God says that we will tread on *all* of the powers of the enemy—no matter how loud and bold, sneaky and deceptive or imaginary the fears may be. God has given us authority over all of them!

No longer are we to put up with the paralyzing fears that, at one time, gripped our hearts and left us powerless at the sight of the evil that was striking all around us. God has given us His *Power of Attorney,* and these problems now have to submit to the authority of His Name.

The word *tread* gives us a good visionary. I think of a tank crossing a brushy plain. Where the tank treads go, everything is crushed and left flat on the ground. It is a great picture of our authority over these spiritual enemies as well, treading like a tank and crushing all that is evil in our path. That is a strong description of our authority in walking over the lion, young lion, cobra and dragon.

Chapter 14

Because I Love Him

Because he has loved Me, therefore I will... –Psalm 91:14a

I N VERSES FOURTEEN THROUGH sixteen the author of the Psalm changes from talking in third person *about* God's promises to God speaking to us personally from His *secret place* and *announcing* promises in the first person. It is a dramatic shift in tone as it moves to God speaking prophetically to each one of us directly, denoting significantly more depth in the relationship. In these three verses He gives *seven promises* with as much open triumph as a man has when a woman accepts his proposal. A commitment to love involves choice. When you pick that person out of all the others, you set your love on that one and you embark on a deeper relationship. That is the picture of how God sets His love on us. In the same way, this passage challenges the reader to set his love on God. When he does, the promises come into effect and God is indulgent with His promises to the one who loves Him.

Love is the cohesiveness that binds man to God, and God will be faithful to His beloved. Love always requires presence and nearness. Special memories are birthed out of relationship. That is why this section cannot be explained, but has to be experienced. Let me give you an illustration…

Ole Red would allow herself to be picked up while in the process of laying her egg and deposit it right in Angie's eager, little hands. The children had some merit to what they advertised as the *freshest eggs in town*—a few times the egg never hit the nest. Nesting season had its own special fascination for the children as they watched Ole Red try to hatch out more eggs than she could sit on. The kids would number the eggs in pencil to ensure that each egg was properly rotated and kept warm. They would wait out the 21 days and then, with contagious delight, call me out to see the nest swarming with little ones. That ole hen had a brood of chicks that was hatched out of eggs from every hen in the henhouse.

Observing a setting hen this close had its own rare charm as one could witness the protection she gave those chicks in a way most people never have the chance to observe. I remember her feathers as she fanned them out. I remember the smell of the fresh straw the kids kept in the nest. I remember that I could see through that soft, downy underside and watch the rhythmic beating of her heart. Those chicks had an almost enviable position—something that all the books on the *theology of protection* could never explain in mere words. This was the unforgettable picture of a real life understanding of what it means to be *under the wings*. Those were some happy chicks! This lets one see in a much more intimate way that true protection has everything to do with **closeness**.

Some people acknowledge that there is a God; others *know* Him. Neither maturity, nor education, nor family heritage, nor even a lifetime as a nominal Christian can make a person "*know*" Him. Only an encounter with the Lord and time spent with Him will cause one to lay hold of the promises in these verses of Psalm 91.

We need to ask ourselves, "*Do I really love Him?*" Jesus even asked this of Peter, a close disciple, "*Peter, do you love Me (John 21:15)?*" Can you imagine how Peter must have felt when Jesus questioned him three times, "*Peter, do you love Me?*" Even so, we need to question ourselves, because these promises are made only to those who have genuinely set their love on Him. Take special note of the fact that **these seven promises are *reserved* for those who return His Love.**

And, remember that the Lord said in John 14:15, "*If you love Me, you will obey Me!*" Our obedience is an extremely reliable *telltale* sign that shows us that we really love Him. *Do you love Him?* **If you do, these promises are for you!**

Chapter 15

God Is My Deliverer

Because he has loved Me, therefore *I will deliver him...*
                                                    –Psalm 91:14a

A PROMISE OF DELIVERANCE is the first of the seven promises made to the one who loves God. Make it personal! For instance, I quote it like this: "*Because I love You, Lord, I thank You that You have promised to deliver me.*"

When I was young I personally needed deliverance. I almost destroyed my marriage, my family, and my reputation because I was tormented with fear. One incident opened the door. I can remember the very instant my happy life changed into a nightmare that lasted eight years. And, one verse walked me out of this living mental hell: "*All who call on the Name of the Lord shall be delivered (Joel 2:32).*" Many of you desperately need God's promise of deliverance. The Word worked for me and it will work for you.

There are also other types of deliverances. There is the internal and the external. Ask yourself, "From what is He going to deliver me?" Remember the external deliverances discussed in previous chapters.

God will deliver us from *all* of the following:

- Lion problems
  (life threatening attacks)
- Young lion problems
  (constant harassments)
- Cobra problems
  (sneaky attacks which seem to come out of nowhere)
- Dragon problems
  (imaginary fears, past horrors, vain imaginations)
- Terror by night
  (evils that come through man—war, terror, violence)
- Arrows that fly by day
  (enemy assignments sent to wound)
- Pestilence
  (plagues, deadly diseases, fatal epidemics)
- Destruction
  (evils over which man has no control)

In other words, God wants to deliver us from every evil known to mankind. What a promise. I thank God that He is the God of deliverance! Deliverance is all encompassing. It happens internally and externally; in fact, it surrounds us.

Thou art my hiding place; Thou dost preserve me from trouble; Thou dost surround me with songs of deliverance.
                                                  –Psalm 32:7

Nothing is impossible with God!   –Luke 1:37

Chapter 16

I Am Seated
With Him On High

Because he has loved Me... I will set him securely on high because he has known My Name.   –Psalm 91:14b

TO BE SET SECURELY **on high** is the second promise to those who love the Lord and know Him by Name. *What all is there to know about a name?* When God wanted to show the people something important about Himself, or about His promises in the Old Testament, He would make it known by revealing another one of His covenant Names. His Name revealed Himself: Jehovah Jireh is above lack, His Name Jehovah Rapha is higher than sickness, His Name as Jehovah Shalom is above a revved up, restless mind. We see this theme of *His Name above all other names* also in the New Testament,

> *...which He brought about in Christ, when He raised Him from the dead, and seated Him at His right hand in the heavenly places, far above all rule and authority and power and dominion and every name that is named, not only in this age, but also in the one to come... and raised us up with Him, and seated us with Him in the heavenly places, in Christ Jesus.* –Ephesians 1:20-21; 2:6

It is interesting that God pulls us up to where He is! Things look better from higher up. Our vantage point is greatly improved when we are seated with Him on high. God's perspective from on High is, in fact, the only answer. Overwhelmed from viewing life at eye level, the concept of God's promise to lift us on High is not only a fresh perspective, but, it is in reality, the only answer that works.

The Bible often refers to the unique situation of being positioned *on high* illustrated in everything from Moses stationed at the top of the mountain (Exodus 17:8-16) to God's admonition for us to mount up on wings of eagles (Isaiah 40:31) to the command to lift up our eyes (Psalm 121:1).

Notice that this verse Psalm 91:14 uses the word *"known"*. *Do you know Him by Name?* These promises come out of a *"knowing"* relationship. This is not an "impersonal" God with whom you don't interact. This promise is connected to knowing His Name.

In the first two sentences of Psalm 91 alone, the psalmist refers to God by four different names. The writer refers to God as *The Most High,* revealing that He is the highest thing that exists. This implies much more significance when we realize we are set *securely on high* with the One who is Most High.

Secondly, in the opening of Psalm 91, God is also called *The Almighty,* denoting that He is "all" mighty—the most powerful. Next, He is referred to as *The Lord,* revealing ownership. Then, the writer calls Him *My God,* making it personal. We see God unveiled in these four unique ways to the man who has known His Name. This promise of being seated securely on high is, therefore, reserved for the one who *experiences God intimately.* God says that the promises are ours—simply, because we *know His Name.*

It might sound strange if someone said, "I serve 'High'". Yet, this is the way Psalm 91:1 first introduces His Name. God is "Most High". And, we are positionally placed with Him by dwelling and taking refuge—in our God named "The Most High." When you were a little child, did you ever go to a parade and find yourself unable to see the passing floats because of the throng of people in front of you? That happened to me once, and I remember my father picking me up and putting me on his shoulders. It was wonderful. From that high up, I was able to see the whole parade—not just what was passing right in front of me. I could look down the street and see what had already passed and what was yet to come!

This psalm has built a case for the benefits of being in the shadow of the "Most" High. Verse by verse we see what this entails. Verse 14 connects His Name to the Promise. Out of all the promises, it is the only one connected to His Name. How interesting to think that "the **Most** High" *sets us* on High. This gives us the concept that the Most High pulls us up *so high* with Himself that it makes harm unable to reach us.

I will set him "securely" on high...(NASB). Besides "securely" being a good promise for those afraid of heights, there's a lot more being said. The adverb *securely* holds a lot of promise. It literally means you can't be toppled. When you are positioned securely it takes away the fear and you begin thinking and operating from a different perspective.

Corrie Ten Boom tells a story of a man who certainly acted on the protection of the Most High! An Englishman, in World War II, who was held in a German prison camp for a long period of time, came to know the Lord. One day he read Psalm 91. "Father in heaven," he prayed, "I see all these men dying around me, one after the other. Will I also have to die here? I am still young and I very much want to work in Your kingdom here on earth."

He received this answer: "Rely on what you have just read and go home!" Trusting in the Lord, he got up and walked into the corridor toward the gate. A guard called out, "Prisoner, where are you going?"

"I am under the protection of the Most High," he replied. The guard came to attention and let him pass, for Adolf Hitler was known as "the Most High." He came to the gate, where a group of guards stood. They commanded him to stop and asked where he was going. "I am under the protection of the Most High." All the guards stood at attention as he walked out the gate.

The English officer made his way through the German countryside and eventually reached England, where he told how he had made his escape. He was the *only one* to come out of that prison alive.[1]

There was a lot going on *from on high* that made the difference. Let's not forget to look for our answers from a higher perspective by getting so locked into our eye-level circumstances.

Paul refers to this in Colossians…

> *So if you're serious about living this new resurrection life with Christ, act like it. Pursue the things over which Christ presides. Don't shuffle along, eyes to the ground, absorbed with the things right in front of you. Look up, and be alert to what is going on around Christ—that's where the action is. See things from his perspective.* —Colossians 3:1-2 (The Message[2])

This unique concept resounds through the entire psalm as God makes the promise to those who **know His Name** (verse 14) that we are seated *securely* on High, *sheltered* with the Most High (verse 1), *dwelling* with Him in both a Most High home and place of safety (verse 9).

---

[1] Corrie Ten Boom's book: *Clippings from My Notebook,* pages 41-42.

[2] Copyright © 1993, 1994, 1995, 1996, 2000, 2001, 2002 by Eugene H. Peterson. Used by permission of NavPress Publishing Group.

Chapter 17

God Answers My Call

He will call on Me, and *I will answer him*...

–Psalm 91:15a

G OD MAKES A THIRD promise here in verse fifteen that **He will** *answer* those who truly love Him and call on His Name. Are we aware of what a wonderful promise God is making to us here?

> *This is the confidence we have before Him, that, if we ask anything according to His will, He hears us. And if we know that He hears us in whatever we ask, we know that we have the requests which we have asked from Him.* –I Jn. 5:14-15

Nothing gives me more comfort than to realize that every time I pray in line with God's Word, He hears me. And, if He hears me, I know I have the request for which I asked. This one promise keeps me continually searching His Word in order to understand His will and His promises, so that I can know how to pray more effectively.

Sometimes we have no power to rescue ourselves and we have to rely solely on His faithfulness. I saw this illustrated during one of the floods we had in our town. Our son Bill, in his twenties, had a herd of goats on land near the bayou. As the bayou water began to rise and overflow its banks, some men saw Bill's goats being overtaken by the flood. They hoisted the goats up into the loft of a barn to keep them from drowning. By the next morning the water was like a rushing river—a mile wide—washing away uprooted trees and everything else in its path. Bill had been told about his goats, so, in spite of the roadblocks and rapids gushing by, he set out in an old tin bottom boat across those swift flood waters to rescue his flock. He knew that in another few hours they would die from thirst and suffocation.

Little Willie was the most precious of all the herd because of the time Bill had spent bottle feeding him. The cry of that little goat was the first Bill heard when he got close to the barn. And, as you might expect, once Bill forced the loft door open amid the rushing waters, Little Willie was the first to jump into his arms. Then, boat load by boat load, goat by goat, Bill was able to get every one of those animals out of the loft and rowed to safety.

It was a heartwarming story, but every time I think of Bill rescuing those goats that were in trouble, I think of how God sees us in our troubles and finds ways to rescue us.

Bill had to risk his life to save Little Willie when the goat had no means of rescuing himself. This reminds me of the verse where Jesus talks about the times a shepherd must leave everything to go after the one sheep—which is, in fact, the

Gospel in a nutshell. When I think of Little Willie crying out above the rest, and the trouble Bill exerted to rescue him, I understand this verse. The shepherd lifts that sheep onto his shoulder and carries him back to safety. In the same way, *God's faithfulness* reaches us in our deepest moment of need.

God is faithful to watch over us using every means possible. My mother-in-law had accepted the Lord late in life, although she had been a church goer all her life. A petite, friendly and independent woman, at eighty-seven—she lived on her own so we regularly checked on her. Angie taught Mamaw the concept of crying out to the Lord, if she ever found herself in a place where she couldn't reach us. Days later Angie was visiting Mamaw and when she left Mamaw was in for the night. However, Mamaw thought of something in her backyard to do right at dusk.

Way at the back of her property, she fell and couldn't get up. That night there were no sounds from her neighbors. Mamaw cried out for help but no one heard her. Rocky, the three-year-old boxer from next door was already in the house for the night. It turned out to be very cold, and she laid on the grass, knowing that it was getting worse by the minute. Her pleas were useless. As she thought about the horrible way this could end up, she remembered what Angie had made her promise, and she began crying out to the Lord to help her.

Rocky, locked in the house for the night, began to whine and bark, scratching at the door to be let out. His owners reluctantly decided to let him go out, but he would race back to the door, whining louder than ever. They were about to put him up again but he displayed more frantic behavior until they felt the urge to follow him. He led them to the back fence where they could hear Mamaw calling for help. There is no end to God's ways and means of providing protection for those who trust His Word.

Jack and Bill, not knowing there was an old underground gas well at the back of our 300-acre property, were burning brush. When the fire got over the gas well it literally exploded, sending fire in every direction and igniting a nearby, tall, dry, grass field. Immediately, the fire was out of control. With no water hoses, they were fighting to no avail. The barrel of water they had in the pickup didn't even make a dent in the flames.

Seeing that the fire was getting dangerously close to other fields that led right in to the surrounding homes, Jack flew up to the house to call the fire department (cell phones were not yet available). He then dashed back—only to find that the fire was out. And, Bill, looking like he had been working in the coal mines was sitting on a tree stump trying to catch his breath. Jack said, *"How on earth were you able to put out the fire—there was no way."* His hair singed on his arms and face, Bill's next words—*"I called on God"*—said it all.

You, too, can be delivered from *destruction*. For those out-of-control days, God is always there.

Chapter 18

God Rescues Me From Trouble

...I will be with him in trouble; *I will rescue him*...
–Psalm 91:15

T HE FOURTH PROMISE—to *rescue from trouble* those who love the Lord—is found in the middle of verse 15. It is a well-known fact that human nature cries out to God when faced with trouble. We've all known men in prison, soldiers in war, people in accidents... who call out to God when their lives get into a crisis. Even atheists are known to call on *the God they don't acknowledge* when they are extremely afraid. A lot of criticism has been given to those kinds of *court of the last resort* prayers. However, in defense of this kind of praying, we must remember that when one is in pain, he usually runs to the one he loves the most and the one he trusts. The alternative is not calling out at all, so this verse acknowledges that calling out to God when we are in trouble is a good place to start.

If a person has never felt danger, he never thinks about needing protection. It is the one that knows he is in imminent danger who will appreciate and take the words of this psalm to heart. God has a great deal of variety in His plentiful means of protection and modes of rescue from trouble.

This verse also reminds me of what I read about a U.S. Senator during the pre-Civil War days. While some of the facts are missing the story is said to be true. The Senator had taken his son to the slave market where the boy noticed a black mother crying and praying as they were preparing to sell her daughter on the slave block. As he walked closer, he overheard the mother crying out, *"Oh, God, if I could help You as easily as You could help me, I'd do it for You, Lord."* Thankfully, the young man was so touched by the prayer that he went over and bought the girl off the slave block and gave her back to her mother.

God answers our prayers and rescues us in so many different ways. I am so thankful that He is creative and not limited by our seemingly impossible situations. But, we have to ask in faith and not confine Him to our limited resources. God says, *"If you love Me, I will be with you when you find yourself in trouble, and I will rescue you."* But we have to trust Him to do it *His* way.

> *When you pass through the waters, I will be with you; and through the rivers, they will not overflow you. When you walk through the fire, you will not be scorched, nor will the flame burn you.* —Isaiah 43:2

I read a story several years ago about a woman who had a son in a war zone in World War II, and she wrote out Psalm 91 and sent it to him—explaining that those promises in Psalm 91 would be his protection. The son took it to his commanding officer who assigned his whole outfit to read the entire psalm out loud together every morning. She said that when the war was over—this was the only outfit she knew of in the war zone that reportedly had not one casualty.

Our son, Bill saw the rescuing power of God when he found himself in serious trouble after attempting to swim across a lake—a distance much wider than he calculated. With no strength left in his body and having already gone under water twice, Bill experienced all the sensations of drowning. Miraculously, a woman appeared on the opposite bank, seemingly from nowhere. She quickly located a life ring and threw it towards Bill. With Bill still far from land, it missed him by a wide margin, yet, when he inexplicably resurfaced a third time, his almost lifeless body, was within inches of the float. That was certainly Bill's day of trouble, but I thank God that He was with Bill, and rescued him.

Although some people might call happenings like these a coincidence, the negative situations that we encounter can become *God-incidences* when we trust His Word.

Chapter 19

God Honors Me

...I will *honor* him.   –Psalm 91:15

T HE FIFTH PROMISE—to *honor* those who love
God—is in the last part of verse fifteen. All of us like
to be honored. In school, at work, in the military…we can
all think of examples of seeing someone honored or think
of times when we received an honor. But, being honored by
men is nothing compared to being honored by God.

It is truly a mind-boggling concept to think that God
would tell us that He would honor us. A person who has
God's honor on his life really stands out. *Let's think about
what it looks like when God places His honor on someone's life.
Have you had a time where you have been favored by God?
Interestingly, sometimes it can be challenging for a period of
time.*

Why would God in a dream tell Joseph about the
coming honor He would give him?

He [Joseph] said to them, "Please listen to this dream which I have had; for behold, we were binding sheaves in the field, and lo, my sheaf rose up and also stood erect; and behold, your sheaves gathered around and bowed down to my sheaf...Lo, I have had still another dream; and behold, the sun and the moon and eleven stars were bowing down to me." Genesis 36:6-7, 9

Yet, when Joseph told the dream, it looked as though the opposite effect had taken place. The honor on our lives can be challenged to such an extent that it creates new problems for us.

Not only did God have His hand on Joseph, but Joseph also experienced honor by man when, out of all his brothers, he was given a coat of distinction. Yet the favor of his father created a spiraling downhill chain of events for him.

However, Joseph matured, and passed through some very difficult times, but found that favor wasn't just for a fleeting moment but it lasted for a lifetime (Genesis 37-50).

In Jesus' famous parable in Luke 15:11-32, one of the highpoints is also about honor. The prodigal son was given extreme amounts of honor by his father when he decided to come home. And, it was so much honor that the older brother questioned the injustice of his brother being honored.

Of all the concepts and promises in Psalm 91, honor, by far, is one of the most unusual. The Bible doesn't always say what we might expect. It seems almost irreverent to even speak of in ones' own personal life, let alone write a whole chapter on it. It is very difficult to give an illustration on honor without sounding like Moses who penned the words: *"Now Moses was the most humble man on earth."* To put honor in words is more challenging than you would think.

Yet, we cannot afford to lose the impact of this verse by trying to tone it down. Like Joseph and like the prodigal, it is truly shocking when you think about honor from the God of the Universe. I can recall countless memories of times God has honored me, in spite of myself. It is a fabulous promise. Through the years I have received some testimonies that touched me deeply; I wanted to share a few as illustrations…

> *Peggy, I wish I could give one [book] to every person everywhere. This book is so alive, so real. I only got through half of my first one and knew completely I would never be afraid again. First time in my 88 years.* C.B.

> *Peggy Joyce, I first read your Psalm 91 [book] a few years ago while being incarcerated. I had consequences from my actions. But I know that it kept me safe through some very difficult and dangerous times through my addiction. I've been to prison twice and jail over 20 times in three different counties… I am about to celebrate 20 months*

sober which is a miracle after 26 years of IV meth use and full-blown alcoholism. I serve at an amazing church and will be leading my first connection group and this will be my study... I can't wait to share this and lead this. I know the awesomeness and divinity in the way God spoke to you through a dream is amazing...people don't realize the power in this. And especially with the terror going on. I want to share this book with the whole world... Thank you so very much for this life-changing book and testimonies. F.B.

Peggy, It was an honor to finally meet you! I'm sure people tell you that your book was an inspiration in their lives, but for my Marines, your book and the Lord saved their lives. Thank you! Semper Fi! Rusty Baker,
SgtMaj - USMC (Ret.)

What an honor it is when people write me, sharing their personal Psalm 91 stories and the impact the book has had on their lives and others they know.

These precious notes are like treasures to me. I love hearing how God is moving in others' lives. The letters from people who have read the book have more meaning to me than I can adequately express.

Honor is sometimes hard to give, but we certainly like receiving it. A book could be written on what a powerful spiritual tool it is to give honor. However, let's start at this level of first receiving it from the Lord, as we begin to think about all the ways in which God honors us. It's very humbling that God trusts us with a promise like this.

Honor is a unique gift God gives us—simply because we love Him!

Chapter 20

God Satisfies Me With Long Life

With a long life I will satisfy him.   –Psalm 91:16a

THE SIXTH PROMISE—to *satisfy* those who love Him *with a long life*—is found in verse 16. God does not just say that He will prolong our lives and give us a lot of birthdays. No! He says that He will *satisfy* us with a long life. There are people who would testify that just having a great many birthdays is not necessarily a blessing. But, God says that He will give us many birthdays, and as those birthdays roll around we will experience satisfaction.

It has been said that there is a *God-shaped vacuum* on the inside of each one of us. Man has tried to fill that vacuum with many different things, but nothing will satisfy that emptiness until it is filled with Jesus. That is the true satisfaction to which God refers to in His Promise. God is making the offer. If we will come to Him, let Him fill that empty place on the inside and allow Him to fulfill the call on our lives—then He will give us *a long life* and *satisfy* us as we live it out. Only the dissatisfied person can really appreciate what it means to find satisfaction.

It is a fact that God wants us to live a satisfied life, but let's also not neglect the promise of a long life. King David was Israel's most valiant, daring warrior, yet he lived to be a ripe old age, *"full of days"* as the Old Testament authors liked to say. His life was filled with combat, high-risk situations, and impossible odds. Yet, he did not die in battle; his head went down in peace in his old age. Long life is a great concluding promise of protection.

Paul lets us know in Ephesians, however, that we are in a fight. We can't flow with the wide road—with what feels good, and still win this battle because the enemy will make the wrong path extremely easy to take. Eddie Rickenbacker, the World War I flying ace, who had near-death experiences throughout his life, once wanted to let himself die, but later said this about death—

"I felt the presence of death, and I knew that I was going. You may have heard that dying is unpleasant, but don't you believe it. Dying is the sweetest, tenderest, most sensuous sensation I have ever experienced. Death comes disguised as a sympathetic friend. All was serene; all was calm. How wonderful it would be simply to float out of this world. It is easy to die. You have to fight to live. And, that is what I did. I recognized that wonderful, mellow sensation for what it was—death—and I fought it. I literally fought death in my mind, pushing away the sweet blandishments and welcoming back the pain. The next ten days were a continuous fight with

the old Grim Reaper, and, again and again, I would feel myself start to slip away. Each time I rallied and fought back, until I had turned the corner toward recovery." Captain Rickenbacker should know how death feels! Death came toward him many times during his service as a soldier in both world wars: when he survived two plane crashes and when he was lost for twenty-four days in the Pacific Ocean.

Sometimes the spirit of death makes a bid for our very life. It is these inner dynamics that are at work when a person is wounded, facing a serious illness, wracked by pain from an injury or sensing impending doom. It is easy to give in to it. We think of the ugly side to destruction, but the danger is when it comes with a pretty face. It is a fight to break free from the enticing call of death, persevere to victory and receive this covenant promise of a *satisfied, long life.*

Once, in a boat on the Sea of Galilee, the disciples cried out in fear that they would drown in the storm. Jesus, however, had said that they must go to the other side. If they had thought through what He'd said, they would have known that the storm would not harm them because they had His word on a mission across the lake. In the same way, if you have been promised a satisfied, long life, then you know you will make it through the present circumstances.

God wants us to claim the promise of long life, but He also wants us to use that long life for Him. Ask yourself, "What *am* I going to do with my long life?"

Chapter 21

I Behold His Salvation

...and let him *behold My Salvation*.   –Psalm 91:16b

ALLOWING THOSE WHO LOVE Him to *behold His salvation* is the seventh promise found in the last part of verse 16. *Behold* simply means to see something and *take hold of it and make it our own*. God wants us to take hold of His salvation.

The movement of this last line in Psalm 91 describes our ultimate, final victory. The order of this sentence gives us promise that we will see salvation face to face DURING AND AFTER our *long, satisfied life*. This moves us beyond an intellectual knowledge of salvation to relationship. It secures our future, but it starts now. Jesus constantly reminded us that, "Salvation is Now! Today it has come!" Many people are surprised when they look up the word "salvation" in a Bible concordance and find that it has a much deeper meaning than just *a ticket to heaven*. We often miss the richness of this promise.

According to *Strong's Exhaustive Concordance,* the Word translated *salvation* includes health, healing, deliverance, rescue, safety, protection and provision. What more could we ask? God promises that He will allow us to see and *take hold of* His Life, His Health, His Healing, His Deliverance, His Protection and His Provision!

Many people read Psalm 91 and simply see it with their eyes, but very few *behold* it in their lives. My prayer is for that to change. One of my biggest thrills, after teaching this truth of God, is having different people write or call, describing the ecstatic joy of having it come alive in their heart. I love to hear the extent to which they have actually taken hold of this covenant and started experiencing it as a vital part of their existence.

In the testimonies that follow, your heart will be encouraged by those who have beheld firsthand the salvation of the Lord. Read their stories in their own words. The truth about God's salvation—His protection, deliverance, health and provision—is more than just wishful thinking. It is a promise of which one can actually take hold.

SUMMARY

Nothing in this world can be relied upon as confidently as God's promises, when we believe them, refuse to waver and decide to make His Word *our final authority* for every area of life...

I believe that Psalm 91 is a covenant (a spiritual contract) that God has made available to His children—especially in these difficult days. But, there are some who sincerely ask, *"How do you know that you can take a **song** from the psalms and base your life on it?"* Jesus answered that question. The value of the psalms was emphasized when He cited them as a source of Truth that must be fulfilled.

*Now He said to them, "These are My words which I spoke to you while I was still with you, that all things which are written about Me in the law of Moses and the Prophets **AND THE PSALMS** must be fulfilled (emphasis added)."* –Luke 24:44

When Jesus specifically equated the psalms to the Law of Moses and the Prophets, we see that it is historically relevant, prophetically sound and totally applicable and reliable.

At a time when there are so many uncertainties facing us, it is more than comforting to know that God not only knows ahead of time what we will be facing, but He also made absolute provision for us.

Someone once pointed out, *"It is interesting that the world must have gotten its distress 911 number from God's answer to our distress call: Psalm "91-1."*

It seems only a dream now to think back on the time when my mind was reeling in fears and doubts. Little did I know when I asked God that pertinent question—*"Is there any way for a Christian to escape all the evils that are coming on this world?"*—He was going to give me a dream that would not only change my life, but also change the lives of thousands of others who would hear and believe.

Our minds cannot even begin to comprehend God's goodness.

TRULY, WHAT A MIGHTY GOD WE SERVE!

What Must I Do To Be Saved?

We've talked about physical protection. Now let's make sure that you have eternal protection. The promises from God in this book are for God's children who love Him. If you have never given your life to Jesus and accepted Him as your Lord and Savior, there is no better time than right now.

There is none righteous, not even one.   −Romans 3:10

...for all have sinned and fallen short of the glory of God.   −Romans 3:23

God loves you and gave His life that you might live eternally with Him.

But God demonstrates His own love toward us, in that while we were yet sinners, Christ died for us.
                                                                    −Romans 5:8

For God so loved the world (you), that He gave His only begotten Son, that whoever believes in Him should not perish but have eternal life.   −John 3:16

There is nothing we can do to earn our salvation or to make ourselves good enough to go to heaven. It is a free gift!

*The wages of sin is death, but the **free** gift of God is eternal life in Christ Jesus.*   −Romans 6:23

There is also no other avenue through which we can reach heaven, other than Jesus Christ—God's Son.

> *And there is salvation in no one else; for there is no other name under heaven that has been given among men, by which we must be saved.* –Acts 4:12

> *Jesus said to him, "I am the Way, and the Truth, and the Life; no one comes to the Father, but through Me."*
> –John 14:6

You must believe that Jesus is the Son of God, that He died on the cross for your sins, and that He rose again on the third day.

> *...who (Jesus) was declared with power to be the Son of God by the resurrection from the dead...* –Romans 1:4

You may be thinking, "How do I accept Jesus and become His child?" God in His Love has made it so easy.

> *If you confess with your mouth the Lord Jesus and believe in your heart that God raised Him from the dead, you shall be saved.* –Romans 10:9

> *But as many as received Him, to them He gave the right to become children of God, even to those who believe in His Name.* –John 1:12

It is as simple as praying a prayer similar to this one—if you sincerely mean it in your heart:

Dear God:

I believe You gave your Son, Jesus, to die for me. I believe He shed His Blood to pay for my sins and that You raised Him from the dead so I can be Your child and live with You eternally in heaven. I am asking Jesus to come into my heart right now and save me. I confess You as the Lord and Master of my life.

I thank You, dear Lord, for loving me enough to lay down your life for me. Take my life now and use it for Your Glory. I ask for all that You have for me.

In Jesus Name,
Amen

Jennifer McCullough

Howard Payne University
Southwestern Baptist Theological Seminary

Missionary in Uganda to Children with AIDS

Murders in the Village

Before leaving for the mission field in East Africa, I was being discipled by Angie Schum, my college Bible study teacher. It was a crash course in *everything you need to know before entering "the Bush!"* I ran into her friend Donna one night at church. She said, *"You do know about Psalm 91, don't you?"* When I said, *"No!"*—she said, *"Angie must not love you very much if she hasn't told you about Psalm 91!"*

I began intently studying the chapter and memorized it before I left. I had no idea the power this passage has until the following January. I lived in a village in the bush with the Ankole tribe (cattle herders), working with orphans with

AIDS and teaching at the village school. I often found myself praying Psalm 91 while walking the circumference of the village. I had gone to the city the day before on the milk truck. That night I was lying in my hut and heard gunshots. I ran to a fellow missionary's hut and sat in a small room praying Psalm 91 over and over. The husband was out investigating, so it was just a 24-year-old mother, her two-year-old child and me.

In the meantime, a group of rebels were raiding our village. Men were shot, a pregnant woman was beaten, villagers were robbed and cattle were stolen. The villagers were laid out in a line on their stomachs with guns and machetes pointed to their heads, while they were being threatened not to say a word. The raid was well planned as they had been watching us for days from the bushes.

Here is the miracle! Village people know that white missionaries have more in their huts than Ugandans make in a lifetime. Yet, the rebels never came to our hut—in spite of the fact that everyone else's hut was raided. After the fact, the rebels admitted to the police that they had followed the milk truck through the bush the night before the raid. I had been on that truck sitting next to the driver who was carrying two million shillings—the villagers' monthly income from the milk sales. They did not attack the truck in route because we had returned before dark that night. This was the first time we had ever returned before dark in the six months I had been riding the route.

The day after the attack it was very intense. I walked through the village, praying for villagers who had been robbed and beaten. They had looks of pure terror on their faces, knowing that the rebels were still hiding in the bush nearby. While talking to the villagers, no one could believe that I was not attacked. My interpreter, Segambe, said, "*It was as if your hut was not even there.*"

God is faithful! He has a perfect plan for your life! God is all knowing! He will give you weapons to fight the battles you face.

God did not give Psalm 91 only to missionaries in the African bush. He gave it to everyone so that we can daily claim His promises to us as Christians. I find the words of Psalm 91 in my daily prayers: "*...He will cover me with His feathers, and under His wings I find refuge. His faithfulness is my shield and rampart...*"

Don't miss the chance to see the power of God's promises in your life. Claim them, memorize them, pray them, and live them. He is faithful!

Dane Kaley
Miracle told by Vicki Jackson

Author's Note: *Our good friends, Vicki and Gerald Jackson, live in Fort Worth, Texas. Vicki called to tell me this amazing story that happened to one of their fellow church members, Dane Kaley.*

Dane Kaley developed a small growth in his ear seemingly overnight. The doctor decided to remove it in day surgery, however, the *minor* surgery turned out not to be so minor. A biopsy revealed the growth to be squamous carcinomas, a very dangerous and aggressive form of skin cancer. He was told to go immediately to an oncologist. Vicki began spending two to three hours every day encouraging Dane and his wife, Diana, with God's covenant promise in Psalm 91. The prognosis from the oncologist/surgeon was grim and frightening. Dane was then sent for a PET scan that showed the cancer had metastasized into the bones in front of and behind his ear. It had also spread to the lymph nodes on the left side of his neck and surgery was immediately scheduled. Two CAT scans were done the day before the surgery. Vicki said she had never interceded so much for one person before Dane. The Lord even woke her in the middle of the night to pray, and He gave her a vision of how He was going to use Dane to touch his church and usher in a fresh outpouring of the Holy Spirit.

On the day of the surgery, Vicki and Diana were permitted to go into a restricted area to pray for Dane, and as they prayed everything came to a complete stop. Even the doctors joined them in prayer. Then, three hours later one of the doctors came out to share THE GOOD NEWS! They had begun the surgery by removing the cancerous growth along with surrounding tissue. The tissue was sent to pathology to make sure they had reached the outer parameters of the unhealthy cells. They also made an incision down the left side of Dane's neck to prepare to remove the lymph nodes along with "all other glands" to ensure the disease would be contained.

Can you imagine the surprise of the doctors when the report came back from pathology and the test showed the very dangerous and aggressive skin cancer wasn't squamous at all, but basal cell carcinomas—which very rarely spread to any other part of the body! The doctors closed Dane's neck and did not remove the lymph nodes.

In addition, the doctor told them that the CAT scans prior to surgery had shown a completely different story from the

PET scan the week prior. The first CAT scan indicated there was no cancer in the nodes, so the second scan was done—this one indicating there was no cancer in the nodes or bone! The disease was retreating before their very eyes and by the time they did the surgery, the threat of death had been rebuked by the Lord.

The doctor was confused and kept saying, "I don't know how this happened!" It was all Vicki and Diana could do to keep from just running and praising through the hospital. Dane was supposed to be in the hospital for several days and then have chemo and radiation treatment, but he went home the day after surgery, cancer free. Thank God, *the things which are seen are temporal and subject to change…,*" according to 2 Corinthians 4:18.

* * * * *

Hayley Platt

Psalm 91
Protection from Chemo

I have read the Psalm 91 book so many times and I love it. There are different lessons for different seasons, but Psalm 91 is for every season. I still pray it out loud every morning. The part that stands out is the fact that angels are there escorting us through our every day, bearing us up in their hands in order that we not even stumble. God is so committed to escorting us that He furnished us with bodyguards. He certainly sent angels to escort me through my time of taking chemo and birthing a baby in the middle of those treatments.

The drug I was being given was bright red. For some reason, I think because of the color, it was very scary watching it come down the IV tube and enter my veins. As the bright red liquid got closer and closer to my arm, I started to panic. I remember that I began demanding to have my Bible. I heard myself saying, "Where is my Bible! Where is my Bible?" I got so panicked that even the nurse became frightened and started saying, "Someone, get her a Bible." My husband, Jonathan, and the nurse were digging through my things desperately trying to locate one. When they finally found it, I started thumbing through the pages until I got to Psalm 91 and began reading it as fast as I could. I was watching the IV and looking at my Bible and just as the red liquid reached my arm, I finished reading the passage. Instantly, my peace came back and I began saying, "I can…drink any deadly poison and it will not harm me…" (Mark 16:17-18). Chemo is a poison, intended to eradicate the cancer, but it can also be deadly to other parts of the body. However, God had promised me in His word that this deadly poison would not be able to harm me. It could only harm the cancer. Normally, all of this procedure takes place while one is under anesthesia, but they couldn't put me to sleep since I was pregnant. I had to be awake for every course of action and all they could give me was a local of Lidocaine. It didn't help that I could hear the doctors in the next room talking about what they ate for lunch. You feel desperate to have them focus on your situation, but I had to remember they do this all day. Nevertheless, to you, it is the most serious thing in the world at that moment.

The next procedure I had was the installation of the port placement so that I could receive chemo directly to the area. Thankfully, they allowed me to listen to whatever music I chose during the procedure. Sadly, that day the speakers were broken. The room is sterile and you're not allowed to bring anything in with you, but I kept telling the Lord, "I cannot do this without worship music." I was really scared because the tubing is threaded up and down close to your heart. I was nervous having anything put that close to such a vital organ. I am sure it was no big deal to the nurses and doctors, but it made me very apprehensive. I was still telling the Lord that I needed worship music when the nurse said, "If you want to take your phone in with you, sneak it under the pillow and you can listen to your worship music." I was so grateful. It was a totally sterile room, yet she let me bring my cell phone in. I had the volume turned down really low and I just lay there and listened in a supernatural cocoon of peace.

I had an MRI done, and the lady who did it was a believer and realized that I was panicked at what it might do to my baby. I was on my back with a board on top of me and they were getting ready to put me through a 'kid' tube since all the adult tubes were taken. It was a tiny little opening and I had a very big belly. With that thought, I started compulsively shaking, unable to control my body. It got so bad that the table I was lying on began shaking the machine. When the nurse saw what was happening, she just leaned over me and began saying over and over, "God is good! God is good! Breathe in! God is good! Breathe out! God is good!" That went on for an hour and twenty minutes, and I was fine. Then, I started singing to the Lord, "You are the famous One." I couldn't remember anything except that one song, so I just sang that over and over—"You are the famous One! The famous One!"

God had put a nurse with me who perfectly demonstrated God's kindness and His awesome peace. It was as though the Lord was touching me through her touch to bring me through the chemo miraculously.

Then, the birth! I could tell the doctors were highly concerned about the birth. The cancer had appeared during the 20th week of my pregnancy, so I had been receiving chemo treatments during the second half of my pregnancy, and now 20 weeks later, it was time for Gabriella to come into the world. They were worried I wouldn't have the strength to push her out. However, God is an awesome God and He gave me a supernatural delivery. My water broke and an hour and ten minutes later, my baby was born—pain-free! To add to the miracle, I had my baby with no medication. There was no time for medication. I had some slight discomfort with the contractions, but once it moved over to pushing contractions, I felt nothing. Even when I pushed Gabriella out, I felt nothing! (According to my friend Cathy, it was nothing short of a miracle because her description of giving birth was the worst thing she had ever experienced in her entire life. She said it felt as though her loins were being ripped out of her.) Even though I wanted medication, there was no time for it. Not long before the birth, I told the nurse that it might be time for the epidural. She made the call, then checked me and excitedly proclaimed, "Honey, you are a 'ten'. You went from a zero to a ten in ten minutes. I have never seen this happen before." Instantly, she then picked up the phone, and said, "Cancel the anesthesiologist and call the doctor. The baby is coming right now." Upon hearing the nurse's excitement, there was a moment when fear tried to grip me. I have heard people talk about liquid fear, and suddenly, I knew what liquid fear felt like. It was hot and I could feel it try to enter me, but during my quiet time the day before, God had spoken to me, "Perfect love will cast out all fear." Out loud I said, "Lord, You said that perfect love casts out all fear and You love me perfectly, therefore, I will not fear." I kept saying, "It is just You and me, Jesus." The whole time I was saying that, the nurse was just typing and looking at the monitor. I wondered if she thought, "We've got a crazy one on our hands."

The moment I said, "Perfect love casts out fear because the Lord loves me perfectly, it went fine." All the fear was gone! For a moment, all I could hear in my head was Cathy telling me that it felt like her loins were being ripped out, so I had to get that voice out of my mind and, instead, begin concentrating on what God was saying. The doctor didn't even have time to wash his hands. I heard the nurse say, "She's coming out. You need to turn around now!" And, instantly, she was delivered with no pain!!

I was told that because of the chemo, my baby would be underweight, but to everyone's surprise, my precious little "underweight" baby weighed 8 pounds and 10 ounces!

Another interesting thing happened when I went in to get the PET Scan. The PET Scan nurse, who had been in cancer remission for ten years, said, "How long have you been in remission and how many years ago did you stop doing chemo?" I responded, "Oh, I'm right in the middle of chemo now". She was shocked and just kept touching my arm, saying, "Oh my! Your skin is so beautiful. You look absolutely great!" She thought I had been through chemo years ago and I was just coming in for an annual PET Scan. Before that, I hadn't realized that chemo almost always changes the skin color.

On one visit to the doctor, I asked, "Is this just a light chemo treatment?" She laughed and said, "First of all, all chemo is rigorous. No chemo is light. The plan we have you on is quite an intense form of chemo. And, I have to tell you that most of my patients lose their hair and most of them do not handle it well. She said that they do fairly well on the first treatment and some do well on the second treatment, but, from there it is always downhill." She told me that I was discussed every day in the conference room because I confused them. "We don't know why you are doing so well, but I have to say that you have baffled us." I found I was on a very strong chemo treatment. It is a common treatment, but strong. My blood count was also amazing—it was off the charts, even for a healthy person. And, especially, for a pregnant person, it was unexplainable.

What an awesome God we serve! I stand amazed at His miracles—no cancer now, baby birthed perfectly and painlessly, no hair loss, no funny coloring, and the chemo poisoning didn't harm me or my precious baby...God is indeed an amazing Father! I can do nothing but give God all the honor and glory during this period of my life because it has been a miracle every step of the way.

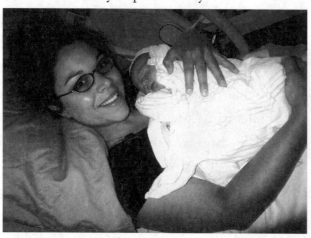

Hayley's Dream 2 Days Before She Went to the Doctor...

In my dream, I was in Brownwood, Texas (where I lived while I was going to college at Howard Payne University) and my car broke down or I ran out of gas. I pulled over and got out of the car and started walking. I had no idea where I was supposed to go. This voice said, "Turn left here. Peggy Joyce [Ruth] lives down this street. You need to go down this street." I passed by the 3M company and the closer I got to their house the more I started to recognize where I was. All of a sudden Peggy Joyce "PJ" comes out on her front porch and points at me and says, "Come inside. Come inside." I told her my car had broken down and I didn't know where to go and this voice told me to come down this street and there you are.

So she said, "Come on in. We have been waiting on you." So I went inside and we were in the living room and a bunch of my family members are there. I went out in the back yard and there are two crocodiles—a large one and a small one. They were trying to get me and I ran back into the living room and then into the kitchen. The crocodiles were after me and I got up on the counter and PJ said, "Use your Scripture. Use your Scripture." Then, I said, "Psalm 91 is my Scripture." So I picked up a frying pan. Psalm 91 was the frying pan. I started beating the large crocodile and killed it with the frying pan. Then the small one started trying to get to me so I started beating it with the frying pan. I kept saying Psalm 91 but I couldn't kill it so I put the frying pan down. Then PJ said, "Your Father has it taken care of." You beat it but it is still alive but Your Father will sever its head. It will be ok. Your Father will take care of it."

Then I went to the doctor. I didn't know at the time that I had two tumors: a large one and a small one. It was a couple of days after the dream that I found out about the two tumors. The large tumor was easy to get rid of but the small one was not as easy to kill. They are both dead now and taken care of. The cancer is gone but when I found out that I had the two tumors I had peace. I knew I had my Psalm 91 Scripture and that it was going to be beaten so it wasn't as shocking or fearful when the doctor delivered the news. I felt prepared in

my spirit for it. I used my Psalm 91 Scripture and it worked.

When the doctor told me about the two tumors, I thought—"Those are my two crocodiles." It was kind of funny that I was hitting them with a frying pan. But I knew in my dream that the frying pan was my Scripture. Like I said, "They are both dead now and taken care of. The cancer is gone, but God was so good to give me the answer before I even knew I would fight cancer."

Alma Reyes
Psalm 91 - At Gunpoint

God's Psalm 91 Covenant of Protection works for anyone, at any time, under any circumstances if we run to God and determine to declare His protection promises in faith. But, too often fear or the world's influence causes us to waver in our faith and miss our miracle. However, that was not the case with Alma Reyes! While we were in Bacolod City in the Philippines we found out about this remarkable testimony that had taken place right in the area where we were ministering. Bacolod is a large city, bustling with activity while jeepney mini-buses and bicycle carts carry people to their destinations.

On one particular day, less than a year after Alma had accepted Jesus as her Lord and Savior, she got a chance to prove the faithfulness of her God. As usual, she was in a jeepney on her way to work. It was routine for the van to stop many times along the way, picking up other passengers until the driver had a full load, but this particular morning Alma had such an uneasiness that she began to pray silently. When the van reached a more secluded area two men suddenly commanded the driver to stop, stepped off the van, drew out a gun and pointed it to the man sitting next to Alma. Perhaps, it was the scripture, "I will not die but live and proclaim what the Lord has done for me," that God had given to Alma just a month after she got saved that gave her so much confidence that she felt no fear. But, when the gunman fired his gun, hitting the man sitting next to Alma in the shoulder, she was the only one on the van who didn't begin screaming hysterically. The panic was so great that an old Chinese man began having a heart attack just as the gunman put his gun to the already wounded man's head, shot and killed him instantly. That was too much. Instead of cringing in fear, a confident boldness in God's protection rose up on the inside of Alma and she turned to look straight into the eyes of the killer, making him so intimidated that he turned his gun to point it directly between Alma's eyes. But, before he was able to pull the trigger, she was taking her authority in the Name of Jesus, commanding Satan, in Jesus' Name, to loose His hold on the man. It was obvious that the man was trying to pull the trigger, but his hand was paralyzed and he couldn't move his finger. He tried three times to shoot Alma, to no avail. The driver finally took off, leaving the killer standing in the road with his gun raised and still trying to shoot it, but it was not until they were out of the killer's range that they heard his gun fire.

By this time everyone's attention was directed toward the old man who was having the heart attack. Alma called to the driver to take the man to the hospital, but as they were going she took his hand and began praying. At that moment the power of God surged through her and he was instantly healed. He was so well that by the time they reached the hospital the old man wouldn't let them take him in because he said that there was no need since he was completely well.

Psalm 91 speaks of the authority that we have been given over the powers of darkness when we decide to use it. Alma is a living testimony to that truth.

* * * * *

Audra Chasteen
Son is Miraculously Healed from a Broken Neck - Skylar

About 7:30 p.m. on a hot July evening, three of my sisters and I, along with our children, were visiting my parents. Skylar, my four-year-old, was riding bicycles with the older boys out in the pasture about a half mile from the house. I had just turned to warn my older son not to ride down the hill because of the steep incline, when I realized that Skylar had

already started down. The next thing I knew the bicycle was out of control and he had gone over the side of a cliff. When I got to him he wasn't moving and he wasn't crying. He was tangled in the wheel of the bicycle, lying on his stomach with his chin twisted past his shoulder, resting on his shoulder blade. It was a terrifying sight to see Skylar's head bent almost backward. His left arm was back behind him with his wrist above his right shoulder. His eyes were half open, in a fixed position, down and to the corner. He was blue and not breathing.

When I saw Skylar in that distorted position and not breathing, I didn't have to be told that it was bad. I just started screaming. In spite of the obvious head and neck injury, I turned his head forward so that he could breathe. But, when he still didn't start breathing—I turned his whole body straight, hoping that would help. When that didn't work, I became hysterical. My three sisters and I are nurses, one RN and three LVN, but we couldn't seem to pull ourselves together to know what to do medically. It was as though none of us had one brain cell functioning. My sister Donna just picked him up and stood there.

When my oldest sister, Cynthia, finally got to the scene of the accident, the first thing she did was to lay her hand over on Skylar's head and start rebuking the enemy. She kept saying, "I rebuke you, Satan, in the Name of Jesus—you get your hands off Skylar—you cannot have him!" Then she started pleading the Blood of Jesus and quoting Psalm 91 over him. Hearing

God's Word coming out of Cynthia's mouth pulled me back to my senses. I sent one of my sisters for her car, and we headed for the nearest hospital—which was about seventeen miles away.

On the way to the hospital, we did some rescue breaths on Skylar, and he would breathe for a few minutes and then stop. I tried to hold his head and neck straight, but the whole time his eyes were still fixed. Cynthia and I continued to speak Psalm 91 over Skylar and to command his body to line up with God's Word—but nothing was coming out as eloquently as I wanted. All that I could say was, "Bones, be like you're supposed to be—Body, be like you are supposed to be—in Jesus' Name."

I remember thinking—"God, how can you ask us to praise You in *every* situation—how can I praise you when my child is in danger?" And I felt like the Lord impressed me, "Just do it— you don't have to know why—just do it!" I was able to give God one sentence—"Lord, I give you the Glory and the Honor and the Praise." (I wasn't giving God the praise from thinking that He sent this situation—I was giving God the praise because of *who He is* and because His Word said to praise Him in all things.) The whole way we prayed in the Spirit and quoted Psalm 91 over him.

When we got to the hospital in Comanche, Texas, they immediately put a neck brace on him, but he still wasn't responding. By then he had started breathing on his own, but his eyes were still fixed. Then he started throwing up— another sign of a bad head injury.

As soon as they had Skylar in X-ray, I called one of our pastors to get some of the intercessors praying. I knew we needed help. As much as we had been taught, I was still unprepared when the tragedy actually happened. As he prayed, peace came over me and I suddenly knew that everything was going to be OK.

The X-rays showed an obvious break in the C-1 vertebra (the first vertebra under the head) and Skylar still wasn't responding. He was immediately, with the X-rays, air-flighted to Cook's Children's Hospital in Fort Worth, Texas.

Since I was still in my scrubs from working all day, they didn't realize at Cook's Hospital that I was the mother, so they had me helping to draw the blood on Skylar. I was listening as the trauma nurse reported to the doctor when he came in —"he has a C-1 fracture, his eyes are deviated and down to the left, he stopped breathing, etc." The doctor was shocked when he discovered I was the mother. I could never have been that peaceful without all the prayers.

The only thing that seemed to calm Skylar while we were waiting was to put my hand on his forehead and pray Psalm 91 over him. Even though Skylar was not awake through all of this, once when I paused in my praying, Skylar said, "Amen!" From the moment that he responded from an unconscious state—giving his agreement to that prayer—I knew he would be fine, in spite of the seriousness of his condition. Finally, they wheeled him in for more X-rays and for a CAT scan to see if there was any bleeding in the brain cavity.

When the doctor finally came in he had a very strange look on his face, and all he could say was, "He's going to be all right!" Then, after consulting with the radiologist, they came in saying, **"We don't know how to explain this, but we can find no head trauma (brain swelling or bleeding) and we cannot find a C-1 fracture."** They had the Comanche hospital X-rays with the obvious break, but their X-rays showed no sign of a break.

There are no words to describe the joy and the gratitude and the excitement that we felt at that moment. All the nurses were pouring in to tell us how *lucky* we were and all I could say was, "Luck had nothing to do with this. This was God!" I was not about to let Satan have one ounce of glory. I knew that it was a miracle and that it was God who had healed him, however, he still wasn't responding very well so they put us in the pediatric ward of the ICU to monitor him. The next morning the nurse came in and scratched him on the head, assuming she would get the same response (nothing) that she had gotten the day before. But this time when she scratched him and called out his name he said, "What?" Everyone, including the nurse, jumped—and then rejoiced!

From that point on he was able to wake up and respond. The doctor was just amazed. He said, "I don't know what to tell you. There was definitely a break on that other X-ray, but he is obviously OK now. I don't know how to explain it." He didn't have to explain it. I knew what had happened. God is so good!

Skylar has always been very close to my mother, and I found out something very interesting after we got home. Two weeks prior to the accident, Skylar had been telling her that it was time for him to go be with Jesus. And, mother would say, "No, Skylar, why would you say that? It's not time for you to go be with Jesus." But he would emphatically say, "Yes, it is! I've got to go" And she would argue with him, but she said she didn't think too much about it since he's only four years old. But, after the accident my mother knew that there was warfare going on, and it was God's promise in Psalm 91 that finally won the battle.

Since the day we left the hospital, Skylar has been a perfectly normal, healthy little boy with no problems and no side effects from the accident. He is truly a miracle!

* * * * *

Rene Hood
Psalm 91 and Six Months To Live

I will begin my testimony in July 1998. At this point in my life I had eaten almost nothing for approximately two months—yet I continued to gain weight. I could not go outside in the direct sunlight for any length of time without my face becoming irritated to the point that if you placed your hand on my face the print of your hand would remain there. I had also begun to develop black spots on my face, arms and legs. Later, a red rash appeared throughout my body. Bruises would appear without my falling or having been hit.

During the month of July, my energy level was so low that it was a challenge to just clean the bathtub after bathing. My body became racked with pain—even when trying to perform a task as simple as brushing my teeth. One particular night is still fresh in my memory. For the past week or so, I had been choking when I would lie down at night. This night was the same but when I got up that morning I made the shocking discovery that I couldn't perform normal bodily functions. Knowing that something had to be done quickly, I called my doctor early that morning. After his examination, he referred me to Scott and White Hospital to see Dr. Nichols, a nephrologist.

The night prior to my seeing Dr. Nichols my body aches had reached a new level and it had become a norm for me to have a fever of 103 or more. I felt like my brain was frying and I would lie on my bathroom floor in misery. My brown body transformed before my eyes into a gray color, covered with perspiration and rolled up in a fetal position. I told the Lord that it would be so easy to give up the ghost and just go home to be with Him, but I said, "Lord, I know that You are not finished with me. Lord, I hurt so badly and yet I know that there are people out there that You have called me to touch. My kids need me! I know I am walking in the *valley of the shadow of death, but I will fear no evil.* You promised me, Lord, in Psalm 91 that *only with my eyes would I see the reward of the wicked—that a thousand would fall at my side and ten thousand at my right hand, but it would not come nigh me.*"

My 18-year-old daughter was home for the summer at the time and since my husband wasn't concerned, and told me so, she took me to the hospital in Temple, Texas. I was so weak that I could barely walk. After about a 25-minute examination the nephrologist, with no bedside manner and no sense of caring, said, "I give you three months and you will just go 'poop'." I was very angry that he would speak such words to me in the presence of my daughter, without any sensitivity. Then he said, "It will not be easy because you will be in a lot of pain, but (as he pointed to my daughter) she's big enough—she can take care of herself." Then he walked out the door. I looked at my daughter and assured her, "Mom is not going anywhere."

I was hospitalized, running a high fever and unable to eat. I would have involuntary shakes that I couldn't control and my right lung had collapsed because of the mass of protein my kidneys were now throwing into my system. I looked like a seven-month pregnant woman. My kidneys were shutting down, my joints ached and were swollen, and the doctors had found a mass on my liver. After twelve days of their making one mistake after another and causing me more suffering without my getting any better, I asked my daughter to help me dress and take me back home to Bangs, Texas because God was going to give me a miracle.

I am a living testimony of His faithfulness to His promises. I went to my parent's house and I would sit up and walk as well as I could—reminding God of what He had promised—

"You will not be afraid of the deadly pestilence. It will not approach you."

My local doctor would call and remind me that those specialists said I was dying and that I needed to be in a hospital. I wouldn't! I couldn't! I knew that *"greater is He that is in me than he that is in the world."* I had a supernatural peace that I was well and that the healing would manifest itself soon—so I kept pressing.

Since I would not go back to the hospital and my condition, by sight, was no better, my doctor encouraged me to go to a nephrologist in Abilene, Texas. I finally agreed but refused the medicine because of the side effects. Not one doctor gave me one ounce of hope, but I was determined to receive the healing that Christ had provided. Then, the miracle started manifesting. It was during that next few months that I gradually started feeling better and my strength started returning. Finally, after seeing the Abilene doctor for two months and once again being put through a battery of tests, he stated, "I'm looking at your paperwork and I'm looking at you. If you had let us do what we wanted to do— and you wouldn't—we doctors would be patting ourselves on the back, saying we had gotten you in remission. All I can say is—whatever you have been doing, just keep doing it." Then he told me that I was a "miracle."

My doctor had a liver specialist meet me at the nearby hospital in Brownwood and after a CAT scan and two sonograms, he could not find any mass in my liver. I was then sent to a blood specialist, and after reading the reports he repeated twice that I was "a wonder." I have seen almost twenty Christmases since being told that I would not live to see another Christmas.

My prison ministry didn't suffer and souls continue to be saved, delivered and set free because I abided in God's Word and trusted Him to be faithful. I have a book out called *"Being Found in His Word"*. We all need to be in His Word—refusing, no matter what—to be driven from His promises. I know that this battle and subsequent victory give honor to a "faithful, loving, and caring God" who desires to be embraced by each one of us.

James (Jimmy) M. Stewart
Air Force Combat Pilot and Bombardier Trainer
Brigadier General, USAF

An Actor is a Real Fighter

Jimmy Stewart stands out for his one difference, he wasn't trying to get out of the war! He joined the US Air Force in 1941, even before the emotional Pearl Harbor attack made most men angry enough to sign up nine months later. At 32, and already a pilot himself, he'd been the first Hollywood star to enlist for World War II. From the start, Jimmy had to "fight to fight". The famous actor drew the press—pushing for interviews and photos while girls lined up at the gates to get a glimpse of him at every training base.

Jimmy stood out as one who was first in and who was driven to stay and finish the war. While others *tried to go home* sooner, he tried to fly *all* missions. He wasn't just a survivor, he understood how to overcome. Every mission he flew, earned him the respect of his men and it earned him the nickname, "Lucky".

Many of the men kept combat diaries of their harrowing experiences, numbering off each mission as one step closer to getting them to their required number of 25, which would send them back home. It was nothing short of a miracle when a man was able to return back to his family. His commander once quipped about Stewart: like the star who was no better than his last movie, an air commander was no better than his last mission. On his own orders, Stewart's missions into Nazi-occupied Europe went uncounted. Although the official number is recorded at 20, the true number will never be known.

Trained for the Real Thing

As girlfriends and wives came to say goodbye to the deploying men, Jimmy had a surprise visit by his parents, Alex and Bessie, to attend the farewell ceremonies. The visit served to just let him know how serious and strenuous the next part of his life would be.

On November 11, 1943, the day of Stewart's departure to active combat in the war, his father, a veteran of World War I himself, waited for the last few moments of time with his son to do something that would impact Stewart for the rest of his life. Grabbing Jimmy in a final hug, his father slipped something in Jimmy's pocket. Jimmy described the moment in these words: "We were very self-conscious with each other, talking in generalities, trying to conceal our awareness that, starting tomorrow, he could no longer walk with me. At the time of the greatest crisis in my life, he would have to stand aside. We were both afraid. We embraced, then he turned and walked quickly away. Only after he was gone, did I realize he had put a small envelope in my pocket. In it was a handwritten note from my dad and a small booklet titled *The Secret Place—A Look at the 91st Psalm.*" Jimmy read the words by himself on his bunk and cried himself to sleep. His dad had been so overcome by emotion he couldn't get the words out of his mouth, but he had slipped something in Jimmy's pocket that would now carry him through the war.

My Dear Jim Boy,

Soon after you read this letter, you will be on your way to the worst of danger. Jim, I am banking on the enclosed copy of the 91st Psalm. The thing that takes the place of fear and worry is the promise of these words. I feel sure that God will lead you through this mad experience. I can say no more. I only commit to pray. Goodbye, my dear. God continue to bless and keep you. I love you more than I can tell you.

Dad

Stewart once remarked about the Psalm 91 passage his dad had handwritten out for him, "I carried the worn and creased piece of paper always, and each time I read it, I learned something new. *I will say of the Lord, He is my refuge and my fortress... His truth shall be my shield and buckler. Thou shalt not be afraid for the terror by night; nor of the arrow that flieth by day... For He shall give his angels charge over thee, to keep thee in all thy ways. They shall bear thee up in their hands, lest thou dash thy foot against a stone'...* Before every bombing raid over Europe, I read some of the booklet, and with each reading the meaning deepened for me." Stewart spoke of the impact of the words of Psalm 91, "What a promise for an airman! I read those comforting words as a prayer."

In the War Zone

A cot on a drafty concrete floor, in a cold Nissen hut in Tibenham, northeast of London was a far cry from growing up in Indiana, Pennsylvania, surrounded by a warm and loving family and definitely a world away from his career in movies in Hollywood and his life before the war.

Jimmy had no illusions as to what a death from the air would look like because of what he saw in training when he cleaned up wrecks after losing friends. Yet Stewart pushed to fly deeper and deeper toward the enemy.

Hole in the Bottom

In the early morning briefing of February 25th, 1944, Colonel Terrill entered the room. "Attention! The target today is…" The curtain was pulled back and the red ribbon strung way across the map—"Nuremberg Germany", to the gasps and groans and moans of the petrified crews. Probably the closest Stewart came to becoming a war casualty was on this raid over southern Germany. Stewart was group commander, flying as co-pilot in the *Dixie Flyer*. As group flier, he had 17 planes under his command. The men knew Stewart wanted to go on *all* the missions, but high command was keeping as tight a leash on him as they could for his own protection.

As they would take off, the Brits would wave to the American pilots. Many of the locals whispered prayers as they saw the men take off. Flying over this dangerous route where they had lost 130 men the day before was almost too much for them. Morale was dropping. The group had lost 25 crews out of the original 62 crews and planes that had come over with Stewart. A day like yesterday surely made the numbers add up!

Stewart looked down on rows of brand-new German fighters parked on the airfield. At least 200 or more planes were on that airfield. It was everything that the briefing promised. Lt. William Robinson, his bombardier, ordered *Bombs Away!* Destruction arose as buildings collapsed and metal twisted and smoke belched out of the airfields.

Bull's eye! Bull's eye! Bull's eye! Perfectly dropped bombs blew to smithereens the parked aircraft below. To Stewart's right were formations of B-17s and behind him B-24s as far as you could see passing over the target. An assault rained down. A lot of lives were saved that day with those planes being destroyed before they could wreak terror in the air.

Bam! Everything shuddered including the co-pilot's chair upon which Major Stewart sat. The ship reacted to the 88mm shell that had punched up into the bottom of the ship and detonated. The explosion rocked the plane, filling it with the smell of cordite. It was all smoke, confusion and noise as the crew fought back within the convulsion of the blast. For a split second, the crew braced themselves to see if the craft would stay in the air.

Stewart's ship sustained a direct hit right between his feet and exiting out through the top of the plane leaving a gaping two-foot hole at his feet. That one seemed aimed right for him!!! His map case of the mission fell out the hole, straight to Germany and he was shocked he didn't fall out, as well. It can't be a good feeling when you see your parachute sucked right out through the hole.

The whole plane tremored and Stewart could look down on what was left of the target from a new viewpoint. Things started falling out of the hole in the plane. Major Stewart peered down between his feet. It was enough to make your stomach drop out of the plane, free-falling to the ground.

Inside the plane, the air was already 37 degrees below zero, without the frozen blast coming from this gaping hole in the cockpit. The missile hit so close, the bombardier in the front wondered if the nose would break off from the plane. The crew around Stewart all felt the impact of one single blow that almost took him out of the war! The formation strained to watch to see if Stewart could hang on.

Even the plane directly beneath Stewart's tail turret couldn't withstand the urge for a closer look. Flying only 20 feet back, the pilot moved up to take a better look.

A hole opening up beneath your pilot's seat is unnerving, but even more so—when 18,500 feet below is bombed out Germany. The ship managed to stay in formation, but their problems were far from over.

"Alarm! Me109s at *ten o'clock*. One! Two! Three! Four! Five! Still coming at Sixteen!" Nazi fighter planes came swarming in for the kill, with our promised fighter-pilot protectors nowhere in sight. "Where are our fighters?!!" Two B-24 Bombers, burning and falling, dropped out of the sky in a mass of smoking chaos. The formation squeezed tight. Almost too tight! They had destroyed an airfield of German aircraft on the ground, now they were getting a chance to destroy it in the air! The day before at Gotha, it was a massacre! How could this day not be a repeat of the disaster? What could make it any different? The lumbering bombers advertise their vulnerability. Each are wide-open targets at best, but if one is wounded, it is near finished. Nothing can quite explain how they untwisted out of this trap of Nazi attackers and made it to the safety of the coastline.

Stewart was coming in for a landing with his plane that was shot to pieces, like hamburger meat. Jimmy fought hard to keep the Liberator in the air. Eventually, the welcomed sight of the runway at Tibenham appeared. Robbie Robinson, the bombardier of *Nine Yanks and a Jerk* witnessed the crash landing. Stewart's plane hit the runway hard. Its neck was broken and pointing up with its tail sticking up at the other end. Sergeant Wright touched down behind him, riding the brakes and making a swift sharp turn to the right, trying to avoid a major disaster.

With the fuel gauge sitting on empty, Stewart crash-landed on the runway with skids. The plane was cracked in half, smoke was coming out of Stewart's ship, the hydraulics were damaged, the tail was shot up, and the fuselage was cracked like an egg. No one could believe he survived that landing, let alone the fact he was almost a singled-out war fatality in his own plane. He was blue from the cold. Yet Stewart walked away without a scratch, while the opposite could be said over the plane.

Years later Frank Managan would write a letter to his friend Robbie Robinson, "I am not overly religious, but I learned to be sincerely religious at 20,000 feet in the air. I could recite the 91st Psalm to myself on many missions. I could relate it to our situation." The men had many stories to relate that night and would talk about this the rest of their lives. You can be assured the reality of Psalm 91 stayed with Stewart's men.

As Stewart stood back surveying the wreckage, and taking it all in, he said to Robinson, dryly, "Sergeant, somebody sure could get hurt in one of those darn things!"

Answered Prayers

Alexander Stewart kept in touch with his son by writing regularly to encourage him. His dad didn't just hand him Psalm 91 written out for him but wrote him letters each filled with prayers for his protection and safety. These letters reminded him of home, to continue the fight and a reminder about the future life which awaited him.

He was flying combat mission after combat mission—without injury to himself or any member of his crew. What others called *luck* was the power of a praying family who believed the words of this psalm. One generation of soldiers handed it to the next and Jimmy flew missions into the heart of danger against impossible odds.

The Big "B"

On March 15th, Jimmy led a second strike on Brunswick. He was in the lead plane of the entire division—157 aircraft on that strike. His orders were to bomb the primary target visually. If the target was obscure he was supposed to bomb a second target in the center of the town, by radar.

As he approached the target, he felt uneasy. The flak concentration was missing them by 400 yards. Meticulously aware that all the signs were slightly off, he felt that they would drop their bombs a half-mile off course. When he checked with the navigator, he was complaining the sensitive radar scope was acting up and he wanted another shot at it.

Stewart found himself in an instant dilemma. He could miss the target and get all his pilots back home or he could make a second loop around the target which would give the enemy time to accurately take the big bombers out of the sky. It was an almost impossible assignment since a second loop would take 8 minutes. Eight slow minutes to lead these heavy bomb groups around in a 360-degree circle. Eight long minutes to give the enemy who had been firing anti-aircraft guns at them furiously to get their settings correct. He would be exposing three groups of bombers to anti-aircraft fire and enemy fighters.

What was he to do? Stewart made his decision to hit the target and make the loop. That terrible feeling of having made the wrong decision plagued him. He had time to think about what the newspaper headlines would say—*Stewart missed his mark and led all his men to their death*. The bullets made it up from the earth within 23 seconds of firing. *What did Stewart do?*

He prayed. Stewart prayed before missions and he prayed during missions. "*In my day of trouble, I will call upon you...*"

His navigator reported a good reading from his scope. They put their nose down as they cut through the black smoke. Three groups of bombers followed Stewart's lead and rained death down on Brunswick's Panzer armored vehicles. The bombers were battered with flak when they returned, but they had not lost a man. It was clear to the generals at Division that Stewart had been a driving force to making the 445th a success.

All Roads Lead to Berlin

On March 22, Stewart was Wing lead with 200 B-24s and 2,000 men behind him. With the responsibility of lead pilot and commander, every move he made was followed. In a group that large it is hard to do anything fast, yet because of weather and lack of visibility, he had to switch his target. The lack of visibility would risk the death of scores of civilians. It was all moving parts and jagged edges to lead one of these missions, and Stewart made his decision—switch to the secondary target, Berlin. The thing that had been withheld from him was now within his grasp but he was making split-second decisions. As commander, he had five minutes to decide where to bomb in Berlin with no clearly defined target and then direct the strike. He had been ordered in his briefing that the secondary goal was to demoralize the city. He quietly let loose his bombs and at his leadership command, over 950 tons of incendiaries and over 500 tons of high-explosive bombs fell on Berlin. Hitler would not have believed who had just dropped all of this on him.

When most men had been shipped home, if they lived through their required combat flights, Stewart was committed to a seven day a week working and flying schedule. Jimmy Stewart was one of only a few Americans to rise from private to colonel in four years as the war ended. He was the highest-ranking actor in military history. During World War II, he earned the Air Medal, the Distinguished Flying Cross, the Croix de Guerre and seven battle stars. Active in the Air

Force Reserve, in 1959 Stewart achieved the rank of Brigadier General and later flew combat duty in Vietnam.

Back Home

Back in Hollywood after the war, movie director Frank Capra wanted only one man to star in *It's a Wonderful Life.* Stewart was still recovering from the shock of war and what he had seen of *thousands falling by his side* when Frank read the script to Jimmy. Jimmy would play a man who mentally crashed and suddenly thought it would have been better not to have been born. The redemption occurred when the man was given another chance after witnessing what life could have been if he were never born. It is the movie that Frank and Jimmy are most famous for. If Stewart had been killed in World War II, we would not have Stewart's movie *It's a Wonderful Life.*

And even though for his entire life, he refused interviews to NY Times and major outlets about the war and his hero status in combat, even refusing contracts to act in war movies, or even discuss the war, he did an article in Guideposts. We have to ask why? Jimmy had something he wanted to say to us that he learned from the war. He did not speak as an actor but someone who had to face death day after day. In this article, he tells us the secret of how he survived and kept his sanity.

He told of a night before combat when he had a premonition of death. There was no use to try to sleep, he was restless and fitful. He thought of the worst thing that could happen. And faced it. He began a mental game of worse case scenarios. He listed everything that could go wrong and how he would respond to every emergency the plane could have: every possible scenario to save his crew, how he would have to parachute from a burning plane, what it would be like to be captured, what he would say to his captors and how he would handle a Nazi interrogation. It was better than just being idle and moving toward everything his mind pictured which could go wrong. It was like he was facing his death.

Then he did something that turned the situation around. He prayed.

Reaching for Psalm 91, he read the words again. Over and over he had read those words. Jimmy said, "I read those comforting words and I relinquished to the Lord my fears for the coming day. I placed in His hands the squadron I would be leading...I had done all I could. I had faced each fear, and I handed it over to God..."

Jimmy didn't quit carrying his dad's letter with the copy of Psalm 91 after the war. He carried it in his wallet for the rest of his life until he died on July 7, 1997. Engraved on his tombstone is his favorite verse: *For He shall give His angels charge over thee to keep thee in all thy ways* (Psalm 91:11).

Although angels did indeed keep Jimmy Stewart, his life could also be summed up in many aspects of Psalm 91—of the protection from terror, the arrows by day, the pestilence and the destruction.

The promise found in Psalm 91:14-16... *I will set him securely on high, because he has known My name... I will rescue him and honor him... and give him a long life* testifies about his life. God delivered Jimmy Stewart from almost certain death and honored him with success, a good name and a long life.

For Jimmy Stewart, it was a wonderful life...
Because of a *wonderful promise!*

Freeman, Roger A., *The Mighty Eighth War Diary.*
Culver, Scott, *Nine Yanks and a Jerk.* With kind permission.

"A Life of Prayer"

Spencer January

Impossible Battles

Spencer January slid to the ground in the dense German forest, leaning against the rough tree bark.

Appalled, he admitted to himself...

This would be where he met the end.

It just seemed like yesterday when he had been on a motorcycle with his girl clinging on to his waist, headed to Turner Falls, Oklahoma, on June 13, 1943, for his honeymoon. He knew Maymie was the one for him since he had a vivid dream of her even before he had met her. Within a few weeks, he had met the girl of his dream and six months later they were married!

In late December 1944, as a member of the U.S. Army's 35th Infantry Division, 137th Infantry Company I, Spencer landed in France, disbursed with a rifle and a government issued New Testament. He was inserted into World War II active combat, never giving the oozing blisters on his feet from his regulation boots a chance to heal. He had to remain on high alert to stay alive. Beginning the fighting at Roer

River in France, he and the 35th Division carved their way into Nazi Germany.

Machine gun fire ripped through the calm. It was March 1945 and the Allies pushed for Ossenburg where Hitler had factories manufacturing gunpowder. The Germans were bunkered in and waiting for them. A large stone house was the last shield before the men were forced to cross 200 yards of open field. Already it held the bodies of wounded soldiers who'd tried to cross the clearing and were surprised by an ambush. Bleeding men were dragged back to the house for safety. It made for an ominous sight to behold when you considered the insane prospect of attempting the same dash.

Three nests of German machine guns riddled the tree line, spitting dirt and tree bark in the face of everyone who pondered the situation. The American troops tried taking them out, but the Germans were out of range of their guns. The Germans had the advantage of being settled in behind a hill with each machine gun nest strategically placed 50 yards apart from the others so each could control a portion of the field.

Spencer answered to the nickname of "Sunshine" to both his captain and company because of his contagious optimism. However, he couldn't muster up any shred of hope for this situation. They were trapped. It was going to be a massacre.

The Germans knew they had them in a Catch-22. To cross that field meant certain death, and they had strategically blocked every other route into town. The Americans were trapped with no alternative, throwing their lives away as easy targets for the machine guns. They were given no choice except to advance even though no one was making it across the field without being mowed down by a bullet. *Will anybody survive?* A necessary moment in time, yet so senseless.

What does the end feel like? The last moments on earth? How could Spencer make a rational decision to end it here and now as if he had nothing to live for?

Looking up through the trees, Spencer saw a clear blue sky. Thinking through those final moments of his goodbye, he had the sinking realization that he had just begun his marital life. It would be a tragedy. People claimed that he and Maymie were the happiest married couple they had ever met!

Spencer remembers being utterly appalled at the situation. Twenty-four years old, he felt overwhelmed at the thought that he would never see Maymie and his son again. Maymie would be a widow at the tender age of 19. This thought gripped him with such pain that he could barely breathe. Only God could save him now.

Spencer reflected how his home church in Dallas had prayed over him before he left. It all seemed so far away now. His pastor, Carl Alcorn, had asked that all the men deploying to come to the altar for prayer. He stepped forward with other young men. The people at Oak Cliff knew how to pray and intercede—and to pray through until they knew they had the "victory". Countless voices were appealing to heaven for protection for these young men who were leaving to serve their country. A gathering of people joined in at the altar. Prayers were offered up in the most heartfelt unity by the entire church: *Lord, be a shield to these men. Lead them away from evil and traps... Let them abide in your secret place and under your wings find refuge... A thousand may fall at their side, but don't let it approach them... Let your angels guard their every step... Nothing is impossible with You.* Psalm 91 and every protection scripture promise they knew came pouring out of them. They anointed each of them with oil. It felt good to have his church behind him praying that he would come back home.

Maymie's letters reminded him of all he loved back home. She wrote that she had learned how to continually intercede in prayer. Communication for soldiers seemed as if it sometimes stood still. The government had strict privacy for communication not allowing the enemy to intercept any information. The return letters were so scarce Maymie had to trust the Lord when letters didn't come as she pushed through for him in prayer.

In a few minutes he would know if prayer could turn the impossible, hopeless situation, he was facing. What if the physical battle could be turned by the spiritual one? Would that prayer time hold good for what he faced now? Was anyone still remembering to pray for him now that he was long gone and so far away from home? He didn't have the luxury of pondering the issue. They were about to advance— right into a barrage of German machine gun fire.

Dropping to his knees, Spencer prayed a gut-wrenching prayer for his life. "God, you've got to do something! *Please*, do something!" "Advance!" The order came moments after he prayed.

The Edge of Eternity

Grasping his M-1 rifle, Spencer crept to the edge of the clearing. Before he stepped out of the cover of the trees, he pictured Maymie's face. Closing his eyes, he breathed in his son's sweet baby scent.

Then, glancing to the left, he stopped. A long, fluffy white cloud appeared from nowhere in the heat of the day. Dropping from the cloudless sky, it concealed the open field. Things like this don't happen on clear days.

There wasn't time to think, only react. The white foggy mist blocked the German's vision and obscured their line of fire.

The only sound was combat boots thudding against soft earth. The fog from the cloud which had dropped down was so thick that they could hardly see the man in front of them. With renewed spirit, the American soldiers bolted from cover and raced for their lives through the midst picking up wounded men from the former crossings.

200 yards!

150!

100!

50!

I'm almost across! Spencer thought, his legs pumping like pistons, and his heart beating in his ears like a snare drum. The far off trees grew closer and closer. Lunging into the thicket, he threw himself behind a tree, his pulse still pounding in his ears.

Turning, he could make out the other soldiers as they cleared the opening. Those coming in last carried and dragged the wounded. It was enough to make a grown man cry to see the desperation in those carrying their wounded friends.

This is God's doing.

He stood by the tree watching. The moment the last soldier ran past the stone house and crossed the field disappearing in the trees, the cloud lifted. The day was again bright and clear with blue skies. *I can't believe this!*

Moments later, a bomb rocked the earth spitting fire and rubble into the air. The Germans had radioed their artillery. There weren't words to describe what Spencer felt when debris exploded in every direction as he watched the building disintegrate. Unaware that the American soldiers had escaped, the German artillery had blown the stone house to mere rubble. He just had seen a series of events, he couldn't explain. In war, there is no time to process, his company was ordered to move on.

Moment of Truth

Reaching Ossenburg, they cleared the area of all enemy soldiers for the Allies. All the while, Spencer kept the image of that cloud in his mind. He'd seen smoke screens set off to obscure troop activity, but this one had been different. It hadn't been a smoke screen. It was a thick cloud. Not in the early morning, but at midday on a bright sunny day. That appeared out of nowhere. Just for the amount of time they needed.

Two weeks later, bivouacked in eastern Germany, Spencer tore open a letter from his mother in Dallas, Texas.

"You remember Mrs. Tankersly from our church?" she wrote. Who could forget her? Spencer smiled at the thought of her. Folks in his church called her a prayer warrior. He'd thought there were times she took her intense prayers a bit too far. Now he eagerly read the words that his mother wrote him from the other side of the ocean. What was the connection to him that his mother would write to ask if he remembered her?

"Well, she phoned one morning to say that the Lord had awakened her in the night at 1:00 a.m. to pray for you. God said, 'Spencer January is in terrible trouble! Get up and pray for him now!' Mrs. Tankersly prayed hours before the burden lifted. She prayed for you until six o'clock the next morning when she had to go to work at the defense factory. Before getting off her knees, she added in one more punch, 'Lord, whatever danger Spencer is in, just cover him with a cloud!'"

The letter trembled in Spencer's hands. He sat there frozen in thought as the pieces were coming together. Calculating the seven hour time difference, Mrs. Tankersly's praying would have corresponded to the time they were approaching the ambush. With that time difference, her prayer for a cloud would have been uttered at one o'clock in the afternoon in Germany. His mind started to race. A chill went down Spencer's spine. Just when he'd been about to step into enemy fire. Just at the time they were poised to make the suicide dash.

Not only had the cloud itself amazed him, and how it stayed a certain length of time—now Spencer held a letter that pinpointed the exact time that prayer had reached all the way around the world to him.

Spencer explains, "I'm convinced that there is no substitute for the power of prayer, even those in the valley of the shadow of death."

Spencer January believed that the fervent prayer of one woman not only saved his life, but the lives of every soldier who passed through the cloud. She had answered the call of God to pray—in the middle of the night for five hours until she felt the danger had been averted. Spencer claimed that he could actually *"feel"* people back home praying. During their time in combat together, the soldiers in his company had questioned the fact he *felt the prayers* literally. Because of his job of carrying the radio, it made him the first target which was always over him yet he escaped time and time again—only because of the prayers continually being prayed. When they questioned him, Spencer mentioned that he could constantly feel the prayers from the "west"—being America.

Taking him to task over it, the soldiers doubted that he could truly "feel" those prayers being prayed, so they would ask him from time to time, "Sunshine, point to the west!" He never failed to get it right. They still weren't satisfied. In order to try to trick him—or prove him wrong—the soldiers blindfolded him. They turned him around and around and asked him to point to America where the prayers were coming from, knowing that he was certainly dizzy and could not. Well, he directed them straight to America without a doubt. YES, the prayers were very strong, well and alive!! He could actually sense the protection from Psalm 91 and God's Word over them.

Spencer and his company weren't the only ones who benefited from those prayers. The church had all their prayers answered from the time they had spent down at the altar and daily interceding. And the scriptures they prayed over those young men had a lasting impact. During the war, the most wrenching and heartbreaking moment was when a family would receive news of their young son, or brother or loved one who had fallen in battle. The grief of losing a courageous man, so young, and so in his prime, was like a kick in the gut to a family that never left the family-consciousness. There was the special recognition when the government sent the gold star to hang in the window to honor the sacrifice of the family. People who passed by acknowledged the family's sacrifice. Yet it didn't make up for the pain or the hole that the death would leave of someone dying so young with his whole life ahead of him. Spencer January's church family prayed at the onset for each family who sent a son to war—and all of them had returned safe and unharmed! Cozadene Martin, who was there when Spencer was prayed for, remembers "Not one family we prayed for received one of those stars."

But Spencer had a unique story. No one had returned with the testimony of the power of *specific prayer* like Spencer. His journal testified to the accuracy of Mrs. Tankersly praying—asking for *exactly* what he and his fellow troops needed at the *exact* moment they needed it.

After being discharged from the Army, he continued to fight. This time he fought the good fight of faith, and he fought on his knees in prayer. When Spencer came home, it was then that he and Maymie made their life together one of fervent prayer.

"From the time God rescued us with a cloud, I spent the next 60 years getting up early every morning to pray for others," Spencer explains. **There is no substitute for prayer.**

[Read about Spencer's remarkable family life after the war, including his documented story of saving a child's life through his unrelenting powerful prayer in *Psalm 91 God's Shield of Protection Workbook*.]

Michael Payne

Freelance Writer - Five Times to Iraq

In 1998, at the age of forty-eight, I was constantly dogged with hopelessness and despair. I felt I was never going to smile again. I had spent thirty-three of those forty-eight years drinking, drugging, gambling and committing multiple adulteries in vain attempts to grab temporary moments of what I thought would bring happiness. These things no longer brought any satisfaction or respite from the depression, thoughts of suicide and other symptoms attributed to PTSD that were now hounding me constantly. My second marriage was falling apart and my sons from my first marriage could no longer stand to be around me.

In the fall of 1998, a Christian from Guatemala, seeing the pain and distress in my face, said to me, "Brother Michael, I read Psalm 91 every day before I come to work!" He did not elaborate, but the Spirit of the Lord was at work and He gave me ears to hear. I started reading Psalm 91 several times a day. Eventually, it brought, not only a smile to my face, but also a smile in my heart. I knew that the Lord was speaking directly to me and that He was keeping all His promises in Psalm 91. There is not one part of Psalm 91 that I did not grab hold of and believe as a covering from the battles in my life. It not only saved my life, but the Psalm lead me to believe in God, and, one year later, I gave my life to Jesus.

I carry a handwritten copy of Psalm 91 in my wallet. It reminds me of the power of God's Word as I traveled through Iraq, Afghanistan and even right here in the U.S. I have been to Iraq four times as a freelance Christian radio reporter. I know the Lord saved my life on several specific occasions, and, many times, when I was not even aware. God is sovereign over every bullet and every piece of shrapnel that flies. He gives me victory and peace and if we but stand in the shadow of the Almighty, He will deliver us, without fail.

I am set free from alcohol, drugs, sexual sin, gambling, and worldly ways. I am not recovering from any of these; I am set free. I am a new creation in Christ Jesus! I owe it all to God and I owe it to the truth, the way and the life expressed in Psalm 91 and Jesus Christ.

MICHAEL PAYNE, Winchester, Virginia

www.takeastandministries.org

Sergeant Harold Barclay
Brownwood, TX - told by his daughter, Janie Boyd

Sergeant George Harold Barclay served in World War II in General Patton's 320th Infantry of the U.S. Army, Company E. Continuous fear eliminated any expectation of ever returning to his wife and baby daughter. The same fear kept his wife terrified when she would see a Western Union truck delivering letters of war casualties. Once a Western Union messenger came to her door by mistake and she said that she froze with terror. Sometimes as many as six weeks would go by without a letter, during which time the News reported that half of Harold's company had been killed. The Battle of the Bulge saw his whole outfit cut off from the rest of the army.

Finally, however, a letter came from Harold saying that God had given him Psalm 91, and he now had absolute certainty that he would come home without even an injury. So certain was he of this promise in Psalm 91, that when the medics said they needed volunteers to go to the front lines to bring back the injured, Harold volunteered and made repeated trips under extreme enemy fire, saving many lives.

The citation for the Bronze Star Award that he received said "...for bravery", but Harold insisted that it wasn't bravery since he knew nothing would happen to him because of the covenant promise God had given to him in Psalm 91. When he came home without a scratch, it was obvious that *angels had indeed borne him up in their hands, allowing no evil to befall him.*

* * * * *

John G. Lake's Psalm 91 Testimony

I have often read accounts of the time when John G. Lake took foam from the Bubonic Plague in his hand and placed it under a microscope where people watched in amazement as the germs literally died instantly on contact with his hand. I was puzzled for years, wondering what kind of anointing he had on his life to bring about this supernatural phenomenon.

Nothing could have pleased me more than when I learned Mr. Lake's secret—his wholehearted belief in the Psalm 91 protection that God has provided.

Mr. Lake made the statement that confirmed the secret to his supernatural protection—"For many years God kept me so that sickness and death could not touch me, **from the day that I saw in the ninety-first Psalm a man's privilege of entering into God, not only for healing, but *health* and having God and the life of God in every fiber of his being."**[1]

[1] *John G. Lake: The Complete Collection of His Life Teachings*, Albury Publishing, Tulsa, Oklahoma, *p.340*. [Reprinted with kind permission]

* * * * *

Mary Johnson
Kidnapping Testimony

After just returning from a five-day Red Brangus Cow sale where we also met our daughter to buy clothes for the soon-to-be-birthed, first grandchild, I had gotten an early start that morning to catch up on my chores. We lived 12 miles in the country, so I was surprised to be interrupted by a young man in an old van—supposedly lost—asking for a drink of water. But, the pretense was over when he pulled a gun and told me to get in the car. My surprised scream was soon stifled, however, when he threatened my life if I did that again. I was thrown into the back of the van and a man wearing a nylon stocking on his head put athletic tape over my mouth and hands and covered my head with a black windbreaker. Black shag carpet covered the sides, floor and roof of the van and the windows were covered with black curtains.

I couldn't tell where they were taking me. I know that we crossed railroad tracks and ended up on a gravel road. I had never been so frightened in my life. All I could think about was that I was soon to be 50—soon to be a grandmother—and, I wasn't sure I would live to see either; but my greatest fear was being raped. Finally, however, I came to my senses and started claiming my spiritual covenant promise of protection. I suddenly realized—*I was a child of God—fear was of the devil— and I was trusting God that nothing would happen to me.*

By this time we had stopped and with a wool cap pulled down over my face, I was led over a barbed wire fence and across a pasture to an old abandoned ranch house where I was handcuffed to the bathroom lavatory and asked, "What would be the best way to get your husband to cooperate without alerting the police." Then I was warned that if he went to the police he would never see me again—alive! A phone call with all the usual kidnapping threats and instructions was planned, and then I was left to my dilemma.

Still quoting my promises, singing hymns of deliverance and thanking God, I was frantically working to get the pipes loose, but they wouldn't budge. God said in Psalm 91:15: *"In your day of trouble, call upon Me and I will answer."* I started praying, "Lord, I am calling on You! I can't do this, but You can. Show me a way to get loose." Then, for the first time I noticed a tiny pipe coming up the back of the sink. I don't have any idea how I was able to break through, but I know it was a miracle because later the FBI agent couldn't believe I was able to do what I did.

Feeling sure the kidnappers would make their call to Don and be back shortly, I was out the back door and over the fence in no time. I had no idea where I was, but I was confident God would get me where I needed to be. Twelve miles later I came to a house with every door locked except the front door. (I later found out that the lady never left her doors unlocked, except on this particular day.) After several calls the Sheriff was on his way to get me, but my husband had already left for Goldthwaite, Texas, with the ransom money.

The kidnappers skipped that first meeting but called at 12:30 that night with a new appointed place to meet in Austin, Texas. Obviously, they didn't know I had escaped. This time it was the Texas Rangers who met and took the first man into custody, and later, the second one was apprehended. I was called to Austin by the FBI to pick him out of a "line-up." All I asked was for the men in the line-up to wear a ball cap and say, "Would you get me a glass of water?" With that, I was able to successfully pick him out of the group and my job was over.

I thank God for His covenant of protection in Psalm 91. We do not have to be afraid of the *"terror of what man can do to us—it will not approach us when we run to God and dwell in His Shelter."*

[*The man who was convicted of this crime was no amateur criminal. According to police investigation, he had a habitual crime problem since his youth and had previously been convicted and imprisoned for robbery, indecency and sexual assault. For this present offense he was sentenced to 99 years in prison. The sheriff told Mrs. Johnson that they had never had anyone in their local jail as malicious as this man. The FBI was shocked that Mrs. Johnson was able to escape and even more shocked that she had not been beaten, raped or murdered. One of the FBI made the comment, "We cannot believe we are sitting here today with you and that you are alive and well."*]

Tornado Protection Miracle

By Nikki McCurtain
Moore, Oklahoma

Smiling, I put the finishing touches on a gift. It was May 2013, the weekend before the last 4 days of school, which marked the end of my first year as a teacher at Plaza Towers Elementary School in Moore, Oklahoma. Call me sentimental, but I'd made gifts for all of my 26 students. I *loved* my job and knew I would never forget this class. I'd made each student a portfolio of their work, hoping they too would cherish the memories.

Humming, I walked across the room in our house in Norman, Oklahoma and froze. A picture freeze-framed in my mind's eye. I saw what looked like a war zone, and *I was walking through the debris*! I realized I was seeing a disaster, but what kind? Here in Oklahoma, we'd suffered a terrorist attack in 1995. Might there be another? It looked like *war.* Whatever it represented, I knew one thing for certain; God wanted me to pray.

Already alarmed, when the picture flashed in my view a second time, I knew for sure that some kind of disaster was about to happen. "Preston," I said to my husband, "we've got to pray!" I described the vision I'd seen and we began praying in the spirit, pleading for understanding.

The next day, Sunday, May 19, tornado sirens wailed in the afternoon as we took cover in a friend's storm shelter. Several tornadoes touched down north and east of us bringing death and destruction. I was tired by the time we got home that evening and turned on the news. It wasn't good. Meteorologists said that conditions were ripe for supercells. Most of the time those conditions don't fulfill their potential, but we've learned to keep an eye on the sky and stay abreast of the storm warnings.

On Monday, May 20, only 23 of my 26 students arrived for class. Some had been kept home because of the uncertain weather. Many of them had taken shelter the night before and that's all they wanted to talk about.

During journal time I said, "Okay, let's get out our journals and talk with our pencils."

The classroom fell quiet for a few minutes except for the scratching of pencils against paper. Taking care of some paperwork, I thought about the women's mentoring group I attended which was led by Rev. Barbara Stumprud and Julia Pickard. Back in February, they suggested we read *Psalm 91 God's Umbrella of Protection* by Peggy Joyce Ruth. Although I was familiar with the Bible, I'd never studied that psalm of protection. I loved reading about the secret place of the Most High.

The 4th verse read, *"He will cover you with His pinions, and under His wings shall you trust and find refuge…"* The author explained that pinions are the strongest part of the wing. She compared this verse to a mother hen scooping her chicks under her wings for protection. For some reason I'd gotten stuck on this verse, reading it over and over. I couldn't seem to get past it.

The children finished journaling and around noon we had Café Time. I used my SmartBoard to project an image of a café on the wall, complete with coffee and biscotti. Students gathered around me and each one took a turn with the microphone, talking about things they'd written in their journal.

During recess, Preston showed up to take my car. "It's going to be bad," he said. *How bad?* I thought, looking up into dark, ominous clouds. I always prayed protection over my students and I'd anointed their desks with oil early in the school year. But, today was unusual; I'd spent every spare moment praying and listening for God.

Returning after recess, our 4th grade classes rotated and my class was much smaller in the afternoons. Parents picked up their students at a steady pace, and by 1:35 I only had 10 left. We all settled on the floor for reading time. The students were excited about our next chapter. I was reading *The Magician's Nephew*, one of the books in the *Chronicles of Narnia* series. The world of Narnia was in darkness, still in the process of being created. As Aslan sang, brilliant green grass sprang up out of the ground piercing the darkness with new life.

I paused and whispered, "This is such a powerful comparison between good and evil and how new life always grows out of darkness." Enrapt in the story, for a while we almost forgot the dark clouds gathering over our comfortable little world. Thunder bellowed outside our classroom shaking our walls as the hail began to fall.

There weren't many children left at school by 2:30 when the principal's words crackled over the loudspeakers instructing everyone to take tornado precautions. We'd practiced enough over the school year that the kids knew the drill by heart.

They also knew this *wasn't* a drill.

The noise I heard approaching the school was louder than any train I'd ever heard. The ground vibrated like a train approaching the station. But, as it closed the distance to the school, it felt like an earthquake.

Scared and weeping, they formed a line in the hall. Outside tornado sirens shrilled as the children knelt and held a book over their heads just as we'd practiced. As we waited, calming the kids, more parents arrived...but it was too late to leave. They were trapped with us.

There were only about 40 people in our hall, 30 of them children. When the school is full, there are too many children to take shelter in the bathrooms. However, part of our disaster plan is that if we think that students might be in danger from breaking glass, we can move them into the restrooms. Our hall was dotted with large square lights which the other hallway didn't have. After a brief consultation with the other teachers, we decided to squeeze our group into the girl's bathroom.

"Scoot up! Scoot up!" I urged. As the tornado sirens screamed again, children crawled under the sinks and stacked like cordwood in the stalls. My back was facing the doorway and I was holding hands tightly with my co-teacher. We had to survive this together. Just then my cell phone rang, and I hadn't had reception before.

Preston had been watching the path of the tornado and was horrified to watch it tracking straight for the school. "I love you so much," he said, choking back tears.

"I love you too." As Preston and I said goodbye, fear and grief threatened to overwhelm me. *Would this goodbye be forever?* My cell phone went dead. Gasping, I jumped to my feet trying to get a breath. Swirling around, I stood facing the doorway to the hall—and watched, frozen in shock—as the tornado came near us. I took cover again hovering over a couple students. Massive brown, violent, swirling debris moved past us down the very hallway we'd just vacated. In my life I'd never felt a more demonic presence. The sense of evil was so overwhelming that a startling truth crossed my mind: *tornadoes are not an act of God!*

I didn't know if I had the spiritual strength for what we faced. "Lord, give me one verse to pray!" I cried.

The answer was delivered to me as I stayed in a prayer position. *"Psalm 91:4."* Personalizing the verse I prayed, *"He will cover us with His pinions and under His wings we will trust and find refuge!"* I prayed that verse over and over until someone pressed their hand to my back. Had another parent arrived and needed to squeeze inside? I turned to see who it was.

No one was there.

The fear was palpable. "These are my students!" I declared. "They *aren't* dying!"

The rumble of the approaching tornado was deafening, but I heard an assuring whisper. *Nikki, you're going to be okay.* Suddenly it felt like the earth shifted on its axis. Walls crashed, the roof lifted away. Pipes broke. Children screamed. Cement blocks flew through the air like twigs. Nothing prepared me for what came next.

The cacophony of sights and sounds indescribable, the building that had been our refuge from the world was reduced to nothing more than matchsticks of timber and desolation. My ears still roaring from the sound, I began pulling debris off of screaming children. Many of them had head wounds, cuts, scrapes, and they were all terrified. "It's okay!" I said to screaming children as we pulled them out of the rubble. "You're alive!" Everyone was in shock. The kids were cold and shivering, bloody and caked with mud and debris, but they were all alive.

My brave co-teacher Mrs. Martinez helped our student, Makaila, out of the rubble. With a tear-stained face Makaila said, "I knew I was going to be okay because I asked God to put us in protective bubbles."

As I stepped out onto the debris to view the scene, my breath hitched. It looked like a bulldozer had razed the school. *It was the exact image that had flashed before my eyes twice over the weekend.* I later found out that children in the other hallway were ushered into heaven and into the Lord's glorious light on that day.

I often think back to May 20, 2013. *How did I stand so close to an EF-5 tornado, watching it pass, and not get sucked into the vortex?* It's as though we were in the secret place of the Most High, a place so supernatural that a child might describe it as a protective bubble.

I still recall the pressure on my back. And, I remember how the Lord directed me to pray Psalm 91:4, *He will cover you with His pinions..."* I don't believe that what I felt was a hand. It was the Lord covering us, scooping us *under His wing* for protection.

Don Beason
Testimony of Mother's Prayers

While working on our Psalm 91 military book, I met a precious veteran of World War II who gives his mother credit for praying him through the war. He retired from the service and later began traveling with "God Mobile" ministry to county and state fairs. He would give people a spiritual aptitude test and anyone scoring less than 90%, Don would lead to the Lord and give them a Psalm 91 book. —Here is Don's story:

"When I found Peggy Joyce Ruth's Psalm 91 book it revealed the supernatural protection that we as Christians have whether we are young or old, whether we are in the service during war time or just going through the struggles and battles in everyday life. We do not have to wait until we get to heaven to enjoy the supernatural protection God has provided in our Psalm 91 covenant. It is exceedingly and abundantly more than one can ask or think.

I began going with the Full Gospel Business Men's Fire Teams all over America and in England where we go into businesses, homes, jails, prisons, homeless shelters, churches, on the street or any place else where we find hurting people. It breaks my heart to see so many in the Body of Christ just warming the pews on Sunday morning and living like the rest of the world for the rest of the week, doing nothing to save the lost, heal the sick and set the captives free."

Mr. Beason knew his authority as a believer. It's evident in the newspaper documentation he sent me of the following unique story depicting what took place in the midst of a horrible natural disaster in Grand Island, Nebraska.

Speaking to a Tornado

June 3, 1980, three, possibly four, tornadoes grouped together and slashed their way down the streets of Grand Island. In all, there were at least seven tornadoes all going in different directions, but four of them came together to make a large tornado that did most of the damage.

The tornado was headed directly for Mr. Beason's office and the first of the two erratic, unexplainable turns the tornado made was only a few yards before it reached him. It ruined the office directly across the street, but not even a window was cracked in his office. The second of the two radical changes of direction was just before it would have swept through Mr. Beason's farm. The farms next to his were all destroyed. The city map showing the tornado's path confirmed its going straight to his office, then turning in front of his doorstep and going straight for his farm, then once again, turning just short of his property line. The chart dramatically showed the two major surprise changes of direction were directly related to his real estate. There was no explanation in the natural for the two sudden turns of the tornado—but no one could convince Mr. Beason it was not the direct result of God's Psalm 91 protection he had been claiming—"*I will not be afraid of the destruction (natural disasters) that lay waste at noon.*"

A few years later the TV station reported a mile-wide tornado heading once again toward Grand Island. Mr. Beason said, "I went outside and rebuked it and commanded it to turn away and disappear. A minute or two later when I went back into the house, the TV announcer said the tornado had lifted out of sight." Beason said, "*This was just more of God's Psalm 91 protection!*"

Don Beason has learned to pray. It wasn't only his mother's prayers now.

* * * * *

Stella Marshall

I could hardly believe what my eyes were seeing and my ears hearing as I sat in Ms. Stella Marshall's room and listened to her life story. Watching her have no need for glasses or a hearing aid, while listening to her answer questions with the sharp mind of a twenty-year-old, and noticing that she didn't have to take her teeth out at *night, I was in awe when Stella told me all about her **ninety-fifth** birthday party she had enjoyed the day before. (I would have guessed her to be not a day over seventy years old.) From the moment I heard some of her fellow church members refer to her as the "Psalm 91 Lady" I was determined to get an interview with this beautiful woman.*

*Truly, she is the epitome of someone who has been **"satisfied with a long life"** and **"kept safe"** by the power of Psalm 91.*

Stella Marshall's maternal grandfather came as a young boy by ship to Virginia from Africa where his own people had sold him and his mother and father as slaves. Stella's mother was one of his eighteen children. Stella's father, on the other hand, had a much different background. His mother was Irish and it was his sister who later took Stella and her younger brother and sister to rear when their dad died at age twenty-eight after receiving a head injury at the Ennis railroad yard where he worked. Stella, who picked cotton most of her young life, married at sixteen *for the sole purpose of never having to pick cotton again,* but her dreams of how married life would be did not turn out as she had planned. She had envisioned having a long table with benches on each side where the family would gather for meals—six boys on one side facing the six girls across from them, and she and her husband sitting at each end of the table. Her idea of how a marriage should be was shattered when it ended in divorce and she was left with three children to rear alone. She had been brought up in a Baptist home, but there was no real relationship with the Lord so worldliness quickly took hold of her life. Finally, in desperation, at age fifty-four, Stella stood by the fence in her front yard and said, "God, You see these cigarettes in my hand? When I smoke these, I'm not going to smoke ever again. I'm not going to take another drink and I'm not going to be with another man as long as I live." She kept that promise, but for the next five years she could not find satisfaction for the longing and the hungering in her heart for a deeper walk with God. In August 1971, five years after she had given up her flesh life, she asked Jesus in her heart and to be Lord of her life. She was prayed over to receive the Baptism of the Holy Spirit and everything in her life changed. She said that each night she would go to sleep and see Jesus standing over her with His hands outstretched. Before receiving the Baptism of the Holy Spirit she had read her Bible with very little understanding, but after being prayed for, Stella said that she was getting something new every time she opened her Bible. Every Full Gospel meeting found Stella on the front row. She couldn't get enough of the Lord.

When I asked Stella why her friends called her the *Psalm 91 Lady*, she said, "When I found Psalm 91 I have prayed it over myself and over my family every single day since, and I tell everyone I see about God's wonderful protection." I was curious how she happened to find it and she told me an interesting story. She was asked to go to Dallas to keep the grandbaby of the fifth richest man in Texas. The servant's quarters where she lived was secluded back behind the big mansion. Not being accustomed to staying alone, she began to think about the real possibility of someone breaking into a rich man's property. She got very fearful because she knew that no one would be able to see or hear her if she needed help—so she began crying out to God to take away all her fears. Faithful to His promises, God supernaturally led her to Psalm 91 and she has been saying it every day since. Those angels that God placed in charge of her and the confidence that began to build with the knowledge that God had answered her cry, developed such faith in God's Psalm 91 covenant of protection that she has been kept from harm from that day forth and satisfied with a long life. Stella recalled the time when a flu virus slipped in on her and she began to stand for her healing. When the symptoms didn't leave right away, she said, "*Lord, You said if we asked anything, You would do it. I've been expecting my healing. If I haven't heard from You by tomorrow, I am going to the doctor, but my trust is in You.*" Then, she turned over and went to sleep. About 6:30 a.m. Stella said that something woke her up, saying, "You are healed." She said that there was not a place on her that wasn't well. Where she had been struggling to breathe, she could now breathe with ease. Stella, who has practically raised many of her grandchildren and great-grandchildren, never misses a night praying Psalm 91 over every one of them.

Because of her belief in God and the many blessings He has poured out on her life, Stella wanted to find some way to do something to help others; therefore, in her early 60's Stella started a routine that lasted over 20 years. She would buy bananas bunches with her own money and distribute them to the residents of nursing homes. She was such a regular visitor that the director of one of the homes scheduled "The Banana Lady" as an activity all by herself. No matter what the weather, Stella never missed her Thursday afternoon appointment. She never worried if she would have money for her bananas. When Thursday came, the money was always there. For over twelve years Stella also volunteered at the Casa de Amigos' Health Clinic getting files and signing people in. And, all of that is in addition to helping raise her eight grandchildren and thirteen great-grandchildren.

I have often said that just having a lot of birthdays is not always a blessing. It takes a *satisfied* life to make long life good. You don't have to ask Stella if she is satisfied with her life. Just as obvious as her dissatisfaction with life was before age fifty-four, her satisfaction since then has been just as obvious.

Copy and enlarge this **Psalm 91 prayer** to pray over yourself and your loved ones, inserting his or her name in the blanks.

_____ dwells in the shelter of the Most High and he/she will abide in the shadow of the Almighty. _____ says to the LORD, "My refuge and my fortress, My God, in whom I trust!" For it is He who delivers _____ from the snare of the trapper and from the deadly pestilence. The Lord will cover _____ with His pinions, and under His wings _____ may seek refuge; His faithfulness is a shield and bulwark. _____ will not be afraid of the terror by night, or of the arrow that flies by day; of the pestilence that stalks in darkness, or of the destruction that lays waste at noon. A thousand may fall at _____'s side and ten thousand at his/her right hand, *but* it shall not approach _____. _____ will only look on with his/her eyes and see the recompense of the wicked. For _____ has made the LORD, his/her refuge, e*ven* the Most High, _____'s dwelling place. No evil will befall _____, Nor will any plague come near _____'s tent. For He will give His angels charge concerning _____, to guard _____ in all his/her ways. They will bear _____ up in their hands, that _____ does not strike his/her foot against a stone. _____ will tread upon the lion and cobra, the young lion and the serpent _____ will trample down.

"Because _____ has loved Me, [God said] therefore I will deliver him/her; I will set _____ *securely* on high, because he/she has known My name. "_____ will call upon Me, and I will answer him/her; I will be with _____ in trouble; I will rescue _____ and honor him/her. "With a long life I will satisfy _____ and let _____ see My salvation."

We carry **Psalm 91** Books for the ENTIRE FAMILY!

*My Own Psalm 91 Coloring Book
A Coloring Book and Teaching Combined
My Own Psalm 91 Book
Children's edition available in many languages
Psalm 91 for Youth
*Psalm 91 for Teens
*Psalm 91 for Mothers
Psalm 91 God's Umbrella of Protection
*Psalm 91 Real-Life Stories of God's Shield of Protection
Psalm 91 Real-Life Stories (Hardback Edition)
Psalm 91 God's Shield of Protection
Psalm 91 God's Shield of Protection – Pocketbook size
Psalm 91 God's Shield of Protection Workbook
*Also available in Spanish!

Psalm 91 Coloring Book
Paraphrased version
of Psalm 91 - accompanies
"My Own Psalm 91 Book"
boardbook. Learning
this psalm will be fun and
engaging for young children
and grandchildren. Use in
Sunday School, Childcare
Facilities and at home.

For additional copies of this book and other titles including: Those Who Trust The Lord Shall Not Be Disappointed, Tormented Eight Years and Back, and God's Smuggler, Jr.

 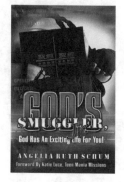 

Visit our website or call us:
www.peggyjoyceruth.org | 325-646-6894 | 877-972-6657
Call us for *special* bulk order pricing!
For donations or correspondence mail:

Peggy Joyce Ruth Ministries
P.O. Box 1549 | Brownwood, TX 76804

Bible Study Teachings by Peggy Joyce Ruth air weekly on KPSM 99.3 and KBUB 90.3 FM—Streaming kpsm.net

CD Teaching Series and Individual CDs available